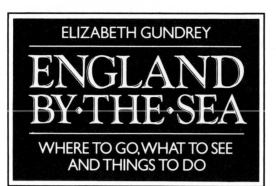

ELIZABETH GUNDREY

ENGLAND BY·THE·SEA

WHERE TO GO, WHAT TO SEE
AND THINGS TO DO

Some other books by Elizabeth Gundrey

England by Bus   (Hamlyn)
Staying Off the Beaten Track   (Hamlyn)
Helping Hands:
The Observer Guide to Conservation   (Unwin)
Sparing Time:
The Observer Guide to Helping Others   (Unwin)

For children:
Send Off For It   (Hamlyn)
250 More Things to Send Off For   (Hamlyn)
All Your Own   (Hamlyn)
Making Decorations   (Hamlyn)

ELIZABETH GUNDREY

ENGLAND BY·THE·SEA

WHERE TO GO, WHAT TO SEE
AND THINGS TO DO

SEVERN
HOUSE

For Pat, with love

British Library Cataloguing in Publication Data
Gundrey, Elizabeth
  England-by-the-sea.
  1. Seaside resorts — England   2. England —
  Description and travel — 1971- — Guide-books
  I. Title
  914.2   DA665

  ISBN 0-7278-2016-8

Published by Severn House Publishers Limited
4 Brook Street
London W1Y 1AA

Text © Elizabeth Gundrey 1982
Maps © Severn House Publishers Limited 1982

Editorial
Ian Jackson
Diana Levinson
Design
Keith Lovegrove

Filmset by Tameside Filmsetting Limited,
Ashton-under-Lyne, Lancashire
Printed and bound by Hazell Watson and Viney Ltd.
Aylesbury, Buckinghamshire.

Contents

Foreword

England has friendly shores. Is it these which soften the coast, and the hospitable people who make their living from receiving urbanites?

Whatever might be the cause, Elizabeth Gundrey captures their spirit and reveals to us a veritable compendium of facts which will motivate visits as well as adding fascinating pieces of knowledge, not normally associated with a guidebook; which this publication is definitely not.

Only a likeable author could put pen to such an amiable read.

I thought I knew a lot about our coastal villages and resorts. Each page humbled and interested me. This is a valuable book for all landlubbers, of which I am unashamedly one, and for those fortunate enough to live upon our bracing coastline.

Michael Montague

Michael Montague C.B.E.
Chairman, English Tourist Board

Preface

This book is for families who enjoy the seaside, but want to get a bit more from their outings than just a laze on the beach. It is not a guidebook. It's a book of ideas and suggestions for having a varied holiday on the coast — or just a day out by car or bus.

In it, I have taken about 30 different aspects of maritime England, and have described what I enjoyed in that particular field. I've visited only places that are open to the general public — nothing 'behind-scenes'.

In most cases I've deliberately explored lesser-known examples, and not the world-famous or most spectacular. The point is that, *wherever* you go round England's coast, there is bound to be something of interest to see. Sometimes, behind an oil refinery you will find a seabird reserve. Or, in the shadow of factory walls, a historic cobbled quayside and old warehouses that take you straight back to the 18th century. Perhaps no country in the world has such variety within so small an area; geology, scenery, wildlife, historical associations and leisure or workaday activities all change from county to county. That means there is a tremendous choice of what to see and what to do, from clifftop to cove, from harbour to headland.

Although this is not a guidebook, but simply intended to whet your appetite, I have listed at the end of each chapter a selection of sites where you are likely to get as much pleasure as I have done from exploring 'England-by-the-Sea'. But these lists are far from exhaustive, and on any coastal walk or drive down those little 'no through roads' marked in white on the edges of the map, who knows what you may find when you set out to make your own discoveries?

Elizabeth Gundrey

Elizabeth Gundrey

Making the most of Tourist Information Centres

Nearly all seaside towns have a Tourist Information Centre, usually near the sea-front. Each Centre is run by the local council and so they differ somewhat in what they offer: for instance, some give information about their own neighbourhood only, others cover a much wider area. Here is how to get the most out of them.

Before you make your visit
A telephone call will bring you whatever free booklets and maps are on offer. For more substantial guides, a charge will be made. Some Centres will book accommodation for you, and all can send you lists of hotels, guest houses etc. from which to make your own bookings.

If you want to time your visit (for example, to coincide with some local event of interest, the quietest time, the best weather or during a sports season) the Centre will be able to advise you. Most have programmes of forthcoming events which they can send and they can also tell you the best road and rail routes.

When you get there
You can pick up information, find accommodation or ask questions by calling at the Centre: their opening hours vary as do their seasons (some close in winter). Every Centre should have reference books — such as bus timetables — and many sell books and maps. Some operate the Book-A-Bed-Ahead service. This means that if you are travelling around they will get you booked into a hotel or guest house at the place where you next want to sleep along your route, provided that it, too, is in the scheme. Small charges are made for booking; and, particularly in high summer, the earlier you can ask for accommodation the better.

Quite a number of these Centres are housed in buildings of historic interest, and some have interesting exhibits, video shows and so on.

The list overleaf covers coastal Tourist Information Centres only.

Coastal Tourist Information Centres

S means open only in summer

CUMBRIA

Silloth	0965 31276
Maryport	090081 3738
Workington	0900 2122
Whitehaven	0946 5678
Egremont *S*	0946 820693
Ravenglass *S*	06577 278
Millom *S*	0657 2555
Barrow-in-Furness	0229 25795
Ulverston	0229 52299
Grange-over-Sands *S*	04484 4026

LANCASHIRE

Morecambe	0524 414110
Fleetwood	03917 71141
Thornton Cleveleys *S*	0253 853378
Blackpool	0253 21623
Lytham St Anne's *S*	0253 725610

MERSEYSIDE

Southport	0704 33133/40404
(and evenings/weekends 0704 33333)	
Liverpool	051 709 3631/8681
Birkenhead	051 652 6106/7/8
New Brighton *S*	051 638 7144

AVON

Bristol	0972 293891
Weston-super-Mare	0934 26838

SOMERSET

Burnham-on-Sea	0278 782377 ext 44
Minehead	0643 2624

DEVON (north)

Lynmouth	05985 2225
Ilfracombe	0271 63001
Woolacombe *S*	0271 870553
Bideford *S*	02372 77676

CORNWALL

Bude *S*	0288 4240
Wadebridge *S*	020881 3725
Newquay	06373 71345/7
St Ives	0736 796297
Isles of Scilly, St Mary's	0720 22536
Penzance	0736 2341
Falmouth	0326 312300
Fowey	072683 3320
Looe *S*	05036 2072

DEVON (south)

Plymouth	0752 23806
Salcombe	054884 2736
Kingsbridge *S*	0548 3195
Dartmouth	08043 2281
Brixham *S*	08045 2861
Paignton	0803 558383
Torquay	0803 27428

Teignmouth *S*	06267 6271 ext 207/258
Dawlish *S*	0626 863589
Exeter	0392 72434
Exmouth *S*	03952 3744
Budleigh Salterton *S*	03954 5275
Sidmouth *S*	03955 6441
Seaton *S*	0297 21660

DORSET

Lyme Regis	02974 2138
Bridport *S*	0308 24901
Weymouth	0305 785747
Swanage	09292 2885
Poole	02013 3322
Bournemouth	0202 291715
Christchurch *S*	0202 475555

HAMPSHIRE

Fareham	0329 285432
Southampton	0703 23855 ext 615
Beaulieu	0590 612345
Portsmouth	0705 26722/3/4

ISLE OF WIGHT

Yarmouth *S*	0983 760015
Ventnor *S*	0983 853625
Shanklin	0983 862942
Sandown	0983 403886
Ryde *S*	0983 62905

WEST SUSSEX

Chichester	0243 775888
Bognor *S*	0243 823140
Littlehampton *S*	09064 6133
Worthing	0903 39999

EAST SUSSEX

Hove	0273 775400
Brighton	0273 23755/26450
Peacehaven	07914 2668
Newhaven *S*	07912 7450
Seaford	0323 892224
Eastbourne	0232 27474
Bexhill	0424 212023
Hastings	0424 424242
Rye	07973 2293

KENT

Folkestone	0303 58594
Dover	0304 820650
Deal	03045 61161 ext 263 or 271
Ramsgate	0843 51086
Broadstairs	0843 68399
Margate	0843 20241/2
Herne Bay	02273 66031
Whitstable	0227 272233
Faversham	079582 4542
Sheerness	07956 5324
Rochester	0634 43666

ESSEX

Southend	0702 49451 ext 228
	0702 44091/49451 ext 556
Clacton	0255 25501 ext 180
Walton-on-the-Naze *S*	02556 5542
Harwich *S*	02555 6139

SUFFOLK

Ipswich	0473 58070
Felixstowe	03942 2122/2166
Lowestoft	0502 65989

NORFOLK

Great Yarmouth	0493 4313
Cromer *S*	0263 512497
Sheringham *S*	0263 824329
Hunstanton	04853 2610
King's Lynn	0553 61241

LINCOLNSHIRE

Boston *S*	0205 62354
Skegness *S*	0754 4821
Mablethorpe	05213 2496

HUMBERSIDE

Cleethorpes	0472 67472
Grimsby	0472 53123/4
Barton-upon-Humber	0652 32333
Goole	0405 2187
Hull	0482 223344
Withernsea	09642 2284
Hornsea *S*	04012 2919
Bridlington *S*	0262 73474/79626

NORTH YORKSHIRE

Filey *S*	0723 512204
Scarborough	0723 72261/73333
Whitby	0947 602674

CLEVELAND

Hartlepool	0429 68366

TYNE AND WEAR

South Shields *S*	0632 557411
Newcastle	0632 610691/615367
North Shields *S*	0632 579800
Whitley Bay *S*	0632 524494

NORTHUMBERLAND

Seahouses *S*	0665 720424
Berwick-upon-Tweed *S*	0289 7187

A directory of Tourist Information Centres for the whole of Britain is obtainable (free) from the English Tourist Board. 01–730 3400. For information about counties with a coastal area, phone the regional tourist boards:

Cumbria Tourist Board	09662 4444
North West Tourist Board	0204 591511
(Lancashire and Merseyside)	
West Country Tourist Board	0392 76351
(Avon, Somerset, Devon, Cornwall and west Dorset)	
Southern Tourist Board	0703 616027
(East Dorset, Hampshire, Isle of Wight)	
South-East England Tourist Board	
(Sussex and Kent)	0892 40766
London Tourist Board	01–730 0791
East Anglia Tourist Board	0473 214211
(Essex, Suffolk, Norfolk)	
East Midlands Tourist Board	0522 31521
(Lincolnshire)	
Yorkshire and Humberside Tourist Board	
	0904 707961
Northumbria Tourist Board	0632 817744
(Cleveland, Durham, Northumberland, Tyne and Wear)	

To help you obtain up-to-date details about opening hours and so on, telephone numbers are given in the text. Please refer to 'England-by-the-Sea' when you telephone. Alternatively, ask the nearest Tourist Information Centre. Every effort has been made to check information in the book, but organisations and their addresses or phone numbers, are constantly changing. The Tourist Information Centres should always have the most recent details.

I am grateful to many organisations named in the text for information each supplied about its own field of activity. In addition, I would like to thank the following for particularly valuable advice or help they gave me: British Ports Association, Cumbria Tourist Board, East Anglia Tourist Board, English Tourist Board, Isle of Wight Tourist Board, Marine Society, Nature Conservancy Council, Northumbria Tourist Board, North West Tourist Board, South East England Tourist Board, White Fish Authority, Yorkshire and Humberside Tourist Board and also the press officers of Brighton, Hull and Poole in particular.

These maps show the principal towns around the coasts of England, all of which have Tourist Information Centres. The telephone numbers of these Centres are listed on pages 8–9. From them you can obtain information about their town and its neighbouring coast.

In the text, wherever sites of interest have been listed, they are in geographical sequence following the coast round from the north-west to the south-west, and from the south-east up to the north-east. I have given telephone numbers of 'sights', from which to obtain information about opening hours, address and admission charge (if any); such information can usually be obtained also from the nearest Tourist Information Centre. In these lists, towns with a Tourist Information Centre, which are on these maps, are asterisked.

If you want information about a small coastal village that does not have a Tourist Information Centre of its own, refer to the Centre of the nearest town that does have one.

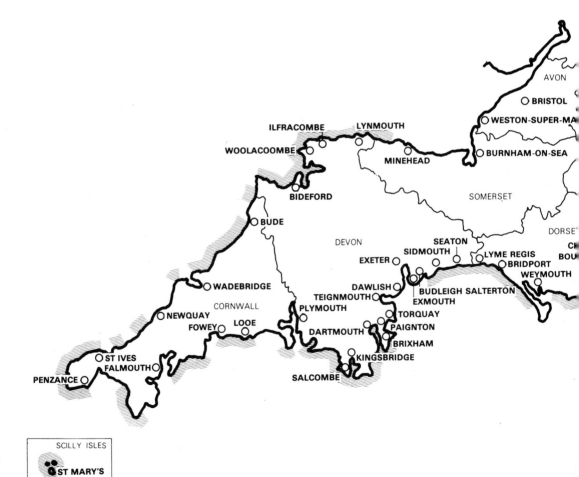

Southern Coasts of England

HUNSTANTON ○
SHERINGHAM ○
CROMER
○ KING'S LYNN
NORFOLK
GREAT YARMOUTH
LOWESTOFT ○
SUFFOLK
IPSWICH ○
○ FELIXSTOWE
HARWICH
○ WALTON-ON-THE-NAZE
ESSEX
CLACTON
SOUTHEND
WHITSTABLE
HERNE BAY
MARGATE
ROCHESTER ○
SHEERNESS
○ BROADSTAIRS
FAVERSHAM ○
RAMSGATE
KENT
DEAL ○
DOVER
FOLKESTONE ○
HAMPSHIRE
SOUTHAMPTON
BEAULIEU
WEST SUSSEX
EAST SUSSEX
HOVE
RYE ○
BRIGHTON
PORTSMOUTH
PEACEHAVEN
URCH
CHICHESTER
NEWHAVEN
UTH
FAREHAM ○
○ HASTINGS
E
BEXHILL
RYDE
WORTHING
SANDOWN
LITTLEHAMPTON
EASTBOURNE
YARMOUTH ○
BOGNOR
SHANKLIN
SWANAGE
VENTNOR
SEAFORD
ISLE OF WIGHT

○ Tourist Information Centres

Areas of outstanding natural beauty

County boundary

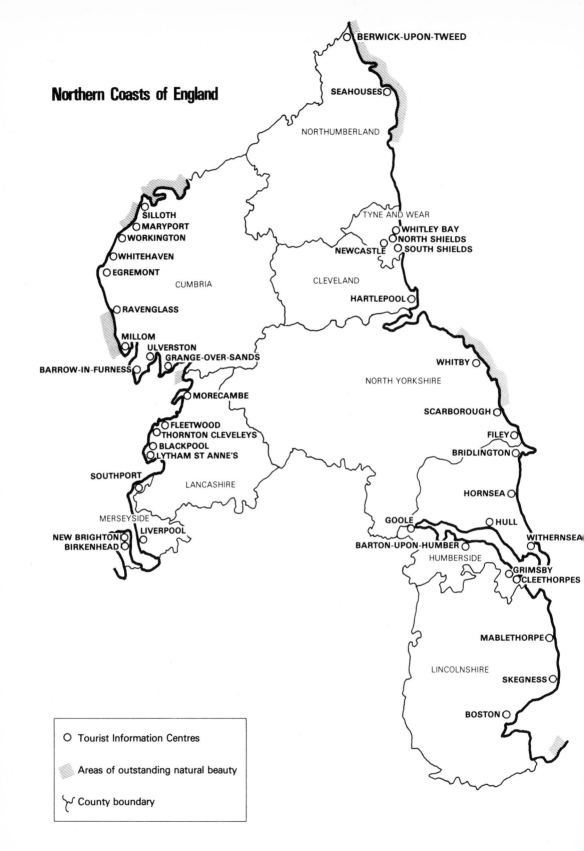

Northern Coasts of England

BERWICK-UPON-TWEED

SEAHOUSES

NORTHUMBERLAND

SILLOTH
MARYPORT
WORKINGTON
WHITEHAVEN
EGREMONT

CUMBRIA

RAVENGLASS

MILLOM
ULVERSTON
GRANGE-OVER-SANDS
BARROW-IN-FURNESS

MORECAMBE

FLEETWOOD
THORNTON CLEVELEYS
BLACKPOOL
LYTHAM ST ANNE'S

SOUTHPORT

LANCASHIRE

MERSEYSIDE

NEW BRIGHTON
BIRKENHEAD
LIVERPOOL

TYNE AND WEAR
WHITLEY BAY
NORTH SHIELDS
NEWCASTLE SOUTH SHIELDS

CLEVELAND

HARTLEPOOL

WHITBY

NORTH YORKSHIRE

SCARBOROUGH

FILEY
BRIDLINGTON

HORNSEA

GOOLE   HULL
WITHERNSEA
BARTON-UPON-HUMBER
HUMBERSIDE   GRIMSBY
CLEETHORPES

MABLETHORPE

LINCOLNSHIRE

SKEGNESS

BOSTON

O Tourist Information Centres

    Areas of outstanding natural beauty

    County boundary

Our maritime heritage

1 Roman forts: invaders and invaded

The centuries that the Romans spent in Britain were equivalent to the span of history from the Middle Ages up to today. At the start of their story, they were invaders and attackers, holding down a rebellious native population. But towards the end it was they who were the defenders, threatened by Saxons crossing from the continent. And when finally they left the British to fend for themselves, aid was sought from Rome in an appeal vividly called 'The Groans of the Britons'. But in vain: the Saxons had come to stay.

So Roman remains around the coasts of England differ greatly in their age and therefore in their purpose. The earliest forts were built to house the invading armies, and from them the occupation of the country was carried out. Inside each fort were stored supplies – not just those needed by the occupying forces but often vast hoards of produce wrested from the natives for export to Rome or other parts of its empire.

Quite different are the much later coastal defences known as the Saxon shore forts: these were built by the Romans to protect the island from invasion by sea-borne barbarians from what we now know as Germany.

I visited Arbeia at South Shields (Tyne and Wear), one of the earliest Roman forts. There could hardly be a greater contrast between 'then' and 'now', for these vast remains are found unexpectedly in the middle of modern housing by the seashore, and a road runs right through the middle.

The size of the fort is fantastic – in it were no fewer than 22 granaries. Archaeologists believe that the hundreds of soldiers along the 120 km of Hadrian's Wall, which ends not far away, and the needs of the army that abortively invaded Scotland in the third century, may have accounted for the need to house such huge quantities of food.

Even now the site is not fully excavated because outside the fort walls a civilian settlement grew up, some of it still under the homes of today. Here British and foreign traders would have lived and there is a temple waiting to be uncovered.

The fort was ideally placed to protect the Tyne estuary, along which ships could bring in more legionaries or take grain back. It began as a typical Roman fort housing only 500 men, but was extended and altered as the years went by to accommodate more and more men and granaries – the ruins one sees are mostly the remains of buildings put up around 300 AD. Later some granaries were converted into living quarters for boatmen brought from what is now Iran (an old record of their origin has survived). The Romans recruited from all parts of their vast empire and may have decided that boatmen accustomed to the shoals of the River Tigris were just what was needed to ferry supplies up-river to the garrisons on Hadrian's Wall. There must have been a Roman port down by the sea but no traces are to be seen now.

I wondered whether any intellectual officer ever murmured to himself as he looked out at the bleak winter waters of the North Sea the words of the Sicilian poet who, around 300 BC, wrote:

> . . . when the roar
> Of Ocean's grey abyss resounds, and foam
> Gathers upon the sea, and vast waves burst,
> I turn from the drear aspect to home . . .

The fort's museum is, like many others run by the county council, extremely good. Unlike some dusty collections of broken pots and rusted iron fragments, this one makes you feel what it was like to have lived in Arbeia all those centuries ago. The fort springs to life when you look at it reconstructed in a model complete with tiny model soldiers; and at the vivid painting of Roman ships with swans carved at their prows arriving at the quay serving the fort. Trivia of day-to-day life have been found during excavations and are now well displayed: enamelled clothes-fasteners, gaming counters, cosmetic pots, iron keys, brooches with dragons and rings with intaglio gems. Life does not seem to have been particularly hard for those in the fort — in fact, it is known that the life-span of the legionaries was much longer than that of the native population.

Recently a new wing has been opened at the museum, with its chief treasures dramatically spotlighted: tombstones carved so delicately that they might be of wood rather than of sandstone. One shows Victor, an Arab, banqueting in a leafy paradise: he reclines on a couch while a wine flagon is offered to him. Victor was a slave who had been freed by his master, a Roman cavalry officer. Another memorial is to Regina, shown sitting in a wicker chair with her jewel box and sewing basket. Regina, a former slave from what is now Hertfordshire, had done well for herself by marrying her master, a Syrian in the service of the Roman empire. There is even a stone monument commemorating the laying-on of piped water to the fort in 222 AD.

Down at your feet is an open grave (under glass), complete with gruesome skeleton lying just as it was found. The Romans accorded death much solemn ceremony; and elsewhere in the museum burial customs have been reconstructed, an urn of ashes is shown in its special lined pit and a Roman funeral is recreated in a painting.

You can see what the Romans ate from a display of excavated shells from winkles, limpets and oysters — clearly the Tyne estuary was cleaner in those days — to stuffed mice and the game that they hunted in nearby woods; boar, bears and wolves. Their weapons are there too, including a particularly fine sword with an inlaid figure of the war-god Mars.

All this was from the heyday of the Roman occupation. Later I was to visit a shore fort where the story was very different when the Romans were on the defensive, soon to abandon England altogether.

Where to see Roman coastal forts

In addition to **South Shields** (Tyne and Wear), **Richborough** (Kent) is well worth visiting: it is one of the earliest Roman ruins in Britain — you can even see the ditches dug around a wooden palisade in the first invasion in 43 AD. This huge, spectacular ruin (with museum), is now inland but was once the principal port in Roman Britain. **Caister-on-Sea** (Norfolk) was also a Roman trading-port; here too the sea has receded. Among other remains of the Roman town and defences are the walls of a seamen's hostel.

There are fewer Roman sites on the west coast: a fort at **Ravenglass** (Cumbria) where bath-house walls still stand over 4 m high; and rather meagre remains at **Maryport** (Cumbria) which had a fort to guard the western end of Hadrian's Wall.

Saxon shore forts are quite numerous, all on the south or east coasts, between the Solent and the Wash. **Portchester** (Hampshire) has Norman additions. **Fishbourne** (West Sussex) was a naval base that later became a magnificent palace, now beautifully displayed, with museum. At **Pevensey** (East Sussex) a mediaeval castle stands within the remains of a Roman fort captured by the Saxons. Once the sea lapped its walls but it is far off now. **Lympne**

(Kent) has overgrown but impressive remains of a fort at Stutfall Castle, again now inland. The shore fort at **Dover*** (Kent) is mostly under a road now but the celebrated 'painted house' (probably that of the admiral in charge of the Roman port) can be seen: it has more surviving murals than any other Roman building in Britain. Up on the hill, within Dover Castle, are 14 m of the octagonal lighthouse the Romans built, using a fire beacon to guide ships through the Channel at night. At **Reculver** (Kent) the sea is constantly eroding and part of the fort (an early one, re-fortified against the Saxons) has been washed away; within the remains an ancient church still stands. At **Bradwell** (Essex) the sea has consumed part of the fort, leaving a remote and picturesque ruin on a promontory. Another Roman site in Essex worth visiting is **Mersea Island**, connected by a causeway, where you can walk right inside a great Roman burial mound. Burgh Castle near **Norwich** (Norfolk) now inland, is also imposing. At **Brancaster** on the Wash (Norfolk) a fort is still under excavation.

Further reading
'Roman Fortifications on the Saxon Shore' (Stationery Office booklet) and 'Roman Remains in Britain' by R. Wilson (Constable). Free leaflets include the 'Saxon Shore Forts Trail' available from Tourist Information Centres.

2 Castles of the Middle Ages

The Saxons left few traces (for often they built in wood). It was only after the Norman invasion that the building of great, stone castles began to spread — hundreds of them. A chronicler wrote: 'They filled the land full of castles'. These were not just forts with garrisons, Roman-style, but the residences of great lords who were licensed by the king to erect such strongholds as bases from which to keep the native population subdued, and most of them were inland. As they were lived in, they contained — usually within the keep (tower) that stood on a motte (mound) within the bailey (grounds surrounded by battlemented walls) — such amenities as kitchens, a well, chapel and garderobes (shafts used as toilets). The fighting men, their horses and, in time of siege, cattle, would be accommodated in huts in the bailey.

One lord might own several castles and estates, moving with his retinue from one to another — probably over some distance, because the king would not permit too great a build-up of power by one lord in one place.

The thick stone walls were intended to withstand sieges which might involve bombardment by stones hurled from machines not unlike huge catapults, or undermining (a moat would help to prevent this) and also scaling by ladders or battering with rams. The main gate, being the weakest point, was usually well fortified and, in later periods, further protected by approach works known as a barbican.

When a siege was successful it was usually because those in the castle were starved into surrendering. So postern gates (small exits at the back) were often added in order that fighting men could get out of the castle to attack the besiegers and so that supplies might perhaps be brought in.

The Norman kings were succeeded in 1154 by the Plantagenets from Anjou, the first being that great king Henry II, who also ruled from Normandy down to the Pyrenees. A fresh wave of castle-building took place during his long reign. Castles continued to develop for another 200 years, becoming increasingly sophisticated. For example, walls were now regularly defended with bastions, projecting towers from which arrows could be fired not only outwards but also towards any enemy soldiers engaged upon scaling or battering the walls. Superb castles were built in Wales by Edward I in the 13th century but in the 14th century, cannon started to be used and castle-building diminished.

The castles of the Norman period were needed both to combat internal strife and for coastal defence; later on, they were used in repelling the incessant raids by the Scots in the north of England. Few had to resist a sea-borne attack; only Dover suffered a long siege.

Threats from across the sea rarely materialised (except for trouble in 1216) until the Hundred Years War (1338–1453), which began because Edward III asserted a claim to the French throne. When visiting old towns on the south or east coasts, one regularly comes across references to churches or other buildings having been burnt or otherwise destroyed in raids by the French during the latter part of this war. Coastal towns' fortifications often date from this time, and the Cinque Ports, with their pre-Navy defensive role, rose to eminence because of the Hundred Years War. Coastal castles, with a few exceptions, did not, however, greatly figure in these events, though Dover had earlier been besieged unsuccessfully by the French while King John was warring with his barons.

Of all the coastal castles, Bamburgh (Northumberland) most vividly evokes the history of mediaeval times. As I turned a bend in the road and it sprang into view, Bamburgh Castle looked almost fictitious. It is so spectacularly sited, perched on a huge rocky outcrop jutting into the sea, a great pile of bastions and towers with battlements and loopholes, that it looks as if it has been designed as the backdrop for a Verdi opera: particularly when floodlit at night or if seen silhouetted against a glowing dawn sky. No wonder the Saxon kings north of the Tyne had previously chosen this place for their capital, and no wonder that legends of King Arthur have attached themselves to it. If he did not hold court here, he certainly should have done! A little gold Anglo-Saxon plaque with a typical writhing beastie is one of the few fragments which have been found from these times — no buildings have survived.

The Normans' mighty keep was soon put to the test by marauding Scots but they found it impregnable. Half-a-dozen kings of England stayed in it; famous prisoners were confined here (Piers Gaveston and David Bruce of Scotland, for instance); Hotspur was once its commander; and here de Baliol submitted Scotland to the English throne. The redoubtable Margaret, wife of Henry VI, held the castle in 1461 against his usurper Edward Duke of York (later Edward IV) but eventually had to flee to France. It was the first castle ever to be successfully attacked by cannon.

In later centuries Bamburgh was neglected and might have become a ruin, had not restoration started in the late 18th century when a variety of buildings, quite out of keeping, were added to it: many were put up for charitable purposes — to educate, feed or nurse the poor. The castle became a military HQ during the Napoleonic scare, and yet again in the Second World War; but it is now — although open to the public — lived in once more, just as it was in the Middle Ages. Not only does the owner, Lord Armstrong, have a home there but a number of the 18th-century buildings have been turned into flats.

The castle is no hollow shell. It is filled with antiques and paintings — many dating from the 18th century when it got its new lease of life. Rather closer to the spirit of its historic past is the collection of armour (much of it lent by the Tower of London), and visitors are equally fascinated by the scale model of the castle on its rocky outcrop, which was carved from wood in the 18th century. But the interior, though very impressive, is more like that of a stately home than of a great mediaeval fortress.

So it was only when I wandered out to the ramparts again — where cannon point out to sea — that I could imagine myself back in the Middle Ages, as I leant on those ancient walls looking out across the sea to Holy Island and to the Farne Isles where seals and seabirds live, or inland to the Cheviot Hills. It was a place of idyllic beauty on that sunny day, but the rocks 50 m below, pieces of old life-saving equipment exhibited inside the castle, and the recollection of Bamburgh's heroine Grace Darling (see Chapter 28) were reminders enough that the Scots have not been the only threat to this wild coast. Yet for the best part of a thousand years Bamburgh Castle has defied man and the elements alike, and its red sandstone walls look equal to withstanding as many centuries again.

Other castles open to the public

The principal Norman castles around the coast of England are listed below. All are in the care of the Department of the Environment, 01-734 6010, except for Hastings. Many are on the sites of Saxon, Roman or even Iron Age forts.

Tintagel near **Boscastle** (Cornwall) Much eroded.
Portchester (Hampshire) Contains Norman church.
Pevensey (East Sussex)
Hastings (East Sussex) Ruins only.
Dover (Kent) The most spectacular: keep dates from Henry II, outer walls were built after abortive French raid of 1216, and, like some others, it was still a military stronghold in Second World War.
Rochester (Kent) Huge keep.
Skipsea near **Bridlington** (Humberside)

Castles dating from the time of Henry II
Orford (Suffolk) Huge polygonal keep.
Scarborough (North Yorkshire) Ruins only.

Later castles
Dartmouth (Devon) 15th-century fort guarding the approach to what was then one of England's leading ports. It was built for cannon to fire at water-level. Kingswear Castle (private) is on the bank opposite.
Hadleigh (Essex)
Tynemouth (Tyne and Wear) 14th-century ruins.
Dunstanburgh (Northumberland) Dramatic ruin of late 13th-century castle destroyed in the Wars of the Roses.

This list is not exhaustive. There are more castles on estuaries or a little way inland, such as **Christchurch** (Dorset), **Colchester** (Essex), **Caister-on-Sea** (Norfolk), **Newcastle** (Tyne and Wear) and **Warkworth** (Northumberland) and smaller fortifications on a variety of headlands, waterfronts and islands.

Further reading
A good book on the subject is 'The Observer's Book of Castles' (Warne).

3 Tudor and Stuart defences

Mediaeval castles were designed for defence as much as attack, and to house small communities during a siege. Therefore they were often sited on headlands, difficult for an enemy to approach.

Tudor castles (so-called — they were really forts) are very different. By the 16th century, the range and accuracy of cannon had vastly improved. Henry VIII was quick to grasp the idea of siting forts designed to accommodate a huge array of such cannon, right down on the waterfront and at strategic points where the enemy (France, again) might be expected to fire on ships in a harbour or to invade via an estuary. He appointed commissioners to advise on such sites, and himself took an active part in the design of these novel forts, which were all built around 1540.

They were totally different in appearance from the old castles: very squat and compact, with curved bastions all the way round — often two tiers of these — on each of which cannon were mounted. The very thick, rounded walls had rounded parapets too as curved surfaces were considered harder to damage than flat ones with square corners. As well as the cannon on top of each bastion, there were other guns below, housed inside and firing through big embrasures, some right down at water level. The interiors of these forts are dark and cramped (no baronial halls, or pomp and ceremony here). Officers would live on the upper floor, a dozen or two men and often the kitchens were on the ground floor and a cellar was provided for storage.

Just in case the enemy succeeded in landing despite all this concentrated gunpower the circular forts were as heavily defended at the rear too, with a moat and drawbridge. When you enter one, you can see that there are also small posts for hand-guns within the fort so that, as a last resort, any intruder could be shot at close range.

The commissioners recommended sites for these forts from Portland in Dorset to Sandown in Kent. In the west country, Dartmouth was already protected by a waterside fort, listed in the previous chapter; but later Henry put up castles on each side of the Fal estuary (Cornwall), at Pendennis and St Mawes, to protect Falmouth; Plymouth (Devon) did not get its citadel until the time of Charles II.

By the time he built Southsea Castle in 1544, the last of these defences, opinions on design had somewhat altered. Triangular instead of the stronger circular bastions were used, possibly because the forts now ran less risk of bombardment as their big guns put them beyond the range of the smaller guns carried by ships. The next development was to be the use of great banks of earth merely lined with brick or stone in place of thick stone walls. One can still see these at, for instance, Berwick-upon-Tweed in Northumberland, built by Elizabeth I; and at two forts dating from the time of Charles II: Plymouth Citadel (Devon) and the much more impressive Tilbury Fort (Essex), replacing earlier defences. The elaborate shape was contrived so that each bastion could provide covering fire for the next if it were attacked at close quarters. The rear of Tilbury Fort is additionally protected by a very wide moat. In 1868, it was re-fortified by General Gordon and early in the Second World War was used as the control centre for all the anti-aircraft defences of the Thames and Medway.

The mere presence of these forts was enough to keep the French away — but not the Dutch. The only Tudor fort that ever had to fire a shot in anger was one that Elizabeth I had ordered to be built in the first year of her reign: Upnor Castle. This fort, different in design from Henry's (and not so well known to tourists), is on the Medway estuary, placed there to guard the approach to Chatham dockyard and the Queen's ships. The French never in fact came near it; but a century later, in the course of the trade wars with the Dutch, the English suffered an ignominious defeat in the Medway, despite spirited defence from the castle's guns.

As I walked in the castle grounds, where some of those 17th-century cannon stand on the grassy banks, the view across the water was very different from those days, for now one looks at today's great, grey warships moored in Chatham Dockyard while being serviced or re-fitted. Along the river pass cargo ships heading for Rochester, small boats from the nearby yacht clubs, occasionally a great sailing-barge or the 'Arethusa', the ketch that provides sailing holidays for youngsters. But when the Dutch came sailing in on their notorious raid in 1667, the upper reaches of the Medway were filled with the best of Charles II's fleet: proud ships with great, carved superstructures, brilliantly painted.

Despite appearances, however, the ships were not good for much — they lay unarmed and many of their crew, unpaid for years, had deserted. Although a chain was stretched across the estuary, the Dutch got through, set fire to the fleet and towed off the best ship of all, the gilded 'Royal Charles'. They then made the mistake of waiting for the tide to turn again before pressing on further, which gave time for more arms and men to be rushed to the castle. The increased gunfire was too much, and they had to withdraw, but enough damage had been done to force England to sign a peace treaty favourable to the Dutch. The diarist, John Evelyn, wrote of the raid: 'A dreadfull Spectacle as ever any Englishman saw, and a dishonour never to be wiped off'. It was only after this that Charles II was moved to build the great fort at Tilbury, lest worse should befall in the Thames.

In the following centuries the castle became a naval ammunition store with sentries from the Royal Ordnance Corps. A nearby wall still bears a painted warning to ships not to anchor too close. As I walked inside the castle I noticed the absence of any ironwork. Lest a spark might accidentally be struck off metal, floors were made of loose wood blocks without nails, and the staircase handrail is encased in lead. Windows have heavy shutters, for closing during thunderstorms. The great posts added to give the upper floor extra support were needed because of the weight of gunpowder barrels up there. Now there is nothing weightier than a pictorial display on the subject of the Dutch wars.

Tudor and Stuart defences

Except for Southsea, these are in the care of the Department of the Environment, 01–734 6010.
CORNWALL
Pendennis Castle, Falmouth*
St Mawes Castle
St Catherine's Castle, Fowey* In ruins.

DEVON
Plymouth Citadel*
Bayard's Cove Castle, Dartmouth*

DORSET
Portland Castle

HAMPSHIRE
Hurst Castle Much altered in the 19th century.
Southsea Castle 0705 24584

ISLE OF WIGHT
Yarmouth Castle*

KENT
Walmer Castle
Deal Castle*
Upnor Castle

ESSEX
Tilbury Fort

NORTHUMBERLAND
Berwick-upon-Tweed* Town walls.

Some other Tudor forts were later modernised. For example, **Star Castle, St Mary's*** (Scilly Isles) is a hotel; **Lindisfarne, Holy Island** (Northumberland), converted by Lutyens into a house, belongs to the National Trust and is open to the public.

4 19th-century fortifications

The French Revolution sent shudders of alarm through neighbouring countries, but worse was to come when Napoleon and his armies began to storm through Europe. Fear of invasion led to a fresh crop of British coastal defences: the string of Martello towers dotting the south and east shores, the military canal that runs like a moat from Hythe across the Romney Marshes, the 'Great Lines' on the hill above the naval dockyard at Chatham, and so on. A number of these are accessible to the public, and some have interesting museums (see list at end of chapter).

Even after Napoleon's defeat at Waterloo in 1815, the English continued to view France very warily. When, in 1851, Louis Napoleon (nephew of Napoleon Bonaparte) seized power from the Republic in a coup d'état and had himself crowned emperor, there was considerable alarm. Another despot intent on military aggrandisement was an uncomfortable neighbour to have. Palmerston took swift action: many of the Napoleonic defences were to be re-fortified, and fresh ones built: these included not only land forts guarding strategic waterways, but also a number actually *in* the sea — some are mentioned in Chapter 30. It was later said that Palmerston panicked unnecessarily, for France never attacked after all: but possibly the preparedness of England was deterrent enough. The French started constructing their first ironclad battleships during this decade and building up their naval bases: there were good reasons for disquiet. During this period gun range doubled, and devastating explosive shells superseded solid cannon balls, rendering old-style forts vulnerable. And some of Palmerston's 'follies' were to prove very useful in the two World Wars of the 20th century: for example, the Needles Fort on the Isle of Wight.

I walked along the narrow headland, 130 m above the sea, that leads to the westernmost tip of the Isle, a thin finger of wilderness that ends in a sheer drop and then the white chalk 'Needles' themselves: tall, sharp and jagged, three of the most famous rocks around the coast of England. This is a glorious spot to visit even without the attraction of its historic fort. The grass was dotted with clumps of sea pinks, yellow vetch and sea holly; and butterflies were on the wing. There were superb views of the Solent, calm and blue as the sky above it and broken only by the white sails of small boats. The Hampshire mainland was clearly visible, with Hurst Castle dating from Tudor times on its long spit facing Fort Albert (now flats) on the Isle: sentinels guarding the way in to Southampton and Portsmouth.

The south coast is dotted with Martello towers such as the ones at Hythe (Kent) which were built as defences against Napoleon. Some are now museums.

This exceptionally beautiful headland and the fort on it now belong to the National Trust. When I visited the area, the fort's restoration was well advanced. Much of the hard slog had been done by volunteers — 500 of them, giving a total of 3,000 hours of work.

The fort is typical of many others of its period, with underground tunnels and walls reinforced with banks of earth unlikely to be penetrated by gunfire. To reach it I walked across a wood bridge over a moat (once there was a retractable drawbridge — it would roll back, not rise up) and went into what had been one of the magazines, now equipped as a small museum. High in the wall is a lamp-window: here, behind a thick, sealed pane of glass was placed the oil-lamp that used to illuminate the room in the days when explosives were stored there. There is a lamp-passage (open to visitors) which winds about behind the walls of these rooms, from which the oil-lamps could be filled and lit in safety.

Beyond lie the gun emplacements, known as barbettes. When old cannon were superseded, they were simply thrown into the sea below. The old gun-rails on which they were swivelled into position for action are still there, and guns will be replaced on them when retrieved from the sea. The 12-tonne guns were originally hauled by horses, which dragged them 10 km along rough, uphill tracks: one old man remembered being told by his father how the maidservants in a big house along the way had hung out of the windows, cheering them as they sweated past.

Towards the end of the century, however, there was developed a defence more potent than the guns (which had never fired a shot in anger): the search-light. This was mounted in a cliffside emplacement on the very tip of the head-land, from which position its beam could sweep out to sea or scan the entrance to the Solent. The light was originally powered by a generator that depended upon coal being shovelled into a boiler by stokers working underground: not an enviable task. Visitors can reach the emplacement by clambering down a shaft (a spiral staircase has been put in) and walking along a dim-lit zigzag tunnel — suddenly emerging onto the sunny emplacement, for an unequalled view of the Needles and the lighthouse just beyond them. The searchlight is no longer there, of course.

In years to come, as the restoration progresses, there will be even more to see, for in other subterranean passages and rooms are the old boiler, a lift, engines, and underground emplacements for guns sited to fire at water-level. The museum tells the story of the fort from its beginnings up to its use in the First World War (the very first anti-aircraft gun was sited here), in the Second (when German torpedo-boats were fired on), and even later (in the 1950s, 'Black Knight' space-rocket tests were carried out on this headland).

Within the grounds of the fort is a small coastguard station, flying its blue ensign, and when I walked up the ramp that leads to a viewing-point on top of the fort, I could see in and watch the coastguards at their work — ceaselessly and systematically scanning the sea through a telescope. On such a calm and sunny day, their activity seemed almost unnecessarily conscientious but I was told that two people with a small sailing-boat had drowned only a week before. In winter, force 10 gales are not uncommon here and, up in the fort, can some-times suck as well as blow a walker.

From this vantage-point, I could also see, across the fort's moat, where cliffs were already cracking and would ultimately crash into the sea. Iron tie-bars (some already snapped) span these cracks, put there by government surveyors who come annually to check how much the gaps have widened. Here the gulls perch, and in nesting time are apt to 'dive-bomb' any passer-by who is seen as an intruder.

Of all the 19th-century coastal defences there is none more dramatically sited than the Needles Fort, perched high above the sea and far from the holiday throng; where the menace of war seems only a distant echo now, but where sea and weather are still, at times, savage enemies.

(For opening hours etc, phone 0983 526445. It is possible that a minibus will later be provided for those who do not want to walk the one-and-a-half km.)

The traces left by the two World Wars of the 20th century are slight. Some of the historic forts already described still show evidence of their re-use in modern times; and around the coast are occasional remains of defences — gun-posts crumbling into the sea at Grain (Kent) or tank-traps still on the beach near Seahouses (Northumberland), for example. In a chine (ravine) at Shanklin (Isle of Wight) is a section of the 'Pluto' pipeline that carried fuel underwater for the D-day invasion of Normandy. There are a number of memorials to this epic occasion — a column at Weymouth (Dorset) commemorating the American troops who embarked here, and others at Southsea (Hampshire) and Slapton (Devon), for example. The D-Day embroidery is on show at Southampton (Hampshire). The gate of No 4 dock at Southampton has a plaque commemorating earlier embarkations of the First World War and there is a Road of Remembrance, appropriately planted with rosemary, at Folkestone — the road along which so many marched to embark from the Kent coast. Local churches have other memorials (see Chapter 10). Local museums sometimes have exhibits: the Wishtower Museum (Eastbourne, East Sussex) is good on the anti-invasion precautions and the air raids that affected coastal populations.

19th-century fortifications

Napoleonic
Many squat Martello towers, looking like upturned buckets, can be seen around south-east coasts, some converted into houses. There were originally 74 in Sussex and Kent, built between 1805 and 1808. Later, 29 more were built in Essex. They copied the design of a fort at Mortella (Corsica) which had proved immune to bombardment. The following are, or soon will be, open to the public. Most contain museum exhibits.

Seaford* (East Sussex) 0323 892915
Eastbourne* (East Sussex) As well as a tower, a large redoubt (depot-fort). 0323 35809 and 33952
Dymchurch (Kent) 0892 24376
Harwich* (Essex) 02555 3429

The Military Canal designed by Rennie as a defensive moat across the Romney Marshes in 1804 is most accessible at **Hythe** (Kent).

The Grand Shaft at **Dover*** (Kent) is a triple staircase down through the cliffs to the harbour, built for the use of the 5,000 troops camped on the Western Heights when Napoleon was amassing 130,000 troops and 2,000 landing-craft at Boulogne. 0304 201066

Fort Cumberland, built shortly before the Napoleonic era east of **Southsea** (Hampshire), is to be opened in due course. 0705 811527 There are late 18th-century fortifications at **Berry Head** near **Brixham*** (south Devon).

Mid-Victorian
The only accessible fort in the north is an early one: Fort Perch at **New Brighton*** (Merseyside), built in the 1820s. It houses a museum of wrecked aircraft from the Second World War. 051630 2707

The harbour at **Portsmouth*** (Hampshire) was ringed with defences of which Fort Brockhurst (with audio-visual show) and Fort Widley (guided tours) are now open to the public, 0705 811527; others can be seen from the outside only. On the Isle of Wight there are, in addition to the Needles Fort described in the text: Fort Victoria, near **Yarmouth**,* in a country park, 0983 524031 ext 162, and the remains of batteries in Puckpool Park, **Ryde**.* The fort at **Sandown*** is now part of a zoo; the fort at **Bembridge** will be opened later. Out in the Solent can be seen a number of round concrete-and-steel forts, now deserted.

In East Sussex, the fort at **Newhaven*** is being restored for opening.

To guard the dockyard at **Chatham** (Kent), the Medway estuary had a great many forts and other defences: the Great Lines are mentioned in Chapter 29. Some are crumbling away but can be reached by footpaths; some have been converted to other uses or are being restored. Fort Amherst, above **Chatham**, may later be opened. Grain Tower, in the estuary, can be seen from the shore. The Tourist Information Centre at **Rochester*** has a small booklet describing them all.

The Thames estuary too was guarded by forts. The one at **Gravesend** (Kent) has been destroyed; on the opposite (Essex) bank there is not only Tilbury Fort but also Coalhouse Fort (in a public garden). Shornemead Fort near **Gravesend**, is accessible by footpath, as is Cliffe Fort.

At **Felixstowe*** (Suffolk) the Landguard Fort is being restored for opening.

Anyone keen on exploring old forts can join the Fortress Study Group which has a magazine and other publications, and which organises visits to forts not yet open to the general public. 0734 251954

Further reading
The most comprehensive book on the subject is 'Coast Defences of England and Wales' by I. V. Hogg (David & Charles), but each area has its own book or booklet on sale locally.

5 Historic buildings: palatial and workaday

Coastal towns and villages often have the same kind of ancient buildings as their inland counterparts — the old guildhalls and buttermarkets, almshouses and merchants' homes. But many have buildings of specific maritime interest too. Some of these are monuments to past grandeur, and some once served a humble purpose. They are as varied as fishermen's or coastguards' cottages, the Prince Regent's oriental pavilion at Brighton and the great tower at Blackpool — a people's palace. A large number are the workplaces of the past: quayside buildings, tide mills, warehouses, rope-walks, old Custom Houses, sail-lofts and net-sheds, fish-cellars and lookout towers.

Sometimes it is the very simplest relics from the past that are of greatest interest, because their chances of survival are so slight. It was, for example, almost luck that saved from dereliction an old barge-building yard at Sittingbourne (Kent) on a creek from which at least 500 sailing-barges had been launched since the early 1800s.

Dolphin Yard — perhaps the most complete and unaltered shipyard of its kind — is far down a winding and pot-holed track between muddy inlets half-choked with reeds. Half-a-dozen privately owned sailing-barges are moored in the creek alongside it while their owners work on repairs. For Dolphin Yard is no mere museum: since it was given a new lease of life, it has provided the resources needed for repairing old sailing-barges which are now being carefully conserved (see Chapter 6). The scene is one of 'mud, mud, glorious mud', a litter of timber and tools, and a hum of activity.

A triumph for volunteer conservationists, the old sail-loft at Milton Creek (Kent) is again in use and open to the public.

In its heyday, the yard built barges primarily for the cement trade. They sailed down the creek and along the Swale channel to get out into the Medway estuary. The focal point of the yard was – and still is – the large weather-boarded building with a carpenter's shop on the ground floor and a sail-loft above, together with a nearby forge.

These buildings had ended their working-days and were slowly rotting away when they were discovered by some sailing-barge enthusiasts, who set about the massive task of restoring them to working order. I looked at photographs of the way they were in 1969: the roofs half-gone and elder trees sprouting from the débris in the sail-loft. It is difficult to credit that the present shipshape building was resuscitated by the endeavours of a small handful of amateurs (with only the heaviest parts of the work delegated to contractors, also volunteers). The creek had to be dredged to give the barges passage once more – and in the course of this all kinds of old tools and other finds came up out of the mud, which have been refurbished. They are now on show in the building, along with an ever-increasing number of other exhibits which local people have found in their attics or at the backs of cupboards.

The volunteers' efforts were recognised when they won second prize in one of the BBC's annual 'Chronicle' awards for industrial archaeology. Since then, still further progress has been made and there have been more acquisitions. When I called, Peter Reeves was busy re-rigging a huge old model of the sailing-barge 'Veronica' that had just been presented: a very different activity from his weekday job as an electrical fitter working on nuclear submarines.

Around him in the carpenter's shop were all the traditional shipwright's tools used for barge-making, which had survived inside the decaying building: huge augers to bore huge timbers, a great hand-morticing machine and a foot-operated lathe, for example. Old masts and other timbers from ships had been used in building the big shed, in one corner of which was sited a securely locked nail-store: nails were valuable at the turn of the century, and easily pilfered. Everything smelled slightly of tar. Amongst all the dark wood and iron, only a few exhibits provided a dash of colour – particularly, the painted decorations of the bow badges and name boards that are the sole relics from some long-departed barges.

Up in the sail-loft, Peter showed me how the huge sails are made (one can watch this), using strange tools. Fids are wood tools for making holes, cringles are the holes, and thimbles are eyelet rings. A nauseous red concoction (cod oil, horse fat and red ochre) is used to proof the canvas.

Outside, beyond the barges (some of which can be visited on various 'open days' which the Yard holds each year) are the original steam-chest boiler and forge.

The red-and-black boiler, despite its Heath Robinson look and the crazy angle of its tall tin chimney, is still doing a vital job. It connects with a long box, inside which timbers are steamed. Stand well clear when the moment for their removal comes as helpers lift out the steaming-hot wood and rush to clamp it in position to complete a repair to the hull of a barge.

The forge, on the other hand, has been to a large extent superseded by modern welding techniques. But it is a building well worth visiting even though the huge leather bellows are now still and no fire burns in the hearth. When barges went over to wheels for steering a century ago the great old tillers were discarded. Ten of them – decoratively carved and painted – were used as up-rights in the construction of the shed that houses the forge.

There's much more to Dolphin Yard and Milton Creek than this. The trustees of the Yard have a concern for the wildlife of this small green patch within an area of light industry. They have produced a trail so that walkers can explore the creek and discover its lost wharves, slipways and barge hulks; have planted trees; and are planning a museum on the history of the old brick and cement industries that used to be an integral part of the estuary, which supplied mud for similar purposes right back to Roman times.

Visitors will almost always find owners working on their barges and very ready to talk about them. If you get really interested, you can join the Friends of the Dolphin Trust — membership brings invitations to barge races, barn-dances and suchlike — and if you want to get more involved and start working on the buildings or boats yourself, you will be given a very warm welcome indeed (in fact, volunteer workers are wanted by virtually any of the conservation bodies mentioned in this book). For details of opening hours and events phone 0734 585644 — evenings.

From work to leisure . . . from the humble to the resplendent . . . from the unknown to the world-famous . . . there could be no greater difference than the contrast between the Dolphin boatyard on an obscure creek and the people's palace overlooking a vast beach, the resort of some 16 million people a year: Blackpool Tower. All the two have in common is that they started at about the same time.

1891 saw the laying of the Tower's foundation stone. It took three years to build — a half-size copy of the Eiffel Tower built in 1889. People were singing 'Ta-Ra-Ra-Boom-De-Ay' at the music halls; they were reading the first Sherlock Holmes stories, the first picture newspapers and Kipling's 'Barrack-room Ballads'; and the Labour Party was being formed: the age of the common man had arrived, and the Tower was his symbol.

Over 160 m high, the Tower can be seen 80 km away. But, unlike the Eiffel Tower, this one is not just a landmark: between its four legs, which thrust deep into the ground, is a vast layer-cake of entertainment: amusement arcade and aquarium, bars and bird-garden, cafés and cabaret — but one could go on through a whole alphabet of popular pleasures. A single ticket buys admission to them all.

The Tower is of the very essence of Blackpool: brash, ebullient, totally dedicated to having a good time — and, above all, impossible not to notice.

There are nearly 3,000 tonnes of iron and steel rearing up so airily into the sky. It takes 20 men working all year round to keep the ironwork coated with red lead to protect it from the sea air. Even so, about two-thirds has had to be renewed, bit by bit.

Lifts make some 55,000 trips a year to take sightseers to the top (or almost the top: the highest pinnacle involves a stair climb) and they have never ceased to run except during the two World Wars: in the First World War, the Tower was a lookout post for submarines and in the Second, a radar base.

I entered via the great arena which stands between the four legs: a vast palace, Indian-style, in gold and red where a permanent circus plays to audiences of up to 2,000 several times a day. Having no stomach for the sight of animals compelled to lead such a life, I moved on to the aquarium, laid out as if in underwater caves and with every conceivable kind of fish from piranhas to the eyeless creatures that live in caves without light: 2,000 species in all.

Up and up, ascending staircases decorated with *art nouveau* tiles, until I reached the great ballroom, as spectacular as a *schloss* designed for mad king Ludwig II of Bavaria — all roses and nymphs, curlicues and caryatids. A rota of five organists keep the mighty Wurlitzer reverberating while grey-haired couples waltz on the parquet floor all day long (the ballroom opens at 11 a.m.) and for most of the night too. There are playgrounds for the children, tropical gardens, hamburger bars, a butterfly reserve: in the Tower, there certainly is no business like show business. Spectacle is (literally) piled upon spectacle.

And so to the lift. Up we swayed, through the middle of this great Meccano-kit folly, peering out between the immense and complex girders to gasp at the painters walking so nonchalantly across loose planks hundreds of metres above ground. The lift doors rattled slightly in the wind: these men go on working no matter what the weather. Having survived nearly a century's gales, the Tower is not likely to succumb now. But what if it did? It was so designed, said my guide, that it would topple onto the beach and not the town.

We all poured out, onto the glassed-in viewing platform to look dizzily down at the great panorama far below our feet: at the huge town that owes its existence almost entirely to providing pleasure, laid out like a map down below, and at the kilometre upon kilometre of golden sands where the donkeys plod up and down. The throng of coaches looked like ants, the 4,000 hotels and guest houses were no more than a pattern on a tablecloth.

The Tower cost £45,000 to build: not such a folly after all, for on a wet day some 20,000 people shelter in it and spend-spend-spend. What would it cost to build today? My guide said: 'You'd never get planning permission!'

Blackpool is full of other historic 'monuments' — from vintage electric trams still clattering along the sea-front, to the famous late-summer lights, nearly 400,000 of them (a tradition that started in 1912 in a small way and now fills three km with elaborate illuminations right through to November, keeping four artists and 40 craftsmen in constant employment). Colonel Gadaffi once tried to buy the lot for £2 million, to celebrate his tenth anniversary in Libya; but Blackpool — eager to sell almost anything to anybody — could not spare them. The town invented seaside rock, and this it exports in quantity (also false teeth: cause and effect?).

Its pleasure beach, packed with £50 million-worth of what are graphically described as 'white knuckle' rides, is in its own way a monument too, the nearest thing we have to Disneyland. Three piers, too. Blackpool is full of 'firsts', 'biggests' and 'mosts' — but nothing exceeds its unique Tower in sheer bravura.

Often, however, it is not just one building which stands out as being of maritime interest but the whole of an old part in some historic coastal town. For example, the once down-at-heel seamen's quarter of old Poole has now been declared a conservation area, and strolling round its quiet lanes and busy quay brings back a salty tang of the past. As in so many ancient ports, the quayside was where the workaday buildings went up (warehouses, Custom House, harbour offices and inns). Narrow lanes at right angles to the quay were probably once lined with fishermen's cottages, snugly tucked away from wind and weather. The merchants' houses, guildhall and church were set still further back.

I walked round old Poole with Graham Smith, curator of Poole's museums, including the Guildhall Museum — itself an interesting building, with the former council chamber at the top of an elegant exterior stairway, above what used to be the market hall. Down the cobbled streets are the homes of sea-merchants, dating back to the days when Poole and Dartmouth were premier ports of England and doing a flourishing trade with Newfoundland. Ascribing dates to buildings doesn't really put them in historical perspective for me; when Graham Smith told me the almshouses had been built just before Henry V fought the battle of Agincourt, this was far more meaningful.

High on a wall was a small niche, intended for a lamp — maybe the earliest form of street-lighting. Poole has filled gaps between old houses in sympathetic style — small courts and modern homes deliberately higgledy-piggledy, not imitating the old but of similar materials and scale. Near the church, with its monuments to the great seafaring families of Poole, is the Mansion House — now an elegant hotel — which was once the home of a merchant who grew wealthy from the Newfoundland fisheries; and on one of the fine classical fireplaces the decorative motif in the centre acknowledges the source of his riches: fillets of dried cod. Probably furs and seal-oil contributed, too.

Custom House architecture adds Georgian elegance to many quays and harbours. This one is at Poole (Dorset).

Down to the quay, next, along lanes and past great warehouses, the old town lock-up, a century-old buoy made of wood staves just like a barrel, and the 'town beam' — a massive timber structure with iron rings from which a weighing device used to hang. Here goods from ships could be weighed, and the old notice reads: 'The Bailey shall receive from every stranger or foreigner having goods and merchandises to be weighed, for weighing the same halfpence for every hundredweight. Which half pence shall be the whole duty, as well for the beam as for the porters for the putting in and the taking out.' All of which is far removed from the practices of the modern quays, on the opposite bank of the harbour now, where cars and timber can be seen coming in from Europe.

The so-called Town Cellars stand here (they are not underground — simply a vast mediaeval store for wool, once 40 m long but later truncated to cut a road through). Under the handsome roof-beams are housed relics of Poole's maritime past — a small museum, exceptionally well displayed. Nearby are the old Harbour Offices with the colourful effigy of a former mayor adorning one wall; and the Regency Custom House (still in use) with the grandiloquent coat-of-arms and flagpole which distinguish old Custom Houses in so many English ports.

In Poole, several merchants' houses survive. I visited one of those that are open to the public — even its little courtyard garden has been laid out in Tudor style, and traditional plants grow there. Scaplens Court has a new life of its own, used for recreating old lifestyles. From time to time staff, other adults and children put on old clothes from the museum collection and try their hand at churning butter or Dorset button-making, for example.

And, finally, the most characteristic components of any ancient waterfront — the inns. We went from one to another: 'The Helmsman', with its ship models among the lobster-pots; the 'Poole Arms', to see its collection of ropework, hundreds of knots in every imaginable combination; and the 'Lord Nelson', run by a diver, where we pored over the map of local wrecks and looked at his innumerable finds from them, now decorating the bars.

There is far more than this to old Poole. Warehouses topped with sack-hoists have been turned into restaurants and, in one case, into an exceptionally good aquarium; and an old corn-mill is now used for holiday flats. Other cellars, other beamy lofts, still gather dust, awaiting a lease of life. Old Poole was, not so long ago, in a neglected and decaying state, but gradually new uses are being found for unwanted buildings, which will save them, there as in many other old ports around England.

Some maritime buildings to visit

In addition, see chapters on museums (often housed in historic buildings), piers, lighthouses, forts, aquaria, ports — naval and commercial, churches, inns and restaurants. Many Tourist Information Centres are in interesting buildings.

MERSEYSIDE
Liverpool* Pier head buildings; Titanic memorial; maritime museum. 051 236 1492

SOMERSET
Watchet Historic village.
Minehead* Old cottages, lanes, disused fishermen's chapel.

DEVON (north)
Ilfracombe* Disused fishermen's chapel.

Croyde Bay Thatched cottages.
Bideford* Quayside houses.
Clovelly Historic village.

DEVON (south)
Morwellham Quay near **Plymouth***
Historic port.
Dartmouth* Bayard's Cove; quay at which 'Mayflower' put in for repairs before reaching Plymouth.
Devonport Victualling yard designed by Rennie.

CORNWALL
Boscastle Historic village and harbour.

Newquay* Huer's lookout house: to keep watch for shoals of herring.
St Ives* Old cottages and lanes; fish cellars (many now restaurants etc); disused fishermen's chapel.
Porthcurno near **Penzance*** Minack theatre created out of cliffs. For performances, phone 073672 471.
Mousehole near **Penzance*** Historic fishing village and harbour.
Penzance* Barbican (former defences, now craft workshops).
Cadgwith Thatched cottages.
Falmouth* The old town.
Mevagissey Fish cellars (now restaurants etc) and boat-builder's workshop (now museum).
Looe* Old cottages, twisting lanes.
Cawsand Little houses around quay.
Cotehele near **Saltash** Quay with Georgian and Victorian buildings.

DORSET
Weymouth* Jacobean harbourside house at 3 Trinity Street.
Poole* Town cellars (now museum) and historic houses.

HAMPSHIRE
Bucklers Hard near **Beaulieu*** Shipwright's cottage, and others.
Ashlett Creek near **Fawley** Old coastguard cottages and tide mill, now a club house.
Lepe near **Hythe** Old watch-house and coastguard cottages.
Totton near **Southampton*** Eling Tide Mill. Waterwheel operated by flow of tides, still working.
Portsmouth* Exceptionally interesting old town, full of naval monuments, ancient fortifications etc (obtain Portsmouth Point 'Trail', from Tourist Information Centre.)

EAST SUSSEX
Brighton* Royal Pavilion: Prince Regent's seaside home.
Rottingdean Old village with smuggling connections.
Hastings* Fishermen's net-drying huts on beach.

KENT
Dungeness Old lighthouse.
Dymchurch New Hall court house ('Dr Syn' associations).
Folkestone* Old harbour buildings.
Dover* Maison Dieu: former pilgrims' hostel.
Deal* Time-ball building (housing the Tourist Information Centre), used to signal the time to shipping.
Ramsgate* Old harbour buildings. Granville Hotel designed by Pugin.

Whitstable* Fishermen's cottages and sail-lofts.
Sheerness* Some buildings from former naval dockyard.
Upnor Oldest barracks in Britain, serving waterfront castle.

LONDON
Old warehouses at St Katharine's Dock, some now restaurants. Greenwich: Royal Naval College, very splendid. Tower Bridge: its towers and upper walkway are to be opened to the public during 1982.
Rotherhithe (Brunel's tunnel); exhibition in a tunnel building.

ESSEX
Tollesbury Old sail-lofts.
Harwich* 17th-century treadmill crane.

SUFFOLK
Ipswich* Warehouse being converted to arts centre.
Woodbridge Tide-mill (working).
Aldeburgh Moot Hall on the beach, because of sea's incursion.
Southwold Old houses round harbour.
Lowestoft* Old town.

NORFOLK
Great Yarmouth* Nelson's monument: visitors can go up it. Quays: merchant's house; fishermen's almshouses; lanes.
Cromer* Old part of town.
Sheringham* Old part of town.
King's Lynn* Warehouses. Custom House, watch tower, merchants' houses.

LINCOLNSHIRE
Boston* Old lanes; cells where Pilgrim Fathers were imprisoned.

HUMBERSIDE
Hull* Old warehouses (now hotel, club etc) and merchants' houses.

NORTH YORKSHIRE
Scarborough* Old town around harbour.
Whitby* Old part of town, including house where Cook was apprentice.
Staithes Fishermen's cottages and lanes.

TYNE AND WEAR
Newcastle* Old quay; bridges.
Tynemouth Priory, battery, watch-house etc.
Cullercoats Historic fishing village.

NORTHUMBERLAND
Low Newton National Trust fishing village.

Some of the above buildings can be viewed only from the outside. For details of accessibility, opening hours etc ring the nearest Tourist Information Centre (see list on page 8). Many Centres have 'town trails' (leaflets guiding you around the most interesting streets, quays and so on). For example, **Ramsgate***(Kent) has its harbour trail; **Scarborough*** (North Yorkshire), a smugglers' trail; **Milton Creek** near **Faversham*** (Kent), a sailing-barge trail; and there is a Cinque Ports trail covering all the ancient ports of Sussex and Kent.

In the larger towns you may be able to join a guided walk or bus tour. Hiring a private guide is sometimes possible for a moderate fee.

The historic buildings of the future
Here are some feats of modern engineering — accessible to the public today — which may qualify as historic buildings of the future.

Bridge over the Humber estuary (longest bridge in the world).

Tidal surge barriers at **Hull*** and **Woolwich**. Boat-trips to the latter go from Westminster Pier, London, and in 1983 it will be possible to go on a viewing platform, with audio-visual show etc.

World's largest floating quay (830 m, 10 hinged bridges) at **Liverpool***.

Orwell Bridge at **Ipswich*** (Suffolk), opening late 1982, will be the longest pre-stressed concrete building in the United Kingdom.

Oil refineries. None are open to the public, but you can still drive through the middle of the Grain refinery, on the Medway estuary (Kent) though it is threatened with closure. And you can see the 'nodding donkey' pumping up oil on the cliffs at **Kimmeridge** near **Swanage*** (Dorset).

Power stations are often sited on the coast because they need water. Some allow the public in at certain times: for details, phone the numbers given.

CUMBRIA
Roosecote near **Barrow*** 0229 22482

LANCASHIRE
Heysham 0524 53131
Fleetwood* 03917 4316

AVON
Oldbury near **Bristol*** 027293 416631

SOMERSET
Hinkley Point near **Bridgewater** 0278 652461

EAST SUSSEX
Brighton* 027359 3131

KENT
Dungeness 0679 20461 or 0679 20551
Richborough near **Sandwich** 0304 612909
Kingsnorth near **Rochester*** 0634 271681

ESSEX
Bradwell near **Maldon** 0621 76331

SUFFOLK
Cliff Quay near **Ipswich*** 0473 55921
Sizewell near **Leiston** 0728 830444

CLEVELAND
Hartlepool* 0429 65841

NORTHUMBERLAND
Blyth 06706 3471

6 Historic ships: great and small

Steam-railway preservationists took the lead in demonstrating that it is not just historic buildings which deserve conservation, and it was quite a long time before realisation dawned that old ships and boats, too, are worth preserving. By then, many had been lost for ever. Things are different now, and in any harbour you may come across an enthusiast working on an old fishing-smack or a disused lightship, for instance, determined to preserve a particular vessel of a type no longer being made.

The Maritime Trust is to great ships what the National Trust is to stately homes, and through its efforts many national treasures have been preserved. Other trusts have come into being to save ships or particular types of craft, often helped by grants from the Maritime Trust. For example, when visiting Hull I went to see what the Humber Keel and Sloop Preservation Society was doing.

A keel is a very special kind of craft, well suited to the Humber estuary and east coast. For a start, because it was designed to sail more in shallow waters than in deep sea, and to rest in tidal harbours sometimes empty of water, it has no keel (its name derives from the Saxon word for ship, 'ceol'). Its square sails suit river or canal work and are easier for operation, using a system of small winches, by the husband-wife team which was the usual crew. Humber keels were the last square-riggers of any kind to continue in use — the last cargo carried under sail was in 1949. Humber sloops had a similar hull, but were differently rigged with sails fore and aft, like many other small coastal craft.

The Society owns one example of each type. I went on board the keel 'Comrade', built in 1923 to carry barley to Wakefield and bring back coal to the coast. It took years of hard work and fund-raising by volunteers to get her sailing

Square-sailed and flat-bottomed, Humber keels were designed for navigation in shallow waters. Only one now survives, taking visitors on day-trips.

again in 1976. I found her in her usual mooring at Beverley, but she is often out and about, taking people on trips from the Old Harbour at Hull or for a weekend on the Humber estuary. She occasionally visits seaside resorts on the east coast and goes inland on the canal network too, her sails supplemented by an engine now. Each year, at least one Open Day is held when the public can crowd on to explore the boat and look at the exhibits inside which tell the story of 'Comrade' and the other Humber keels. (Information about her whereabouts can be obtained by phoning 0482 441277, and a folder of old documents and photographs, called 'Humber Keels', can be bought.)

It was early in the season and when I clambered down into her hold I found her skipper, Fred Schofield, busy advising a volunteer who was making new leeboards (the huge paddle-like boards which are let down on one side when needed to prevent the keel-less boat from drifting sideways). A 20 m pine pole specially imported from Norway, which volunteers had turned into a new mast, was waiting to be raised.

Fred says he began his life on Humber keels at the age of three weeks and, except for six years' schooling, has never been off them since. When 'Comrade' ceased work and the Preservation Society took her over, Fred stayed on to handle the ship and train new crew, though he no longer lives aboard in the cosy stern cabin (which is still there, unchanged). He is the Honorary Sailing Master and, at 75, as vigorous as ever. He talked of the great variety of cargoes he had carried in his time, from beets to tractors (for export to Sweden), coal to peanuts, gum arabic to myrabolams — this was a new one to me! A dyestuff from India, he explained, used in tanneries. The only part of his work he never enjoyed was cleaning out the hold when, after a cargo of coal, some wheat or flour was about to be loaded.

A trip on a boat like this is unforgettable. A previous passenger described it — the silence once the engine is stopped, the skill with which the ropes and tackle are used to hoist the sail, the soothing sound of water splashing aside, the heeling over and the furious flapping of sails when the tiller is pulled hard to one side to tack against an unfavourable wind, the landward view slipping gradually past, and at the day's end the sun glinting off the westward waters.

It was also near Hull that I found a very different kind of conservation afoot, on board the paddle-steamer 'Lincoln Castle'. Not until the great Humber Bridge was completed in 1981 did this, the last coal-fired paddle-steamer in the world, cease puffing daily to and fro across the Humber estuary, ferrying passengers between the north and south banks. It was immediately bought by Francis Daly who had it berthed not far from the bridge, and who has now renovated and opened it, not just as a floating museum but as a restaurant and pub too. The steam engines and paddles have been skilfully overhauled and can be seen in motion though the steamer does not leave its berth. For 2,000 years, it is estimated, some kind of ferry had crossed the Humber (remains of Bronze Age dugouts were found on the nearby foreshore, and can be seen in Hull's maritime museum), and it would have been tragic if the 'Lincoln Castle', the last ferry of all, had gone to the scrapyard.

Francis Daly is Hull's most practical preservationist. He came to the city as an engineering student and stayed on, converting old waterfront buildings and winning numerous conservation awards. I found him, black to the elbows in engine-grease, down in the bowels of the boat, which was a scene of frenzied activity (opening day was only a week off). He introduced me to some of his team of workers — with few exceptions they had once been Arctic trawlermen, unskilled in building or carpentry. 'But they're the best and most honest workers in the world', he said. 'Practical, hardworking and versatile.' Many who spent a

Headlands and outcrops were obvious sites for Norman fortifications such as Bamburgh Castle (Northumberland).

Seaside resorts have inspired fanciful architecture: the Royal Pavilion at Brighton (East Sussex).

lifetime in fishing (more dangerous an industry than mining, in the icy conditions of the far north) ended up after years of backbreaking work wearing an iron corset. Even so, men would take the work, despite low wages. But the deep-sea fishing industry largely collapsed after the 'cod war' with the Icelanders a decade ago, and former trawlermen are scattered in all kinds of new fields — such as the restoration and conversion activities which Francis is continually initiating.

What was once the saloon of the 'Lincoln Castle' is now a stylish restaurant open to the public, as are the bars from which visitors can wander, drink in hand, to sit on deck or go below to watch the stately rhythm of the great brass pistons. (To make table bookings phone 0482 647171.)

Sailing-barge races are a spectacular sight on the east coast each summer.

But of all historic vessels, the ones that excite the most interest are not the fishing, cargo or passenger boats but the great naval warships — and there is none of more heroic stature than HMS 'Victory'.

Heroic? I went to Portsmouth (Hampshire) ready to be awed by the weight of history, the story of the battle at Trafalgar, the spot below-decks where Nelson died, the splendour of the ship herself. I came away with very different feelings — of compassion and of horror at the appalling conditions endured by the men who won that famous victory, which was neither happy nor glorious for them.

A young naval cadet showed me round. He described the lot of his even younger predecessors, the 'powder monkeys'. These little boys, seven to 14-years-old, would have been pressganged (just like most of the adult seamen) and snatched from their families to serve on board — bringing gunpowder for the gunners, fetching meals, clearing up, and cleaning spittoons. (These were necessitated by the universal habit of chewing tobacco.)

Over 800 men and boys lived on this ship, and many died on it too — not all of them in battle. Whenever the ship was within sight of land, armed marines were posted to shoot down any sailors who attempted to desert. So abhorrent were conditions aboard that men would feign dead, for burial at sea. It was the custom for a dead man to be sewn into his own canvas hammock before being pitched into the sea, and an escaper could hope to slash his way free with a concealed knife. Eventually, to prevent this trick, officers came to sew 'the last stitch' themselves — passing the needle through the nose of the alleged corpse.

For the most trifling misdemeanours — like whistling on deck, which seamen believe to be unlucky — a man might be brutally lashed. But first, confined in the leg-irons that are still in place on the ship, he would be given a length of rope which he himself had to make into a cat-o'-nine-tails for the flogging — and his 30 or more lashes would be doubled if he did this badly. Each 'tail' had vicious knots in it. 'No room to swing a cat' is an expression referring to the cat-o'-nine-tails.

Even the wounded could be punished. Anyone with an injury was sent below to dress it himself — with salt and a coarse bandage. If he then failed to return to his post, he would be shot.

Finally, my last recollection of the glorious 'Victory': the lifeboats. Three large ones for the 45 officers. One small one for the 800 men.

Where to see historic vessels

Apart from vessels exhibited inside museums, there are plenty still afloat or on quaysides which can be visited. Details are given below with phone numbers for opening hours. You can usually go on board, where there are often exhibitions inside and booklets, models etc to be bought; or even take a trip in some cases.

Collections
Maritime Museum **Liverpool*** (Merseyside)
This has a floating collection in former docks. 051 236 1492
Maritime Trust **Falmouth*** (Cornwall) Here the Maritime Trust has its Cornish vessels, a lugger and an oyster dredger. 0326 311329
Maritime Museum **Exeter*** (Devon) A collection of boats afloat and ashore and some lifeboat exhibits. 0392 58075

Dolphin Museum **Sittingbourne** (Kent)
Collection of sailing-barges at the quayside. 0795 74132. (See also Chapter 5.)
Maritime Trust **London*** In St Katharine's Dock (near the Tower of London) the Trust has Scott's 'Discovery', a sailing-barge and five other vessels. 01–481 0043

Great ships
SS 'Great Britain' **Bristol*** (Avon) Brunel's huge steamship. 0272 20680
HMS 'Cavalier' **Southampton*** (Hampshire) Destroyer from the Second World War. 0703 37522
HMS 'Victory' **Portsmouth*** (Hampshire) Nelson's flagship; in dry dock. 0705 22351 ext 23111

HMS 'Gannet' near **Portsmouth***
(Hampshire) Steam sloop which took part in
an action in the Red Sea. Now being restored;
to be opened later.
'Foudroyant' **Gosport** (Hampshire) A
frigate; open only during its annual fair in
September. 07017 82696
HMS 'Belfast' **London** The last battleship;
moored opposite the Tower of London.
01–407 6434
'Cutty Sark' **London** In dry dock at
Greenwich; the last of the tea-clippers.
01–858 3445
HMS 'Warrior' **Hartlepool*** (Cleveland) The
most important warship of the 19th century
and the first 'ironclad'. Still being restored;
open at weekends. 0429 33051

Other boats

'Shamrock' **Cotehele** (Cornwall) A coastal
barge. 0579 50434
'Gipsy Moth IV' **London** On the quay at
Greenwich; the boat in which Sir Francis
Chichester sailed round the world single-
handed. 01–858 3445
'Favourite' **Whitstable*** (Kent) Fishing-boat.
0227 274736
'Amy Howson' **Hull*** (Humberside) A
Humber sloop. Also 'Comrade' (see text).
0482 441277
'Waverley' **Glasgow** Although based in
Scotland, this paddle-steamer travels round
the English coast every summer taking
passengers on trips. 041 2218152

About 30 Thames sailing-barges survive and
these can sometimes be seen on the estuaries of
the Thames or Medway (Kent) and Blackwater (Essex). It is sometimes possible to
spend a day on one (phone the South-East or
East Anglia Tourist Board, see list on page 8);
anyone who joins the Thames Barge Sailing
Club (c/o National Maritime Museum, 01–858
4422) can sail regularly.

Of all the boats mentioned in this section,
they are my favourites: colossal red sails and a
huge flat-bottomed hull, yet so simple in their
rigging that, through a complex system of
chains, ropes and winches, only two people
were needed to sail them. In Dickens' time,
they carried grain, bricks or entire haystacks to
London, returning with loads of manure from
the cab-horses (valued as fertiliser). Great skill
is needed to manoeuvre a sailing-barge across
strong currents. The red colour of the sails
was no decorative touch; the ochre coating
was essential to prevent salt water from rotting
them. But oil engines superseded the barges
in the '30s and if you explore the creeks and
mudflats of north Kent, you will discover at
low tide the decaying skeletons of dozens of
these splendid boats.

Replicas of old ships

There is quite an industry in the building of
these, sometimes for films and TV before they
continue on a sailing career around the coast.
'Odin's Raven' is a replica of a Viking ship
(normally at the Isle of Man, but may come to
England). There is another Viking replica at
Ramsgate* (Kent) in dry dock. You may come
across an authentic replica of Drake's 'Golden
Hind' at **Poole*** (Dorset) or elsewhere when
she moves about. Other replicas of the ship at
Brixham* (south Devon) and **Southend***
(Essex) are conversions of fishing-boats and
not authentic. Even Victorian paddle-steamers
are being copied now: for instance, the
'Elizabethan' on the Thames.

Whenever you visit a seaside resort, head for
the old quarter and look in the harbour (or on
the beaches if there is no harbour) and you
may well find traditional fishing-boats still in
use – but for how much longer? To take just one
example, if you go to **Bridlington*** (Humberside) you can still see plenty of the old cobles
at work (in some areas, pronounced 'cobbles').
A few take visitors out fishing (phone 0262
72766, 79434 or 76551 for details). The
coble is said to have derived from Viking
ships. It has a broad, flat keel aft which makes it
easier to launch off a beach even when the
waves are breaking heavily. Its planks are often
brightly painted just like those of boats depicted
in the Bayeux tapestry.

Holidays and trips on historic ships

Mariners International is an organisation which
charters traditional square-rigged ships for
this purpose. For membership details write to
58 Woodville Road, New Barnet, Herts. For
information about holidays on sailing-barges
ring the East Anglia Tourist Board; other
Tourist Boards will give information about
different holidays available. Sailing-barge holidays for children are run by the East Coast Sail
Trust at Old Thatch, Hoxne, Diss, Norfolk.
Other ships offering holidays include:

'Provident' **Salcombe*** (Devon) A Brixham
trawler which, along with some traditional
yachts, is available for sailing in if you join the
Island Cruising Club. You can sleep ashore or
on a converted ferry boat. 054 884 3481

'Biche' based at **Poole*** (Dorset) The last
of the Breton tunny-fishers. Tall and fast, made
for Atlantic fishing, she does everything from
day-trips to week-long cruises, some with
sea-angling. 0491 35531

'Malcolm Miller' and 'Sir Winston Churchill'
Gosport (Hampshire) Three-masted schooners
on which you can take sail-training courses.
070 17 86367

'Foudroyant' **Gosport** (Hampshire) On this
1817 frigate, young people can have sail-

training holidays. sleeping in hammocks. 070 17 82696

Friends of the Maritime Trust
An annual subscription to this entitles you to free visits to 'Cutty Sark', the collection at St Katharine's Dock, and HMS 'Warrior', at **Hartlepool*** (Cleveland) and also to a news-letter and other benefits. Details from the Trust. 01–730 0096
Enthusiasts for traditional vessels like those mentioned above can join societies set up to support their continuance – some local, some national. The Old Gaffers Association started as a group of people owning traditional sailing-boats of all kinds – cutters, luggers, schooners, trawlers, smacks, even old lifeboats. Now there are a thousand such boats registered with the Association. Anyone can join and will receive invitations to races, rallies and social events, as well as news about the boats. 0896 2785

The majority of the boats are nearly 100 years old (a few are much older). Most of the races are held during late summer, off the Essex coast or in the Solent, a few in the south-west: colourful spectacles, when 50 to 100 craft gather, ranging in size from 5 to 26 m. The best places from which to watch the start of a race are Essex – **Steeple Stone** or by the nuclear power station at **Bradwell**; Solent – **Cowes** promenade.

Between races, the craft can often be seen going about their business (usually pleasure-sailing, although some still work as fishing-boats) around small waterside towns such as **Bursledon** (Hampshire) and, in Essex, **Bradwell, Maldon, Tollesbury, West Mersea, Rowhedge** and **Wivenhoe**; (also places like Brighton Marina and St Katharine's Dock). The secretary of the Association, John Scarlett, is a fund of information and it is worth phoning him for advice before a holiday, particularly if you are going to be near one of the racing areas.

There is also a Steam Boat Association. Contact B. W. Smith on 04885 795 for details about their annual gathering. A weekend cruise takes place in summer, on a different part of the coast each year, with other gatherings on inland waterways. These are all small boats, under 33 m, an impressive sight when several dozen are puffing away together.

Seeing boats is mostly a matter of chance, but there are almost always sailing-barges to be seen on the Blackwater estuary (Essex); and the pebbly beaches of **Eastbourne*** and **Hastings*** in East Sussex have their luggers (wide fishing-boats with thick bottoms designed for lugging up the beach in places that have no harbour). On the Fal, oyster-boats still fish under sail: in fact, boats with engines are banned in the vicinity of the oyster-beds. Some coastal towns like **Ipswich*** (Suffolk) en-courage other traditional craft to visit: for example, **Yarmouth*** (Isle of Wight) has a 'folk boat' week in late summer.

Paddle-steamers lend themselves to con-version into restaurants: the one at **Hull*** has been described; several are moored in the Thames; and others are in process of conversion, for instance at **Rochester*** (Kent) and **New-castle*** (Tyne and Wear). Two of the great Baltic sailing-traders are currently being re-stored, one at Brighton Marina and the other at **King's Lynn*** (Norfolk): every year sees new conservation projects being started.

Further reading
There are three monthly magazines that have a lot of information about preserved ships, sailing-barge races, paddle-steamer sailings and so forth: 'Ships Monthly', 'Sea Breezes' and 'Coast & Country'. Two informative county-by-county guides you may find helpful are: 'Discovering Maritime Museums and Historic Ships' (Shire) and 'Old Ships, Boats and Maritime Museums' (Coracle Books).

7 Emigrants and refugees

It is not only the great and the good from times past who engage our interest: the traces left by millions of obscure people are still eagerly sought out by their descendants.

Of the many Commonwealth visitors who head for the English coast each year, a great number have a special interest in one particular spot: the point from which their ancestors emigrated centuries ago – for America, Canada, Australia, New Zealand or other colonies (as they were then). Often the actual spot has changed beyond recognition, though many of the quays from which the Pilgrim Fathers stepped are preserved (see Chapter 5). Visitors then turn to the local libraries, churchyards and museums in the quest to trace their origins. For example, many Canadians make for Poole (Dorset) because this port used to carry on trade with Newfoundland — importing dried cod — and so a number of Poole people were among the early colonists there: the curator of the Guildhall Museum spends a lot of time helping Newfoundlanders to trace their ancestry.

The emigrants to North America went mostly via small ports — and, of course, Liverpool. They sailed not only from the east coast but from Plymouth and Southampton too; and, to a lesser extent even from ports as widely separated as Fowey and Hull. The convicts, who were Australia's earliest settlers, were mostly embarked in the Thames estuary, at Portsmouth or at Plymouth — but many were put on board at innumerable ports along the south coast.

English ports have received many refugees from persecution, some famous and many obscure: the Huguenots, for example, who fled here after massacres by French Catholics in the 17th century. Rochester has a small close, called La Providence (off the High Street) where Huguenot descendants still live; and at the Blackfriars gin distillery in Plymouth one can visit the meeting room used by a congregation in about 1680.

At the National Maritime Museum (Greenwich, London), one of its innumerable galleries — they run to $5\frac{1}{2}$ km! — is devoted solely to the subject of emigration (to America only). I found the display totally absorbing. The first thing that strikes one is the tiny size of the ships that battled their way across the Atlantic in the 1820s and 1830s. At that date they were crammed not with refugees from religious persecution or even from poverty: a newspaper from the little port of Appledore (Devon) is displayed, with its comment: 'Formerly it was disappointed politicians or needy adventurers only who thought of leaving, but now it is the middle classes as well as labourers and artificers'. Ships advertised for migrants as passengers out, creating tight-packed dormitories in holds that would be full of timber on the return voyage. Spring was a popular time to go, for ice and storms made the six-week journey hazardous in winter. The migrants (perhaps 200 men, women and children in one ship) would have to stay below decks nearly all the time: a life-size model has been created to show the cramped conditions, where 'Here a grave matron chants selections from a hymn

Emigrants endured intolerable crowding and hardship, confined below-decks on slow sailing-ships.

book, there a brawny ploughboy pours forth a sweet melody'. North America, scarcely populated in 1800, had received 50 million immigrants by 1875.

Steamships speeded up the journey from about 1860 onwards, but even so the crossing was risky. Fire was a constant anxiety, lifeboats were few, infectious diseases spread easily. On the quarantine island near Quebec many emigrants died within sight of their goal. Those who survived might still be bitterly disappointed: a cartoon on display shows an emigrant (dancing-slippers and silk stockings in his baggage) confronted by the 'fine grassland – only 300 m below the snow'.

Another kind of emigrant used to leave from Portland (Weymouth). In the little cottage museum I had rightly expected to find the usual collection of maritime mementos – details from wrecks, collections of fossils and displays of shells – but in addition there are poignant relics of the days when convicts awaiting transportation to Australia were brought here for a year first.

There were two reasons for their presence. They provided free labour during the period when the great stone breakwaters were being built to enclose Portland harbour and create a naval base to counter the threat from France. And those who had worked well would, on arrival in Australia, be selected for a certain degree of freedom and training – so-called 'ticket-of-leave' men. Some convicts became skilled masons while working in the limestone quarries of Portland. The museum has a pair of shoes carved from stone by a prisoner in his cell; and a beautiful piece of work by a banknote forger – a memorial, elegantly incised on a roofing slate, to a chief warder who died in 1881: 'He was seized with apoplexy and amid universal regret expired'.

Mute emigrants of a rather different kind: the 92 stone markers along the Mason-Dixon line, the boundary between north and south in the United States, were hewn here and shipped out.

8 Smugglers through the centuries

Smuggling has a long history. Ever since the idea of levying a duty on imports (or on exports) was invented, there were bound to be attempts to evade payment of duty. In the 13th century, it was wool that was smuggled out. Edward I had imposed a duty on wool exported to the continent: as a consequence, Romney Marsh (Kent) soon became a hotbed of smugglers, secretly loading wool by night, and the smuggling tradition still continued there centuries later. This is where Russell Thorndike placed the smuggling parson who was the hero of his 'Dr Syn' books; and a Dr Syn carnival is held at Dymchurch every other August.

Tobacco had a duty placed on it in Tudor times, and Cornwall then became notorious for its smugglers, who found all those small coves and creeks very handy for their purposes. To check them, a corps of 'riding officers' was established in 1698, later replaced by the coastguards (see Chapter 27). Smuggling reached its height in Kent and Sussex during the 18th and 19th centuries when brandy, silk and tea were brought in clandestinely in vast quantities. (It was estimated that some eight million lb of tea were smuggled in 1784 – far more than paid duty.) Particularly during the Napoleonic wars (1803–15) the trade was brisk: the French government actively abetted smuggling by supplying smugglers with goods in exchange for the gold, cloth and boots needed by the

French army. Spies were smuggled in, too – and emigrés on the run from France: the smugglers were not particular about whom they helped, as long as there was money in it.

Even the most respectable people became involved – the fictitious Dr Syn had his prototype in many a real-life parson. Virtuous Parson Woodforde wrote in his diary: 'Andrews the smuggler brought me this night a bagg of tea 6 pound weight'.

Up in Cumbria, there were, from mediaeval times, smugglers around White-haven and Ravenglass. Goods could be legitimately landed on the Isle of Man where duties were low and then smuggled across (the isle became nicknamed the 'warehouse of frauds'). Among the smuggled commodities was salt, because Man was immune from the 18th-century salt tax as salt was essential to one of its staple trades, salting and kippering herrings. It was to Whitehaven that rum and brown sugar from the West Indies were brought; and the story is told that Cumberland rum butter was invented when smugglers cornered by excisemen for a long period in a cave managed to survive by mixing their smuggled rum and sugar with butter.

Cornwall has its own Museum of Smuggling, at Polperro (for opening hours, phone 03644 3452), and local books are full of smuggling tales about coves and creeks round Newquay, Penzance, Cadgwith, Coverack and Looe. Falmouth still has its 'King's Pipe', a chimney used for burning contraband tobacco. In Devon the cove at Holcombe (near Teignmouth) was another favoured landing-place; and in the Fairlynch Museum at Budleigh Salterton (03954 2666) is a cellar where contraband was regularly hidden. Swanage (Dorset) had its smug-glers (read about them in C. R. Hardy's little book, 'Smugglers' Guide to Purbeck') and even the now ultra-respectable Bournemouth: the Tourist In-formation Centre there has a leaflet pinpointing the smuggling sites that can be visited and telling the stories associated with them – Hengistbury Head, the 'Haven House Inn', the Black House' at Mudeford, and the Custom House at Poole which smugglers once raided, for example.

Sussex and Kent, facing France, were notorious. Eastbourne has its booklet on local smugglers. Peaceful seaside towns such as Worthing and Angmering, and others with caves (Hastings and Margate) were once smuggling centres, used by various gangs. Some hid their wares in church vaults or belfries, others in inn cellars. (See Chapter 32 for inns with smuggling associations.) The Alfriston gang used Cuckmere Haven (East Sussex) and a smuggling festival has now been inaugurated there, together with a 'smugglers' trail'.

On the Medway estuary, Cookham Woods and the disused waterfront fort (built in the late 17th century, and still crumbling gradually away – a good spot for a picnic) provided excellent cover and an easy landing-place for the smug-glers who abounded in the estuary. The 'Nancy Bell' was a typical fishing vessel which, under its cargo of sprats, often carried kegs of brandy or other contra-band. Caught by the coastguards on one of these runs, 'Nancy Bell' was sawn in half and her breaking-up ordered. But so close were the ties among the Medway watermen that, by the time her crew had finished their term in prison, the 'Nancy Bell's' two halves had been joined again and she was ready to sail once more on her illegal excursions.

Going north, Yorkshire's most notorious smuggling centre was Robin Hood's Bay (near Whitby). At Ravenscar, along the Battlement Walks, is a niche cut into a rock slab where a lantern, invisible from land, helped to signal the smug-glers in. Whitby is full of buildings with smugglers' hideaways, including what was once the Old Ship Launch Inn and is now known as the Old Smugglers' Café.

There are few parts of the coast which smugglers have not frequented at one time or another and, because its chines (coastal ravines) provided such well-concealed landing and getaway routes, the Isle of Wight had more than its fair share. I went to see what traces of those events are left today.

Ronald Dowling has been collecting smuggling relics for more than 20 years, and has them admirably displayed in — appropriately — some cellars at the Botanic Gardens of Ventnor. At this unique Museum of Smuggling History you

THE SMUGGLERS ATTACKED.

Smugglers attacked by excise men. Many caves and waterfront inns — even churches — have their stories of smuggling exploits.

can buy his absorbing book 'Smuggling on Wight Island' (or, if the fancy takes you, a smuggler's knitted cap and cutlass). Some of the genuine exhibits were discovered in barns, crypts or caves frequented by smugglers; others are models created after careful research — some creepy life-size ones of, for example, a mediaeval smuggler undergoing the standard punishment (one hand chopped off) and another of a churchyard 'ghost': one smuggler is dressed up to frighten off the inquisitive, while another hides brandy kegs in a tomb.

The Isle of Wight is an appropriate place for such an exhibition. It was favoured for smuggling not only because there were so many hiding-places but also because Kent and Sussex, where much of the wool for smuggling originated, were too closely patrolled. Off the Isle are reefs known only to local fishermen, who could come in and out safely where weighted barrels could be concealed on the sea-bed amongst the lobster-pots. So widespread was smuggling that one visitor commented on the fishermen who never fished, yet always had pockets of money, and the farmers who ploughed only the sea (by night) and spent the days standing like herons at lookout points.

In the museum you can see one of the old collapsible lanterns (as it was a punishable offence to carry a lantern near the coast, it was sometimes very necessary to fold one up and hide it quickly) and a special 'flash-in-the-pan' pistol used for signalling. There are reproductions of smugglers' tricks: tobacco lumps encased in clay to look like potatoes and a brandy barrel in plaster to resemble a chalk boulder; rowlocks padded for silent rowing and horses' hooves padded to prevent telltale prints in the sand (there's even a gadget for faking horses' footprints, going in the opposite direction). Tobacco was wound into 'rope' and left coiled on deck, and casks with false bottoms contained cider near the bung-hole, brandy behind.

All sorts of things have been smuggled at one time or another: rosaries when Catholicism was illegal; letters from political prisoners such as Mary Queen of Scots or exiles such as Charles II (while prince). Napoleon is quoted as saying that all the secret information he needed in his wars with Britain came via smugglers.

The museum has a section on modern smuggling (of drugs, illegal immigrants and dogs evading quarantine). Dolls' heads, oranges, crutches, radios, car tyres and fire extinguishers are among the varied things that have been used to conceal contraband: 'If it's hollow, stuff it with something' seems to be the modern smuggler's motto. (But in case you are thinking of taking to a life of crime, this is no place to pick up tips, for the one feature all these have in common is that they were spotted by the excise-men and their perpetrators arrested.) Nevertheless, one cannot help but admire the car driver who attempted to smuggle gold in by having it sculpted into a car mascot and then chromium plated!

What started Mr Dowling on this unusual interest? Some 40 years ago while serving in the Navy he was involved in contraband control at Aden. After the war ended he himself became a trickster — but an honest deceiver: a professional conjuror and a member of The Magic Circle, performing under the name of Van Dyne. Meantime, he began collecting and reading everything he could about the history of smuggling until, ten years ago, he had sufficient exhibits to open what is now recognised as a museum unique in Britain.

Finally, more vicious than the smugglers were the wreckers. Not content with plundering ships wrecked on the shores by storms, some wreckers actually lured ships to their doom by placing shore-lights in misleading places. And, because the law used to say that no other person could claim salvage if even one of the ship's crew or passengers lived, survivors who got ashore were apt to be murdered. The part of England most notorious for such activities was the Scilly Isles, but it went on elsewhere too: the old Post Office in the picturesque village of Warden (Isle of Sheppey, Kent) used to be an inn called the 'Smack Aground' – a smack was a sailing vessel. For his wrecking activities, the inn-keeper's son was deported to Australia during the 18th century. Warden's Manor House is reputed to have a tunnel that was used by smugglers and wreckers to get their loot away: as usual, even the most eminent in the community had a hand in things.

9 Shipwrecks and marine archaeology

Marine archaeology has developed fast since diving equipment has become more widely available, and since the invention of the air-lift to suck away silt around wreckage. Sometimes the Navy lends its divers or apparatus to help. There is plenty waiting to be discovered near the shores of England, for thousands of wrecks have been charted – ships that foundered on rocks or sandbanks, or were sunk in storms. Around Padstow alone (near Newquay, Cornwall) there are so many known wrecks that a chart of them has been put up on the quay.

Although some wrecks have broken up long ago, others have been well preserved by the silt covering them. In fact, the superstructures of a few are clearly visible at low tide if you are out in a boat: a German U-boat from the First World War in the Medway estuary, for instance, and a number of masts projecting from the 16 km of the Goodwin Sands (off Deal) at low tide, 'where', as Shakespeare said, 'the carcasses of many a tall ship lie buried'. But there are ships of far greater antiquity than this which have been discovered. Some museums have remains of Bronze Age boats and the London Museum has part of a large Roman boat.

There is, of course, little likelihood of seeing divers at work (except on video at Southsea Castle, while the 'Mary Rose' is being excavated): the public has to wait until recoveries have been restored, classified and put on show in a museum. In the 18th-century port of Charlestown near St Austell (Cornwall) is the Shipwreck Centre (0726 3332) which shows some of the latest underwater discoveries, examines the causes of wrecks and the processes of disintegration, and explains how marine archaeologists unravel the past. There is even the entire, salvaged 'Grand Turk', a local wooden vessel which was wrecked. A number of coastal museums and inns have finds from wrecks – see Chapters 11 and 32; and in Penzance (Cornwall) is the Museum of Nautical Art (0736 3448) which has many articles recovered by divers from wrecked ships including HMS 'Association', the ship of a distinguished admiral, Sir Cloudsley Shovell, which sank on rocks in the Scillies in 1707. 800 men died; Shovell was thrown alive onto the shore but was murdered by a woman wrecker – for his emerald ring. The museum also has a full-size reproduction of part of a 1730 warship.

The most exciting display of all, however, was still in the making when I was writing this book. I went down to Southsea (Hampshire) to see what was being prepared for the debut of the 'Mary Rose' in 1982: the fruits of the world's biggest underwater operation, greater even than the raising of the 16th-century 'Wasa' at Stockholm.

The 'Mary Rose' sank over 400 years ago. She was Henry VIII's pride and joy, 'the flower of all ships that ever sailed', and with her were drowned most of her crew of 700. She had been sailing out with 60 others, to engage the French fleet of over 200 which was about to attack Portsmouth, when Henry, watching from the shore near Southsea Castle, saw her suddenly heel over and sink — for no apparent reason: possibly overloading coupled with bad seamanship. Her gun-ports being open, she sank within minutes.

There the ship lay undisturbed, in soft mud only 13 m down, until a few years ago when the marine archaeologists moved in with a team of divers who found that not only was most of her hull intact but also a huge variety of artefacts. Even clothes and shoes have survived, along with pottery, metal and wood objects. The divers' work has not been easy: Prince Charles, President of the 'Mary Rose' Trust, went down, and described the experience as 'rather like swimming about in lentil soup'. Moving along above the ship, which was lying on her side, he looked down into a hole and found himself face to face with a skull. It is presumed to be that of a longbowman because by its side were some 2 m longbows and a quiver of arrows.

The first person to go down had been a self-trained military historian, Alexander McKee, who, nearly 20 years ago, was convinced he knew where to find the ship. Wearing diving gear but using only hands and spades, he and members of the local sub-aqua club had to keep probing through 3 m of mud, in water that was always cold, until they found her. The first major find they brought up, in 1970, was a Tudor gun — and only then was Mr McKee able to

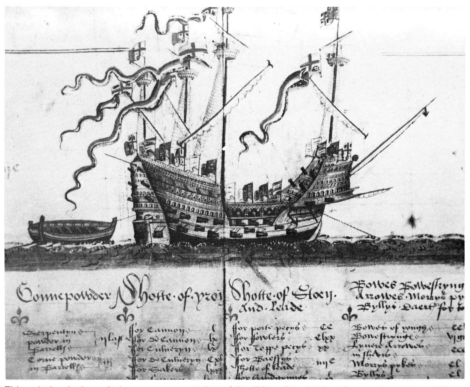

This painting is the only known representation of the 'Mary Rose', taken from an inventory of Henry VIII's ships.

convince the world at large that he had made this momentous discovery, the 'Mary Rose' herself: a structure as high as a four-storey house, over 33 m long, complete with everything needed for daily life in the Tudor period.

It was after this that the professional archaeologists went down — still aided, though, by hundreds of volunteer divers from all over the world. Interest was intense: the 'Mary Rose' is an early, perhaps even the first, real warship — bristling with long-range guns between decks, firing broadsides through gun-ports. Earlier, merchant-ships had been adapted for warfare, with guns up on deck only. The problems of conserving all her equipment were considerable — but trifling compared with those of raising and then preserving the ship herself, to be housed in a special building where her timbers can be kept moist (rapid drying out would cause them to crumble) until a preservative emulsion can be injected gradually. Engineers spent three years devising special lifting gear and a cradle in which the hull, after temporary strengthening has been added to it, can be towed to the shore.

I was shown some of the behind-scenes activity preceding the raising of the great ship, which gave me an idea of what a unique event this will be. All sorts of contradictory reactions have been experienced by those bringing up the finds. The discovery of the first few arrows, for instance, was immensely exciting because hitherto only one Tudor arrow (its provenance disputed) had survived the centuries. But then came an embarrassment of riches: *1,500* arrows so far, and perhaps thousands more to come!

The supple feel of 500-year-old leather (after restoration) makes the centuries seem but yesterday: some leather buckets have survived intact, but one lay on a workbench in a hundred pieces — it would take the technician working on them three weeks to piece the jigsaw together. Clothing, too, is now being discovered.

My guide took me past tanks of soaking timbers and along a row of domestic freezing cabinets, lifting one lid after another to reveal labelled plastic bags stuffed with dozens of combs, barrel staves, the frames of lanterns, pocket sundials (apparently as common as wristwatches are now) and other para-phernalia of life on board. Why in freezers? The conservationists have found that a good way to restore waterlogged finds is first to soak them for weeks in polyethylene glycol (which displaces water and restores natural flexibility) and then to freeze-dry them by the same method as pot noodle snacks. Freezing succeeded by vacuum treatment turns ice straight to vapour, leaving the object dehydrated but not shrunken.

The best is yet to be. Because the ship heeled over onto one side, all her gear tumbled over to that side; and so the deeper the searchers dig, the more numerous their finds. Not only is the ship going to transform historians' know-ledge (she was the very first of a concept that continued in use until the 19th century) but so are her contents. Already theoretical dates are having to be hastily revised — the date of the first English magnetic compass, for instance. And the general belief that our ancestors were shorter than us has been scotched: there are plenty of shoes in size 8 or 9, and 2 m skeletons too. (The skeletons will later be given a sea burial.) The discovery of a complete set of instruments belonging to the ship's doctor (even a jar of ointment with his fingermarks in it!) will reveal a lot about Tudor medical practice.

It will be a great day for Southsea when the ship is raised. There are just two short periods in May and June 1982 when the tide will be right (if this is missed, the operation will have to wait till September). 'Mary Rose' will break surface in a net of nylon straps, for transfer to a 50 m cradle, and it will take two days to manoeuvre her into a specially built, 66 m hall. The public will be admitted, though humidity inside will for a long time have to be kept very high.

Henry VIII, so chagrined by the loss of his favourite ship, would have appreciated the world attention now focused on her! So would the two craftsmen who cast one of her great, innovatory bronze cannons, embellishing it with lions' heads and proudly inscribing on it 'Robert and John Owen, brothers, sons of an Englishman, made this gun'.

Will the finding of this ship encourage a search for others, I asked? There are any number of known wrecks in the Solent alone, I was told; and, with skin-diving so popular now, thousands of people are investigating the world under-water. So there is bound to be a spate of discoveries in the years ahead. But it's very unlikely that another ship as important as the 'Mary Rose' would have gone down in just such a situation, where all the conditions for preservation were right.

Marine archaeology in progress

Some underwater sites currently being worked are at **Salcombe*** (south Devon): Moore Sands – Bronze Age site; **Solent** and **Needles** (Isle of Wight): HMS 'Invincible', 1758, HMS 'Assurance', 1735 and a Dutch East Indiaman; Goodwin Sands, **Deal*** (Kent): Bronze Age site. Would-be volunteers can obtain more information from Alexander Flinder at the Nautical Archaeology Society. 01–794 0292

One of the strangest finds recently has been the cargo of an 18th-century brigantine carrying reindeer hides from Russia to Venice, which sank near **Plymouth*** (south Devon).

To finance further diving, many of the hides – well preserved in the mud and beautifully supple after conservation processes – are being made into bags and belts by a local leatherworker (Robert Snelson) which can be bought.

To find out what maritime archaeology projects are in progress at any part of the coast, ask the nearest Tourist Information Centre which should have details of the local archaeological or marine archaeological society. New finds are most likely to be exhibited at the local museum.

10 Coastal churches

Shyppes that lyith in ye narrow see with
marchandyze, seith at ye hedde of ye cliffe
ye Shrine of ye blue light.

A great many churches, or little headland chapels, were sited as landmarks to help mariners steer their way safely back to harbour in the days before there were lighthouses to help them. The words quoted above were written in 1451 and referred to St Mary's chapel in Broadstairs, Kent.

Often these churches have poignant monuments or windows to local heroes and to fishermen who died at sea; or memorials to great events – storms, battles, expeditions, the Dunkirk evacuation and so forth.

A number incorporate old ships' timbers; and some house ships' bells. There is a particular reason for this: a great deal of tradition and even superstition attaches to the bell of a ship and, although a ship's name may be changed and she may be rebuilt out of all recognition, the name first engraved on a bell is never altered. Old bells were often given an honoured resting-place in the church of their home port – today, a more commercially minded Navy tends to have occasional sales of old bells.

These maritime churches are frequently dedicated to St Peter or St Andrew (brother fishermen, chosen as apostles); or to the Virgin, 'Stella Maris': Mary, the star by which ships could safely navigate. Some are dedicated to St Clement (martyred by being tied to an anchor and drowned), St Nicholas (the Russian saint, original of Santa Claus, who reputedly walked on water); or St Michael (the saint of the winds). A number are to be found inland now, in places where the coastline has receded. Churches dedicated to these 'maritime' saints celebrate their patrons on various dates: St Clement on 23rd November, St Andrew on 30th November, St Peter on 29th June, St Michael on 29th September and St Nicholas on Christmas Day.

It is not always the oldest churches that have the most interesting things to show. For example, St Andrew's (on the Isle of Portland, Dorset) is little more than a hundred years old. It is known as the 'Avalanche' church because it was built as a memorial to a historic wreck: the 'Avalanche', a clipper taking emigrants to New Zealand which collided in a storm and sank — nearly 100 people were drowned within five minutes. Relatives subscribed to the building and presented windows, lectern, pulpit and so on. At the church's centenary a few years ago, New Zealanders came round the world to fill this little church at a special service.

An even more recent church is St Leonard's (at St Leonard's near Hastings, East Sussex), with a pulpit like the prow of a boat and a ship's binnacle (compass-housing) as lectern. In 1944, the old church was bombed. The following night, the then rector dreamed of how Jesus had preached from a boat on the Lake of Galilee and determined to secure a boat from Galilee to turn into a pulpit for the new church. Many difficulties delayed this, but eventually the work was done by a Jewish carpenter on a kibbutz at the very spot where Jesus had preached.

Many headlands have on them tiny chapels with structures on their roof designed to hold braziers (they were early lighthouses): examples are St Aldhelm's (near Swanage, Dorset), St Catherine's (Chale, Isle of Wight), St Catherine's (Abbotsbury, Dorset). Where hermits lived on islands in order to get away from the world there are often commemorative chapels and the most celebrated is St Anselm's in the Farne Islands.

Headlands often have on them the dramatic ruins of great priories — frequently

Many coastal churches have historic associations. Canute's daughter was buried here at Bosham (West Sussex).

destroyed by Vikings raiding the east coast, rebuilt and then destroyed on Henry VIII's orders. They were situated in such places to take advantage of the sea as a highway (the monks were often engaged in trade, or in missionary comings-and-goings) but, as the priories' riches grew, their position made them vulnerable to pillaging by seaborne raiders.

In the south-west, churches' dedications are often to unfamiliar saints — St Mawgan, St Fimbarrus and so on. Most of these were missionaries who came by sea from Ireland and Wales, or from Brittany, and established small churches on the coasts of Cornwall, in particular.

Apart from the churches themselves, there is a lot of interest to be found in the tombstones surrounding them. One of many useful little books for explorers of country churches, published by Shire, is 'Discovering Epitaphs' in which I read these maritime gems:

From Great Yarmouth:

Here lies the body of Nicholas Round
Who was lost in the sea and never was found.

From Whitby:

Sudden and unexpected was the end
Of our esteemed and beloved friend;
He gave to all his friends a sudden shock
By one day falling into Sunderland dock.

and from Ramsgate:

This marks the wreck of Robert Woolward,
who sailed the seas for fifty-five years.
When Resurrection gun fires, the wreck will
be raised by the Angelic Salvage Co: surveyed
and if found worthy refitted, and started on
the voyage to Eternity.

Scarborough, Portsmouth, Appledore — all these and many others have similar memorials to seamen — often decorated with anchors and so forth.

Churches with maritime associations

CUMBRIA
Maryport* St Mary's. Maritime monuments and window. Christ Church. Ship's beams used in structure.

MERSEYSIDE
Liverpool* St Nicholas's. Maritime monuments; services for seamen.

SOMERSET
Minehead* St Michael's. Maritime tombs etc.

DEVON (north)
Clovelly All Saints. Memorial to Charles Kingsley who grew up at the Rectory.

CORNWALL
Zennor near **St Ives*** St Senora's. Mermaid carving and legend.
Lizard St Keverne's. Graves of 400 seamen who perished in shipwrecks.
Gunwallow near **Helford** St Winwalloe's. Timbers from 16th-century wreck used for carvings; many maritime associations.

Fowey* St Fimbarrus's. Pulpit from timbers of Spanish galleon; Maritime windows.
West Looe* St Nicholas's. Roof timbers from ship captured by Nelson.

SCILLY ISLES
St Mary's* St Mary's. Many graves of shipwrecked seamen.

DEVON (south)
Devonport St Andrew's. Ships' masts used as roof piers.
Plymouth* St Andrew's. Sir Martin Frobisher and William Blake are buried here.
Dartmouth* St Saviour's. Brass of Chaucer's 'shipman'.
Teignmouth* St Michael's. A fishermen's church with some maritime memorials.

DORSET
Swanage* St Mary's. Naval monuments.
Poole* St James's. Pillars of pines from Newfoundland where many Poole people emigrated.

HAMPSHIRE
Southampton* Holy Rood (ruin). Memorial to merchant navy, World War II and crew of 'Titanic'.
Portchester near **Portsmouth*** St Mary's (inside the castle). Tomb of Wyllie, the great marine artist.
Portsea near **Portsmouth*** St Mary's. Memorials relating to wreck of the 'Royal George' in 1782.
Portsmouth* Royal Garrison Church. Naval monuments. St Thomas's Cathedral. Naval monuments.

WEST SUSSEX
Bosham, Chichester Harbour Holy Trinity. Canute's daughter buried here, where the 'commanding the waves' incident took place. The church is shown on the Bayeux tapestry.

EAST SUSSEX
Hastings* St Clement's. Maritime memorials.

KENT
Deal* St George's. Tomb of Nelson's much-loved Captain Parker.
Ramsgate* St George's. Dunkirk window (Ramsgate was a principal base for the evacuation).
Broadstairs* St Mary's Chapel. Used by seamen since Norman times; ships used to lower their topsails as they passed the chapel right up to this century, and Broadstairs's coat-of-arms shows a ship with lowered topsails.
Gravesend St Andrew's. Former seamen's church, now an arts centre: ceiling resembles an upturned boat; memorial windows to Franklin's Arctic expedition. Every May there is a service for Dunkirk veterans.

LONDON
Tower Hill All Hallows-by-the-Tower. Mariners' chapel.
Rotherhithe St Mary's. 'Mayflower' memorials.

ESSEX
Leigh On Sea St Clement's. Many monu-

ments to naval heroes and to the Leigh founders of Trinity House (see Chapter 26). Flags commemorate the Dunkirk evacuation which involved many 'little ships' from Leigh.
Southminster St Leonard's. Church furnishings from Nelson's 'Victory'.
Brightlingsea All Saints. For over a century, every local man who died at sea was commemorated by a simple wall-tile (over 200 of them), contrasting with a splendid monument to an 18th-century pioneer of marine insurance.

SUFFOLK
Aldeburgh St Peter and St Paul. Lifeboat memorials; tower used as sea beacon and much else of interest.
Lowestoft* St Margaret's. Fishermen's memorial and other maritime monuments. Bells dedicated to fishermen and to a trawler skipper who won the VC.

NORFOLK
Great Yarmouth* St Nicholas's. Maritime tombs.
Caister-on-Sea near **Great Yarmouth*** Holy Trinity. Window commemorating nine lifeboatmen who perished in a storm.
Happisburgh near **North Walsham** St Mary's. Graves of shipwrecked seamen.
Burnham Thorpe All Saints. Nelson relics.
King's Lynn* St Margaret's. Tide-operated clock.

LINCOLNSHIRE
Donington near **Boston*** Parish church. Window commemorating Matthew Flinders who charted the Australian coast in 1801.
Boston* St Botolph's. Memorials to Australian explorers, Hanseatic merchants, John Cotton and others.

TYNE AND WEAR
North Shields* Christ Church. Graves of shipwrecked seamen.

NORTHUMBERLAND
Bamburgh St Aidan's. Grace Darling memorial. For more on St Aidan see Chapter 23 under Holy Island.

11 Museums of maritime interest

One of my favourite maritime museums is at Hull. It is not only beautifully laid out and crammed with unusual treasures but many of the attendants (always worth chatting to in any museum) are one-time trawlermen. The tales they can tell ...! And as I talked to them, the exhibits relating to fishing really seemed to come alive. One of the attendants even helps run a modellers' club: young and old join in, making new ships' models or repairing old ones.

The Town Docks Museum gets its name from the building in which it is housed (a triangular Victorian edifice with a pepperpot tower at each of its three corners), once the offices of the docks company. The first dock (now a garden) was built late in the 18th century, with others added subsequently — but the dock office building was not put up until 1870. Take a careful look at the building: above various doors you may spot figures representing the River Humber, Neptune or sea-horses; outer walls have anchors, lighthouses and starfish; iron railings are designed like tridents and harpoons.

Hull's real prosperity started in the late 18th century with whaling, not fishing, and a large part of the building is devoted to this. Children make a beeline for the colossal skeleton of a young right whale, 13 m long (an adult might grow to 23 m or more), and for the stairway which leads up and over it. The right whale is almost extinct now, owing to the devastating methods and sheer greed of modern whalers.

Until about 1840, as many as 60 whalers might have been seen at the quays in Hull, bringing in their valuable haul from the Arctic. The blubber was so rich in oil (needed for lamps) that the carcases would float when towed after the rowing boats: a dozen or more behind each. The baleen was highly valued, too, in those pre-plastic days, and in the museum you can see, for example, umbrella-ribs and corset-stays made from it.

Hull was the biggest Arctic whaling port of all, in the 1820s. Then the climate changed, and with it the ice-floes shifted so that the whales were no longer accessible. But the museum has saved a multitude of treasures from the heyday of whaling. There are models of whalers, and of the even smaller boats in which the seamen embarked for their hazardous pursuit among the ice-floes, armed only with harpoons. The tools they used to kill and cut up the great carcases are there — in whalebone and silver, tiny miniatures no bigger than toothpicks, 35 of them in all.

Often the whalers brought back Eskimo craftwork that is now exhibited, and even live Eskimos, too, as 'souvenirs' for presentation to Queen Victoria. Memiadluk and his wife Uckaluk were later put on show, together with their canoe and other gear: 5,000 people paid a shilling a head to come and gape at them.

The seamen themselves created a new craft utilising whalebone or walrus tusks: scrimshaw. Hull has the largest collection in Europe. These lovely objects, delicately carved and with the incised lines filled in with black ink, reflect the interests of Victorian England. Some depict Dickens' characters, a stay-busk has a resplendent Britannia carved on it, and others record events on the ships' voyages: one shows a cannibal feast.

The museum is not concerned solely with the past and I learned a lot about present fishing methods. Five big rivers drain into the Humber estuary, and to this day ships' cargoes unloaded at Hull can be distributed inland via this

The perilous harpooning of a sperm whale. The history of whaling, which made Hull great, is a main feature in the city's Town Docks Museum.

network of waterways. But the rivers pile silt into the estuary, which needs constant clearance; the way in which this is done is shown clearly in yet another gallery of the museum. Navigation charts have to be altered fortnightly to keep up with the continual change in the levels of the sea-bed here; buoys and lights have to be moved; dredgers are continually at work; and local pilots have to go on board the big ships to take them through the shoals. When you walk by the estuary you can see in action what has been explained in the museum.

Children particularly enjoy the galleries devoted to modern shipping. Uniforms and badges of rank are identified, as are the colours of the different shipping-lines. The remains of the earliest known Humber boat (Bronze Age) are there, and innumerable models of famous Hull ships, including the 'Bounty' — but the story is always being kept up to date so you can also see details of the latest container-ships and 'roll-on-roll-off' ferries, a familiar sight making for the North Sea today.

Of all the Museum's many postcards and booklets, I found 'The Great Whale to Snare' the most vivid: a book well worth getting before you visit (for details of this and of opening hours, phone 0482 223111) but perhaps the best reading before a visit is Herman Melville's whaling story, 'Moby Dick', particularly the dramatic climax when: 'A low rumbling sound was heard; a subterraneous hum; and then all held their breaths; as bedraggled with trailing ropes, and harpoons, and lances, a vast form shot lengthwise, but obliquely from the sea. Shrouded in a thin drooping veil of mist, it hovered for a moment in the rainbowed air; and then fell swamping back into the deep.'

Most ports have maritime museums, each with a completely different character, because the shores of England are so varied and what goes on at one place is very different from another. Sometimes there is simply a maritime section within an ordinary local museum, like the ones I visited subsequently.

I went across to the opposite coast and did a museum-hopping tour along the

Cumbrian shore. To the south, there is a small, rather undervalued museum above the library at Barrow-in-Furness, and here the principal maritime interest is the collection of ships' models. Barrow is dominated by Vickers (submarine-builders to the Navy) and the museum collection shows some of their great ship-building achievements from the past, such as a huge model of the super-dreadnought 'Erin', built before the First World War, and of HMS 'Amphitrite', an armed cruiser of 1900 designed to protect colonial shipping from the French. Its sheltered waters apart, it was the nearby iron mining that first made Barrow a ship-building centre (the broken ground that you see around it, and the lakes filling in old pits, show where iron was extracted long ago). In Victorian times, Barrow had the biggest iron mine in the world, the biggest Bessemer steel plant, the biggest dock, and it built the biggest battleships. It really deserves a better museum. (For opening hours, phone 0229 25500.)

Further north is the older port of Whitehaven, where the museum (in an old market hall) is larger, and beautifully set out. Curator Harry Fancy is pleased to answer visitors' questions. Like so many local collections, this one has a delightfully random mixture of trifles from the past — ships' models, of course, maritime paintings and fragments from shipwrecks, but also such curiosities as the jaws of a man-eating shark used as a picture frame, the model of a ship's hull showing the arrangement of water ballast tanks inside, and (inevitably) a ship-in-a-bottle. What look like slabs of iron turn out to be tea, compressed into blocks for easier shipment, which had to be broken into pieces for infusion. A local newspaper of 1792 fulminated against the spread of this imported habit: 'How degenerate is the present age and how debilitated may the next be!'

Whitehaven, once a port second only to London and Bristol, has the doubtful distinction of being where, in 1778, the last 'invasion' of English soil took place, during the American War of Independence. John Paul Jones (a Scot whose apprenticeship had been in Whitehaven) was making a name for himself among the rebels as the 'founder of the American Navy'. He led a raid on Whitehaven, briefly capturing a fort on one of the quays. The museum has a bust of him and a few other mementos.

He is usually thought of as a romantic figure, but he appears to have been singularly ruthless. At 19 he was chief mate on a slaver; then he was accused in Whitehaven of brutality if not murder when a ship's carpenter died; later, one of his crews mutinied, and, unable to get another command after that, he assumed a new name ('Jones' was not his real name).

His stealthy night raid on Whitehaven seems to have been less in order to promote the rebels' cause than to revenge himself on his accusers in White-haven; and it was not very effective. Even American enthusiasm for him cooled eventually, and he entered the Russian Navy; but he wrecked that career too (he was accused of rape). Despite all this, his remains ended up in an honoured grave in the crypt of the US Naval Academy in Nova Scotia. The Museum sells a booklet with the whole story and a replica of the 'Evening Post' at the time of the raid, giving their readers the alarming news: 'All the shipping in the Port was in the most imminent danger . . . diabolical work . . . the scene was too horrible to admit of further description . . . infernal business'. Every other port in Britain was put on the alert, all strangers were arrested on suspicion, the coffee houses were a-buzz with rumours.

(For opening hours of the museum, phone 0946 3111.)

Still further north is Maryport, whose docks and quays have hardly changed since the 18th century — except that now they lie idle and largely deserted, for they cannot take in the bigger ships of today (and the once busy fishing fleet has dwindled to a handful of small trawlers, now that there are fewer fish to be caught). Here the small but well displayed museum is housed in what was once a waterfront inn.

There are several rather special features about this museum. It has one floor devoted to lifeboat history; and it also has a life-size replica of a ship's chart-room with a working radar-scanner on which the visitor will be able to track the movement of local shipping once the installation has been completed. But among the most fascinating features are blow-ups of photographs showing Maryport harbour and harbour-folk early in the century. There's a portrait of Joseph Peile who died in 1790 from a riding accident at the age of – *106*. As a young man, he had sailed with Alexander Selkirk, the original of Defoe's Robinson Crusoe.

One of the most interesting corners is devoted to Fletcher Christian, leader of the 'Bounty' mutineers, who grew up near here. One local primary school teacher recently had the initiative to get her children working on a 'Bounty' project (their relief map of the voyages is in the museum) and another wrote to the Pitcairn Islands in the Pacific – where Christian ended his days – and got a lively correspondence going between the islanders, descendants of the mutineers, and the children. A glass case now houses the carved flying-fish and other crafts which were sent from Pitcairn to the children.

(For opening hours, phone 0900 81 3738.)

Museums these days are often far from being static repositories of dusty artefacts, worthy but dull. They are infinitely varied, well displayed and informative. Of all the ones I have visited, I can think of no greater contrast than that between the Merseyside Museum and Valhalla (see list at end of chapter). The first houses workaday boats in and around the grey, cobbled quays and brick warehouses of the old docks; and the second, a collection of brilliantly painted and gilded figureheads among sub-tropical gardens for which the most apt description is that old cliché, an island paradise. And somewhere in between comes the stylish Bucklers Hard Museum, where you can often watch curator Pat Curtis at work creating yet another exquisitely detailed ship's model for the collection.

Some museums show films or provide quizzes and colouring-books for children – and many have far better postcards to send home than the average stationers. The best way to understand your own particular stretch of 'England-by-the-Sea' is to spend a few hours in the nearest maritime museum – especially when rain or wind make a day on the beach rather less than attractive.

Other maritime museums to visit

For details of opening hours and how to get there, phone the numbers given. Many museums are free, but not all. More specialised museums are listed in other chapters.

LANCASHIRE
Fleetwood* Fleetwood Museum. Fishing. 03917 6621

MERSEYSIDE
Liverpool* Merseyside Maritime Museum. Boats in docks, cargo-handling exhibits, quayside trails etc. 051236 1492
Birkenhead* Williamson Gallery. Shipping. 051652 4177

AVON
Weston-super-Mare* Woodspring Museum. Seaside history.

DEVON (north)
Lynton Lyn Museum. Includes lifeboat and maritime exhibits.
Ilfracombe* Ilfracombe Museum. Ship models and pictures, lifeboat exhibits etc. 0271 63541
Braunton near Ilfracombe* District Museum. Fishing history. 0271 812131
Appledore near **Bideford*** North Devon Maritime Museum. Specialises in fishing and ship-building. 02372 6042
Bideford* Burton Art Gallery. Ship models etc. 02372 6711
Hartland Quay near **Bideford*** Hartland Quay Museum. Wrecks, smuggling, geology etc. 02374 594

CORNWALL
Bude Bude-Stratton Historical Exhibition. Shipwrecks, wildlife etc. 0288 3576
Helston Folk Museum. Life-saving exhibits. 03265 61672
Padstow Padstow Museum. Includes lifeboat exhibits. 0841 532297
Lelant near **St Ives** Lelant Model Village. Also has exhibits of smuggling, wrecks etc. 0736 752676
St Ives St Ives Museum. 0736 795575
Penzance Museum of Nautical Art. Salvaged recoveries. 0736 3448 Penlee House. Fishing, ship models, coastal geology. 0736 3625

SCILLY ISLES
St Mary's Isles of Scilly Museum. Wreck salvage, geology etc. 0720 22337

CORNWALL
Falmouth Museum to be opened shortly.
Mevagissey Folk Museum. Fishing etc. 072684 2511
Fowey Noah's Ark Folk Museum. Underwater diving scenes. Ship models. 072683 3304
East Looe Guildhall Museum. Smuggling, lighthouse, fishing history. 05036 2255

DEVON (south)
Salcombe Maritime Museum. 054884 2514. Overbeck Museum at Sharpitor House. 054884 2893
Kingsbridge Cookworthy Museum. 0548 3235
Dartmouth Dartmouth Town Museum. Ship models etc. 08043 2923
Brixham Brixham Museum. Coastguard gallery of particular interest. 08045 3203
Torquay Natural History Society Museum. 0803 23975
Topsham near **Exeter** Topsham Museum. In an old sail-loft. 0392 56724

DORSET
Portland near **Weymouth** Portland Museum. Wrecks, transportation etc. 0305 821804
Weymouth Local History Museum. Wrecks, ferries etc. 03057 74246
Poole Maritime Museum. Boats, ship models, smuggling, Armada, 'Bounty' etc. 02013 5323
Bournemouth Rothesay Museum. One maritime room. 0202 21009

HAMPSHIRE
Beaulieu near **Lymington** Bucklers Hard Museum. Ship-building, ship models. 059063 203

Hythe Museum to be opened shortly.
Southampton Maritime Museum. Ship models and shipping history. 0703 24216
Portsmouth See Chapter 29.
Southsea Cumberland House. Seashore life, geology etc. 0705 732654 Southsea Castle. 'Mary Rose' finds etc. 0705 24584

ISLE OF WIGHT
Cowes Maritime Museum. Ship-building, yachting etc. 0908 293341
Bembridge Maritime Museum. Ship models, wrecks, diving etc. 0983 223. (There is also a maritime museum within the entertainment complex of **Blackgang Chine**.)

WEST SUSSEX
Littlehampton Littlehampton Museum. Maritime paintings etc. 09064 5149
Worthing Worthing Museum. Seaside history. 0903 39999
Shoreham-by-Sea Marlipins Museum. Harbour and marine history in a Norman building. 07917 62994

EAST SUSSEX
Brighton Brighton Museum. A gallery of seaside history. 0273 603005 Booth Museum. Seabirds, whale skeleton etc. 0273 552586
Newhaven Museum of Local and Maritime History. Marine photos etc. 07912 4872
Seaford Museum of Local History. In a Martello tower. 0323 892915
Eastbourne Towner Art Gallery. Marine paintings. 0323 21635
Hastings Hastings Museum and Art Gallery. Seabirds, fish, marine paintings. 0424 435952 Fishermen's Museum. Fishing-boat, model boats etc in a former fishermen's church. 0424 424787 Museum of Local History. Maritime history, port and resort history, local fishing, models. 0424 425855

KENT
Hythe Local History Room. Cinque Ports history. 0303 66152
Folkestone Folkestone Museum. Port history, ship models etc. 0303 57583
Dover Dover Museum. Cinque Ports history. 0304 201066
Deal Maritime Museum. Wrecks, lifeboat and other marine history. 03045 3865
Sandwich Guildhall Museum. Cinque Ports history. 0304 611160
Ramsgate Ramsgate Museum. Resort and port history. 0732 845845
Broadstairs Bleak House. Smuggling, wrecks, port history. Also Dickens rooms. 0843 62224

Margate* Hoskings Museum. Seaside history; seashells. 0843 25511
Birchington near **Margate*** Powell-Cotton Museum. Yachting and naval exhibits; wildlife. 0843 42168
Herne Bay* Herne Bay Museum. Seaside history; finds from **Reculver** (Roman shore fort). 02273 4896
Sittingbourne Medway Maritime Museum. 0795 76617
Rochester* Guildhall. Ship models etc. 0634 48717
Chatham Medway Heritage Centre. History of Medway estuary. 0634 41540

LONDON
Greenwich National Maritime Museum. This famous collection is in one of the world's greatest and most beautiful museums, for which even a full day's visit is hardly adequate. In dozens of galleries, it covers every conceivable aspect of seafaring from pre-historic times to the present century. There are galleries devoted to Nelson and to Cook, to sail and to steam, to fishing and to warfare, to paintings and to medals, and – and – and! You can get the museum's quarterly 'News' sent to you free if you want information about the numerous events that take place. 01–858 4422

ESSEX
Grays Grays Museum. Thames estuary history. 0375 76827
West Mersea Mersey Island Museum. Oyster-fishing exhibits.
Harwich* Maritime Museum. Lifeboat, naval and harbour exhibits in an old lighthouse. Also another in an old fort.

SUFFOLK
Ipswich* Maritime Centre being set up in old warehouse.
Felixstowe* Fort is being converted into a museum.
Thorpeness near **Lowestoft*** Windmill (working); display on the Suffolk coast. 0473 55801
Dunwich near **Lowestoft*** Dunwich Museum. History of port destroyed by the sea. 072873 358
Walberswick near **Lowestoft*** Heritage Coast Centre. Fishing and coastal history. 0473 5580
Southwold near **Lowestoft*** Southwold Museum. Battle of Sole Bay with the Dutch; ship models. 0502 722711

Lowestoft* Maritime Museum. Fishing, ship-building, lifeboats, paintings, models, Naval Patrol Service. 0502 61963

NORFOLK
Great Yarmouth* Maritime Museum for East Anglia. Fishing, life-saving, ship-building, Nelson, models, slide shows. In a former home for shipwrecked seamen. 0493 2267
Cromer* Cromer Museum. Local history. 0263 513543
King's Lynn* Lynn Museum. 0553 5001

HUMBERSIDE
Grimsby* Whelholme Galleries. Ship models, marine photos and paintings, fishing history. 0472 59161
Goole* Goole Museum. Port history. 0405 2187
Hull* See text.
Bridlington* Art Gallery and Museum. Some historical exhibits. 0262 73769 Harbour History Exhibition. Also includes fishing and seabird exhibits. 0262 70148

NORTH YORKSHIRE
Filey* Folk Museum. Old lifeboat and fishing exhibits.
Whitby* Whitby Museum. Shipping, whaling, Cook, geology etc. 0947 602908 Sutcliffe Gallery. Historical and maritime exhibits. 0947 602239

CLEVELAND
Redcar Zetland Museum. Oldest lifeboat; life-saving and fishing. 0642 8471921
Hartlepool* Gray Art Gallery and Museum. Ship-building and port history; lifeboats. 0429 68916 Maritime Museum. Ship models, fisherman's cottage, working wheelhouse of ship, lighthouse lantern. 0429 72814

TYNE AND WEAR
Sunderland Sunderland Museum. Shipping and lighthouse history, ship models. 0783 41235
Newcastle-upon-Tyne* Museum of Science and Engineering. Huge maritime collection including vessels; lifeboat exhibits. 0632 326789
South Shields* South Shields Museum. Lifeboat and shipping history. 0632 568740

NORTHUMBERLAND
Bamburgh Grace Darling Museum. Lifeboat history. 06684 310

Time off by the coast

12 Seaside resorts: traditional style

Picture-postcards, of scenery or of rude jokes, on twirling racks. Straw hats, buckets and beachballs hanging in clusters over the pavement. Arcades of shops with trashy souvenirs, pink-lettered rock, candy floss and cheap sweets shaped like pebbles and seashells. Shrimp stalls, whelks and fish-and-chips.

A long promenade with regimented flowerbeds, cast-iron lamp standards, wood seats and strings of fairy lights. A clock-tower or fountain or statue of some long-forgotten civic worthy; or — pride of prides — a bandstand. Open-top buses along the esplanade.

Deckchairs and beach huts, donkey-rides and kite-flying, long flights of stairs down cliffs, queues for boat-trips and for ice-cream cornets. Sand in one's sandals, skin peeling off one's nose, legs aching in the pedal-boats.

Clock-golf, boating-ponds, miniature railways, helter-skelters and amusement arcades. Concerts in the winter gardens and bingo on the pier. Street photographers, anglers on the jetty, boats in the harbour.

Hotels with glassed-in verandahs and bay windows facing the sea; guest houses squeezed together in side-streets the sun doesn't reach. Coaches nose-

MERMAIDENS BREAKING MRS. GRUNDY'S LAW NOT A HUNDRED MILES FROM THE NORTH FORELAND.
THE ARM OF THE LAW.—"Hi! you there Ladies are exceeding the Regulations of the Board of 'Ealth. You draw it mild."

1871 seaside frolics at Margate (Kent).

to-tail, bringing in trippers on excursions.

Just a good, old-fashioned seaside resort.

In the 1750s, a Sussex doctor announced that sea water was therapeutic (to drink as well as to bathe in). As a result humble fishing villages, such as Brighthelmstone — now Brighton — were overwhelmed by fashionable ladies and gentlemen coming for purely medicinal reasons. They needed hotels, and they needed entertainment. They also, in those days, needed help in getting themselves into the sea: and about 1760 the first bathing-machines were seen. The bather could undress inside the little hut on wheels, which was then drawn down into the sea where it was easy to descend in comparative privacy (the bathing costume was not invented till later). Queen Victoria's own bathing machine is preserved at her house, Osborne, on the Isle of Wight.

A further impetus was provided by the Napoleonic wars at the end of the century. People no longer able to travel safely on the continent had to find an alternative at home. A few decades later, the spread of railways made it easy for even more people to get to the coast — quickly, cheaply and without effort. Seaside holidays were now firmly established, and not just for the rich.

One of the most distinguished of the early patrons was George III: his colourful statue, commemorating his golden jubilee, stands at the head of Weymouth's esplanade; his house is now the Gloucester Hotel.

Much of Weymouth (Dorset) is still unspoilt; and its wide sands get a good deal of any sunshine that may be going. Here is the stuff of which nostalgia is made: I felt sure the children I was watching on the painted swings that stand on the beach would one day be telling *their* children: 'That's the way seaside holidays used to be!' For though so much that is traditional has survived at Weymouth, it seems too much to hope that modern pressures will spare it unchanged for another generation. No doubt conservationists will ensure the survival of its rows of Regency houses, now hotels, and of its superbly jubilant cast-iron clock-tower with Victoria's profile in gold, its colourful paintwork, and its trimming of fairy lights. But can they preserve also its Punch-and-Judy show, its sand-sculpture artist and the fantasy world of its model village?

Weymouth has every ingredient needed for that rich plum-pudding mixture which adds up to 'the seaside'. There's even a floral clock, with floral hands that tell the time — passing far too quickly. The windsurfers flick across the water, the sedate ferries to the Channel Islands come in and out of harbour, navigating carefully among small yachts, fishing-boats laden with crabs and the water-skiers. At carnival time, all the traditions are properly observed: the carnival queen is crowned, a barrel-rollers race is run, a procession parades through the streets, and the day ends with a firework display.

Weymouth is even one of the resorts that has a free beach club for children (others include Scarborough, Margate and Southport). The clubs are areas of beach fenced off for the exclusive use of youngsters, with organisers of games in charge. As at many resorts, sandcastle competitions are run by the 'Daily Mirror'.

My favourite spot, as in most seaside towns, is around the harbour. The quays are crowded with others strolling too, and the water is lively with the movement of boats. There are little waterfront restaurants and inns, boats unloading fish, even trains wind their way along a track on the quay, bringing people to the ferries. Of course there's a brass band on the pier, a fairground, narrow lanes of small shops, gardens floodlit at night, and — but why go on? I can't think of any of the essentials of an old-style seaside holiday which Weymouth lacks.

There's always something interesting to watch in the harbour (Whitby, North Yorkshire).

Seaside resorts

*Resorts come in every style – from the big and brash (like **Blackpool*** and **Clacton***) to the quiet and sedate (like **Frinton** and **Herne Bay***). In between the resorts are innumerable smaller villages or towns which, although without the same facilities, are often a better choice for those who want something different and quieter – after all, none is very far, by car or bus, from the resorts and their entertainments. Here is a round-the-coast guide to many holiday centres. The ones with ample sandy beaches are marked (SB). Those which started as fishing villages or historic ports often have more character. Towns that are a port foremost and holiday resort second are described elsewhere in this book. Brochures about resorts and their adjacent villages are obtainable by phoning their Tourist Information Centres.*

CUMBRIA
Silloth* Quiet except for high-summer (SB).
Haverigg Quiet and small.
St Bees Quiet and small.
Seascale Quiet and small.
Grange-over-Sands* Quiet (SB).

LANCASHIRE
Morecambe* Large, popular (SB).
Fleetwood* Also a big port (SB).
Blackpool* Huge, popular (SB).
Lytham St Anne's* Quiet (SB).

MERSEYSIDE
Southport* Quiet, rather elegant (SB).
New Brighton* Popular (SB).
West Kirby Quiet (SB).

AVON
Weston-super-Mare* Popular (SB).

SOMERSET
Minehead* Historic parts (SB).

DEVON (north)
Ilfracombe* Sandy coves.

CORNWALL
Bude* Surfing centre (SB).
Newquay* Coves as well as wide beaches. Also a port (SB).
St Ives* Historic parts (SB).
Penzance* Port as well as resort (SB).
Falmouth* Sailing and port too (SB).
Mevagissey Fishing.

DEVON (south)
Salcombe* Many coves (SB).
Paignton* Quieter than adjoining **Torquay*** (SB).
Torquay* Huge resort (SB).
Teignmouth* Sailing (SB).

Dawlish* Quiet resort (SB).
Exmouth* Resort and port (SB).
Budleigh Salterton* Fishing.
Sidmouth* Regency resort.
Seaton* Small resort.

DORSET
Lyme Regis* Historic parts (SB).
Weymouth* See text (SB).
Swanage* Quiet (SB).
Poole* Vast natural harbour; sailing (SB).
Mudeford Fishing centre.
Bournemouth* Huge resort (SB).

HAMPSHIRE
Southsea Quiet, adjoining **Portsmouth***.
South Hayling Quiet.
Keyhaven Small boat centre.
Lymington Sailing.
Hamble Sailing centre.
Emsworth Sailing centre.

ISLE OF WIGHT
Ventnor* Quiet.
Shanklin* Popular resort (SB).
Sandown* Popular resort (SB).
Bembridge Sailing centre.
Ryde* Popular resort (SB).
Freshwater Quiet (SB).

WEST SUSSEX
Selsea Traditional seaside resort.
Bognor* Popular (SB).
Littlehampton* Quiet; sailing centre (SB).
Worthing* Major holiday centre.

EAST SUSSEX
Brighton* Large, sophisticated.
Seaford* Quiet.
Eastbourne* Quite large but unspoilt.
Bexhill* Quiet.
Hastings* Resort with fishing and historic associations.

KENT
Hythe Historic.
Folkestone* With fishing harbour.
Deal* Small; excellent fishing.
Ramsgate* Sailing centre (SB).
Broadstairs* Historic parts (SB).
Margate* Large and popular (SB).
Herne Bay* Quiet.
Whitstable* Good fishing (including oysters).

ESSEX
Southend* Big and popular.
Clacton* Big and popular (SB).
Frinton Sedate (SB).
Walton Small and popular (SB).

SUFFOLK
Felixstowe* Sedate resort.
Southwold Small, historic (SB).
Lowestoft* Fishing harbour (SB).

NORFOLK
Great Yarmouth* Harbour as well as popular resort (SB).
Cromer* Historic parts; fishing (SB).
Sheringham* Small and popular (SB).
Wells-next-the-Sea Small, quaint (SB).
Hunstanton* Sailing centre.

LINCOLNSHIRE
Skegness* Huge and popular (SB).
Ingoldmells Holiday camps (SB).
Chapel St Leonards Small.
Sutton-on-Sea Small and quiet; sophisticated (SB).
Mablethorpe* Popular (SB).

HUMBERSIDE
Cleethorpes* Popular (SB).
Withernsea* Small resort (SB).
Hornsea* Small resort (SB).
Bridlington* With fishing harbour; popular (SB).

NORTH YORKSHIRE
Filey* Popular (SB).
Scarborough* A major, rather dignified holiday centre (SB).
Whitby* Popular; fishing harbour; historic parts (SB).

CLEVELAND
Saltburn-by-the-Sea Rather sedate (SB).
Redcar Popular (SB).
Seaton Carew Popular (SB).

TYNE AND WEAR
South Shields* Sheltered beaches (SB).
Whitley Bay* Popular (SB).

13 Piers for pleasure

To walk underneath a pier at low tide is like walking through some petrified, leafless prehistoric forest. The great girders loom above you, rock-solid it seems and made to last forever.

The truth is sadly different, and one by one England's pleasure piers are being washed away. Each winter storm brings a new threat. In 1978, two piers were wrecked and four badly damaged. Fire, too, is a frequent occurrence, destroying wood superstructures; and quite a number of piers have been sliced in two by a ship at one time or another.

To have a long iron pier (if not two) was the ambition of every rising seaside resort in Victorian times. A mere jetty or harbourside for holidaymakers to walk along was not enough. Needless to say, Brighton led the way. Her first pier had been built in 1823, and it became the subject of a popular song (it was called the chain pier because it was built in the same manner as a suspension bridge):

> Of all the sweet pleasures that Brighton can boast,
> A walk on the Chain Pier delightest me most.
> That elegant structure, light, airy and free,
> Like a work of enchantment hangs over the sea.
> Then hey-derry-derry, be this the toast here,
> George the 4th and Old England, the People and Pier!

Soon Southend, Walton, Herne Bay, Southampton, Sheerness and Deal followed suit and then came the rush: altogether 100 piers were built around the coasts of Britain, but less than half have survived. For instance, Brighton's noble West Pier of 1866 is, at the time of writing, unsafe and closed.

Like a number of others, its deterioration began during the Second World War, when piers were considered a potential aid to German invasion: some were even dynamited to prevent their being used. The West Pier, straining under the weight of sandbag emplacements, had anti-aircraft guns on it, which naturally attracted bombardment. There are plans to get the pier re-opened one day.

The Palace Pier was opened in 1899 to replace the original chain pier destroyed in a storm, and is still going strong. When I arrived there was a shrill hubbub of French schoolchildren at the cast-iron turnstiles. Beyond stretched the white ironwork, a frolic of curlicues; and half a kilometre of wood deck, with feet scampering noisily over the planks to get to the decorative little kiosks (salvaged from the old chain pier) where toffee-apples and candy floss are sold.

Striped deck-chairs. The clairvoyant who tells horoscopes. The scratchy feel of rust and knobbly corrosion underneath the season's fresh white paint. The sea below, dizzily glimpsed through gaps between planks. The sound of waves surging onto the shingle. The anglers patiently waiting. Here were all the familiar components of that most traditional of seaside pleasures, a stroll along the pier.

A thriving pier is a whole community in its own right; its inhabitants have a way of life all their own. Eight thousand sightseers may flow on and off the Palace Pier in the course of a busy day, but the real people of the pier have in some cases gone to their daily work on it for 30 years or more. Nearly 200 people depend on the pier for their livelihood in summer; over 40 work on it all the year round. And that's not counting the shore-based suppliers and contractors, such as the painters whose work has constantly to be renewed.

Down on a lower deck, underneath the big pavilion at the end of the pier, I found Joe and Ted, two of the pier's most essential staff: they are welders. For 35 years they have inhabited a small workshop (with a blacksmith and a plumber alongside) down among the iron underpinnings of the pier, where barnacles form a thick crust on the metal, with mussels and limpets growing on top of one another. Even at low tide, there is nearly 4 m of sea swishing around the pier

Piers are disappearing at an alarming rate, but some keep up their former glory (Eastbourne, East Sussex).

end, and at high tide over 10 m. Joe and Ted go about their work in all weathers, keeping the pier safe for those thousands of feet trampling overhead.

For even longer, the pier has been the workplace of William Everett. General Manager for the last 34 years, he began as an office junior who was expected to work 80 hours a week in summer for £5. He and the pier are married to one another. His office (high up, overlooking the deck of the pier) is full of relics and old documents, some going back to the 1820s, and photographs of famous visitors.

And then there are all the traders and entertainers — the stallholders with their jokes, trinkets and toys, snacks and souvenirs. All the traditional seaside foods are there: ice creams, jellied eels, pink rock, shellfish, strawberries and baked potatoes — and alongside them newer favourites like popcorn and doughnuts, waffles and hamburgers.

You can have your photograph taken or your portrait painted, get lost in the crazy maze or the hall of mirrors, ride on a ghost train or a dodgem car, try your skill in a rifle-range or with a water-gun (or your luck in bingo), get a thrill in a speedboat or on the helter-skelter, go home with a T-shirt or glass goblet embellished with your name — or your arm tattooed with that of your loved one.

Sixty different diversions flourish on this one pier — in summer, that is. When winter comes, and the pier sometimes shudders as the sea flings itself up between the planks, the stallholders put up their shutters and leave. But the pier itself never closes and, for some tastes, it is at its best on solitary, wintry days when the wind threatens to blow you off your feet or snow blankets the onion-shaped domes and the architectural fantasies of the big pavilion at the end.

Once, those domes were kept brilliantly gilded. Once, strings of illuminations sparkled along the whole length of the pier after dark. Those magic touches have gone, and so have some of the pier's other splendours.

The theatre is one. Here (where Tommy Trinder was 'discovered' — Dick Emery and Ronnie Corbett too) all is silent. The huge timber building, with circles and boxes that can seat 1,200, stands empty. The cost of heating, and of insuring against fire, has kept it closed for over ten years. Its stained glass dome, its cherubs and golden garlands are hidden behind locked doors: will these ever open again? Only the exterior can still be enjoyed by the public. There was a particular kind of Egyptian-Indian style beloved of Victorian pier-builders, and the Palace pavilion is a good example of this whimsy.

Another thing that has changed is the amusement arcades. The old-style slot-machines have gone, relegated to a museum above the pavilion. In their place are modern fruit-machines, electronic games and radio-controlled model boats. Fortunately the charm of the old machines ('What the Butler Saw', 'Try Your Strength' and all the rest) was recognised by John Hayward, a young electrician, who began to collect them when they were being thrown out or sold off as scrap-metal. Starting with just one or two housed at home, he has now assembled and restored to working order a collection of over 100, valued at nearly £50,000.

On entering his museum, you can buy the old pennies needed to operate these vintage machines — some dating back to the 1890s. There are 'one-armed bandits' made in Chicago around 1920; a Victorian polyphone (disc music-box), usually seen only in the cowboy saloons of old westerns; optical illusions (the corpse that levitates, the mummy that emerges from a Pharaoh's tomb, and so forth); a coin-operated pianola; the very first electric pin-tables from 1935; and a great deal else to fascinate the nostalgic or intrigue the mechanically-minded.

These machines are now collected by many more people than John Hayward, and there is even a Pinball Owners Association — incorporating the Penny Slot Preservation Society — with a monthly magazine, advice on restoration, social events and tournaments (116 St James' Road, Sutton).

All this is far removed from the first beginnings of the pier, which had its origins in the days when gentry wanting to board the French packet moored off Brighton had to be lifted into boats by seamen: very unseemly for the ladies. That was the sole reason why the chain pier was built; but once it was there it soon became a popular place for promenading — better than the muddy road along the shore. The 1899 pier which replaced it was not only longer but stronger, so that bigger boats could tie up at it; and on deck, under the first out-door electric-lighting in England, there was open-air dancing, classical music and gaiety for the fashionable throng. All gone. But the domes and ironwork scrolls, the lacy arches and oriental flourishes still live on and the turnstiles clack cheerfully round as a million visitors a year stream on and off the pier.

Piers open to the public

Many piers close in winter. For information phone the appropriate Tourist Information Centre, which can also tell you about angling facilities, steamer trips from piers, plays and concerts in their theatres. Those piers with theatres or concert halls often have events like wrestling or roller-skating championships, discos etc.

LANCASHIRE
Morecambe* Central Pier (1868). With ballroom. Stone Jetty (1848). Not a typical pier; with oceanarium.
Fleetwood* Victoria Pier (1910). Amusements include bingo.
Blackpool* North Pier (1863). With an Indian pavilion. Central Pier (1868). Theatre and entertainments. South Pier (1893). With theatre and bandstand.
Lytham St Anne's* The Pier (1885). Fire destroyed its pavilion in 1974.

MERSEYSIDE
Southport* The Pier (1860). Very long; with railway.

AVON
Clevedon (1869). Temporarily closed for repair.
Weston-super-Mare* Old Pier (1862). This connects with Birnbeck rocks, and is the centre of controversy: should it be incorporated in a proposed new marina or not? Exhibition of old slot machines and vintage cars. Grand Pier (1904). Amusements include rail-less train and go-karts.

SOMERSET
Burnham-on-Sea* The Pier (1906). Short; no amusements.

CORNWALL
Falmouth* Prince of Wales Pier (1905). Short; few amusements.

DEVON (south)
Paignton* The Pier (1879). Currently being modernised. Amusements include go-karts.
Torquay* Princess Pier (1891). Fire-damaged; currently being restored.
Teignmouth* The Pier (1865). End part is unsafe; shore end has amusements.

DORSET
Weymouth* Old Pier (1812). Oldest surviving pier in Britain, part of the harbour; with theatre. Bandstand Pier (1939). With theatre/concert hall, etc.
Swanage* The Pier (1896). Mainly used by anglers.
Bournemouth* The Pier (1880). With theatre and big entertainment centre.
Boscombe The Pier (1889, later rebuilt). Usual amusements.

HAMPSHIRE
Hythe The Pier (1880). Railway; ferry to **Southampton***.
Southampton* Royal Pier (1833). Ferry to **Isle of Wight**. Its future is in some doubt.
Southsea Clarence Pier (1861). Hovercraft to **Isle of Wight**. South Parade Pier (1879, later rebuilt). Usual amusements.

ISLE OF WIGHT
Yarmouth* The Pier (1876). Mainly for anglers. Its future is in doubt.
Totland Bay The Pier (1870). Some amusements; used by anglers. Houses the Data Gathering Centre (which supplies oil-rigs with advice on wave-weather conditions).
Ventnor* Royal Victoria Pier (1863, later rebuilt). Usual amusements.
Shanklin* The Pier (1891). Usual amusements and pavilion.
Sandown* The Pier (1878). Usual amusements.

Ryde* The Pier (1813–60). Successive extensions lengthened this to 760 m. With B.R. railway.

WEST SUSSEX
Bognor* The Pier (1865). Amusements, angling, theatre closed.
Worthing* The Pier (1862, later rebuilt). 300 m long. With dancehall and miniature railway.

EAST SUSSEX
Brighton* See text.
Eastbourne* The Pier (1870). With theatre.
Hastings* The Pier (1872). Usual amusements.

KENT
Deal* The Pier (1957, replacing an older structure). For anglers.
Herne Bay* The Pier (1873). Short pier; sports pavilion.

ESSEX
Westcliff-on-Sea Only a jetty.
Southend* The Pier (1889). Over 2 km: longest in the world. Plans are afoot for its resuscitation.
Clacton* The pier (1871). A broad pier with five acres of amusements and various sports.
Walton-on-the-Naze* The Pier (1895). 860 m long. Usual amusements.

SUFFOLK
Felixstowe* The Pier (1904). Amusement arcade.
Southwold The Pier (1900, later rebuilt). Only shore-end pavilion (with amusements) is in use.
Lowestoft* South Pier (1846). With amusements, restaurant and pavilion.
Claremont Pier (1903). With restaurant.

NORFOLK
Great Yarmouth* Wellington Pier (1853). Amusements include Winter Gardens. New developments are being planned. Britannia Pier (1900). With pavilion.

Cromer* The Pier (1901). Amusements and lifeboat station.

LINCOLNSHIRE
Skegness* The Pier (1881). Originally a long pier but storm damage in 1978 cut it in half. Restoration is planned, together with a theatre and monorail.

HUMBERSIDE
Cleethorpes* The Pier (1875). Amusements include bingo, shows etc.

CLEVELAND
Saltburn-by-the-Sea The Pier (1869). Storm-damaged in 1974: amusement arcade now planned for shore end.
Redcar The Pier (1873). Short pier; with ballroom.

To learn more about piers
If you join the National Piers Society (82 Speed House, Barbican, EC2), you will help the piers preservation movement and receive their interesting newsletters together with invitations to, for instance, 'pier weekends'. A number of piers are now listed buildings (officially recognised as being of outstanding historic and/or architectural interest and not to be demolished without a permit). Nevertheless, these may still be rotting away — the particularly fine one at **Clevedon** in Avon is an example – which is why local save-our-pier societies are becoming active on their behalf. The restoration of Clevedon Pier may have started by the time this book is published, solely as a result of action by the local pier preservation society. There are other societies at **Brighton***, **Southend***, **Southampton*** and **Weston-super-Mare***. The Piers Information Bureau (38 Holte Road, Atherstone, Warwickshire) can provide any information on piers.

Further reading
'Guide to British Piers' has notes on the history of each one. This is obtainable from the National Piers Society (see above) which also has stock of an out-of-print book, 'Seaside Piers' by Simon Adamson.

14 Sailing, marinas and races

As fast as piers are falling down, marinas are springing up.

A marina (the word and the idea came to us from America) may be anything from a plank jetty or two, providing moorings for a few small boats, right up to a huge artificial harbour capable of accommodating thousands. Most are accessible to the public, and some of the smaller ones can be as interesting to visit as the smart and larger marinas: for instance, I always enjoy Hoo marina (on the Medway estuary, Kent) because among the smaller craft one can usually see a sailing-barge or two, and there's a rambling riverside path leading to Cookham Woods and the crumbling remains of a 17th-century fort. And the disused canal basin at Gravesend (on the Thames estuary) is interesting for its old quayside buildings, lock and bollards that are the backdrop to the small yachts.

Totally different, in style as well as scale, is the huge modern marina near Brighton which is so large that it even has its own guidebook. It's the biggest marina in Europe, and even Chichester has only half its capacity. There are nearly 130 acres of water, promenades, breakwaters (frequented by anglers), nautical shops, a snack bar, and on board the 'Medina', a former Gibraltar-to-Tangier ferry, a restaurant.

This marina goes out of its way to welcome and cater for families who want an interesting day by the sea (there is a small admission charge), with speed-boat trips or guided cruises and education packs available. There's plenty to see: boatyard, lock, floating jetties, historic vessels as well as modern ones, visiting craft flying the flags of all nations, and a calendar of events throughout the year — races, boat shows and regattas of all kinds, which you can usually watch at no extra charge. (To find out what's on, phone 0273 693636.) Local fishermen use the marina as their harbour, and you can buy fish from the fish farm. Sometimes displays of windsurfing or water-skiing are laid on. Ultimately, the marina will be virtually a small port in its own right, for much more building is planned.

I wandered up and down the jetties where the small boats were moored in disciplined lines, a coppice of masts swaying in a frisky breeze, wavelets lapping at the bright white hulls. Across the water the grey of the concrete breakwaters has already attracted a patina of seaweed: green above, then the dark brown of bladderwrack lower down. It was a bright, colourful scene: masts were reflected, rippling, in the green water; red handrails; bright blue tarpaulins pulled tight over cabins and furled sails. This was in spring; come summer, the boats would be out and about and the marina humming with activity.

The inner harbour houses the underwater cages of spider-crabs, caught offshore and awaiting sale (to buyers from Spain, I was told); and the marina's collection of historic boats. These usually include (when not sailing elsewhere) 'Marabu', a racing yacht sailed by Goering in the 1930s then snatched from Kiel by the Royal Navy, which used her for training purposes until recently, and 'Jester', which once belonged to Colonel Hasler (leader of the 'cockleshell heroes' raid on Bordeaux), which has three times taken part in the single-handed transatlantic races. Very different are the 'old gaffers' such as oyster-smacks 'Speedwell' and 'Gladys' from Whitstable; and the elegant pilot cutter 'Baroque', her red sails once a familiar sight on the choppy waters of the Bristol Channel. The marina also has an early inshore lifeboat from Norfolk, 'Jo-Ann', with oars and sail — quite unlike the modern one based in the outer harbour, ready for use in a crisis. During the summer all sorts of ships call in, such as the brigantine 'Royalist' which is the Sea Cadets' training ship. When I was there, clinker-built 'Seaway' was in the harbour and Sir Francis Chichester's 'Gipsy Moth III'.

What you find from one visit to the next may be quite different: a canoe regatta, a Fleet Air Arm display or perhaps somebody setting off to sail round the world. There is a changing assortment of boats for sale, or for charter. (If you can make up a party of six or so, the cost of your own boat plus skipper can be divided.) Chartering to go sea-angling is increasingly popular.

There is some criticism of the number of marinas sprouting up all over the place, sometimes displacing wildfowl from their natural habitats, and often

Historic ships are restored and conserved by the Maritime Trust: the tea-clipper 'Cutty Sark' at Greenwich (London).

Sailing holidays are increasingly popular. 'Provident', an ex-Brixham trawler, now owned by the Maritime Trust, is used by the Island Cruising Club for sailing holidays to Brittany and the Channel Islands.

costing boat-owners a lot for their moorings. One company has come up with an alternative: the Rotork Boat-Park. So far, there is only one of these boat-parks on the coast (in Poole, Dorset) but the idea may spread. Four acres of derelict industrial land was used, with access to water that is never less than 6 m deep. First Rotork developed a special fork-lift truck ('Big Berther') which is capable of lifting a boat bodily out of the water — any boat up to 9 m and 4 tonnes — and then trundling off with it to its allotted parking space where it is gently lowered onto a steel cradle. Even bigger boats (up to 10 tonnes) can be shifted too, using a special hoist. The berthing operation takes only five minutes including a hose-down, and boat-owners are entitled to as many launchings as they want, at any hour. Charges are much the same as for marina moorings but the big saving is on maintenance: moored boats rapidly become fouled by weed, the clearing of which in dry dock can add up to hundreds of pounds a year. (Rotork's phone number is 02013 81458.)

The big risk in visiting a marina or yacht harbour as a spectator is that you too may get infected with the urge to own a boat. I asked John Perkins, managing director of the Brighton Marina, about this. 'Is boat ownership a rich man's hobby?' I enquired, so our conversation started with some hard financial facts.

A beginner might opt for a secondhand 8-m sailing-boat — big enough to take the family for a summer holiday. The first cost, before buying, would be a survey (by a fully qualified surveyor) to ensure that the boat was sound: say £75. The boat and all its necessary equipment would be unlikely to cost much less than £10,000: mortgages are available but, unlike house mortgages, these do not carry any tax relief. If the boat were berthed at the marina, this would cost £500 a year. As to other running costs, do-it-yourself work can keep mainten-ance low but at least £100 might be needed to have the boat hauled out of the water once a year for her bottom to be defouled. Fuel costs are significant only if the engine is used a lot. Against all this might be offset some savings: the cost, for instance, of holidays in hotels.

As to choosing a boat, the pages of yachting journals are a good place to start. Just as estate agents sell houses, so yacht brokers sell boats (reputable ones have the initials ABYA or YBDSA after their name) and often advertise them in these journals. There is an annual boat show at Southampton and one in London.

Before thinking of boat purchase, learning to sail is obviously vital. Books can teach you about the parts of a boat and how they function; and also the theory of navigation, tides, weather and safety rules. (John Perkins recommended two: the official manual of the Royal Yachting Association and 'The Optimist Book: First Steps in Small Boat Sailing' by Hansen and Aarre.) But a course at a good sailing school is essential. You will be taught — perhaps during winter, at evening classes — to tie knots, read charts, use a compass, set a course, carry out maintenance and repairs, and select the right kind of clothing. When it comes to practical training, usually one instructor takes two novices out at a time: some of these courses are residential.

The majority of sailing schools (and boat builders) cluster around those parts of the coast that provide the best conditions for sailing in safety — such as the Solent, Chichester harbour in West Sussex, West Mersea and Burnham-on-Crouch in Essex, Pinmill near Ipswich (Suffolk), Blakeney in Norfolk, and Poole (Dorset) where I went to see what the Parkstone Sailing School had to offer — in the setting of the second largest natural harbour of the world. Apart from helping to run conventional sailing courses at all levels, John West has had the good sense to initiate a four-hour trial run for those still wondering whether or not they want to get involved. We zipped out in a small dinghy across the choppy waves to where 'Virgo Voyager' was swinging at her mooring, clambered on board and went down into the carpeted cabin. The four-berth cruiser seemed a lot for a novice to handle.

'A good deal easier', said John 'than dinghy sailing which involves considerable balance and control — an exciting sport, but wet and windy. In a boat like this, kept steady by its very long keel of cast iron, you need never fear overturning. People who take up cruising soon treat their boat like a country cottage — it becomes a second home to them.'

John's enthusiasm was infectious as he spoke of the pleasure of sailing along at a spanking 6 knots (equivalent to 7 m.p.h.), smoothly and quietly. The engine would be used only when entering or leaving harbour, so no form of travel could be cheaper than this (and the value of a boat does not depreciate much). He spoke of the relaxing effect of changing to such a very different time scale, of the feeling of independence and self-reliance that goes with sailing. 'You have to learn to alternate periods of idleness with bursts of intense activity. Tides and weather may keep you hard at it during the night, yet there may be hours of the day when you just sit back and relax.'

(Parkstone Sailing School's phone number is 709707 0202.)

Of course not everyone who wants to sail intends to buy more than a little sailing-dinghy, to use for day-trips — but proper tuition is just as essential, and holidays spent learning to sail are immensely popular. Here is what such a holiday might offer. (The details in this case come from the Rockley Point Sailing School, which also operates within the lovely natural harbour of Poole: many miles of waters sheltered by the Purbeck hills, with islands and creeks, sandy beaches and nature reserves.)

The school has different boats to suit different levels of ability and, accompanying them, 20 safety boats with radio links keeping a watchful eye on novices — among whom are children from eight upwards. Though whole families often come along, children are not taught on the same boats as adults. In fact, some members of a family may opt for canoeing, windsurfing or even water-

Setting off to spend a day learning dinghy-sailing.

skiing while others go sailing. There are picnics, occasional barbecues and a good deal of social activity. Children holidaying on their own are accommodated in luxury caravans, with 'house mothers'. Families can book into local accommodation at any level from luxury hotel down to a tent. The school sells off its sailing dinghies every autumn, to get new ones next spring. Students and ex-students often buy these at bargain prices — and ex-students can also hire dinghies on Sundays, when there is no tuition going on.

(For more details of Rockley Point Sailing School, phone 02013 77272.)

While in Poole I went to look at yet another kind of sailing — even more wet and windy than dinghies: wind-surfing. A sport of swerve-and-dip strictly for the lean and muscular young, I supposed, but no — a 95 kg 60-year-old was hard at it too, one of many taught by James Ellis. I watched the wetsuited, life-jacketed figures stepping onto their hulls (similar to surfboards), raising their flexible masts, hauling up their sails — and falling in, again and again. 'It's just a simple matter of technique and balance', said James Ellis airily as yet another splash sent the cold water flying. He reckons to make a competent windsurfer after only eight hours' tuition (half on a simulator, half in the water). Some will go on to master really big sails and achieve speeds of up to 25 knots — the equivalent of 35 m.p.h. although to the windsurfer it feels like 100 m.p.h. It's an exciting and challenging sport, fascinating to watch and it now has its own magazines, association and championships. (Poole Windsurfer Centre, 0202 741744.) The Windsurfer Class Association can supply information about other schools. It is at 489 Finchley Road, London NW3.

In estuaries and round the coast, boats of various kinds are out racing nearly every week in the year. Kent has a mid-winter race on the Medway estuary known as the Hoo Freezer, for obvious reasons: dozens of small sailing-dinghies compete, even in force 9 gales, and even though many are likely to overturn before completing the course.

Racing is no novelty: gig-racing, for example, has taken place in the Scillies and at Newquay (Cornwall) for centuries. (Gigs are heavy, 10-m rowing boats peculiar to the area.) These days, there are races for yachts of all sizes, power-boats, row-boats, sea-canoes, sailing-barges and other historic craft, and even for model yachts. There are hovercraft and hydroplane races, too. As if that were not enough, some resorts organise raft races and even tin-bath races.

The most prestigious races are, of course, at Cowes (Isle of Wight), home of the Royal Yacht Club; but the most spectacular is the Tall Ships Race.

Each summer some 20 nations enter as many big sail training-ships as they can: square-rigged windjammers (these participate in alternate years only), slender schooners and ketches of 10 m or over. These are invariably followed by about 15,000 other craft (from small yachts to steamers) carrying spectators. The tall ships themselves are manned by about 3,000 youngsters, working alongside adults. As to the course, this varies from year to year. The organisers have chosen Falmouth to Lisbon for the 1982 race, with the ships later racing back again, to Southampton. To see this fleet of great ships setting sail is the sight of a lifetime. (Details from the Sail Training Association, 07017 86367.)

And then there are the regattas — a get-together of boats not just for a series of races but for a lively social gathering too.

It would be impossible to list here all the sea racing events that are held in the course of a year: every Tourist Information Centre and regional Tourist Board listed at the beginning of the book has programmes that can be obtained on request. Two of the most outstanding events are Cowes week (0983 524343) and the thrilling Fastnet race (01-493 5252), both usually in early August. The latter starts at Cowes and finishes at Plymouth.

At the other extreme are barges. Those that sail are described in Chapter 6. Some have engines. Most are 'dumb' barges — that is, vessels without any motive-power or steering, which are hauled along by a tug.

There was a time, though, when dumb barges driven along by *oars* ('sweeps') were a common sight on the estuaries and along rivers, particularly the Thames: a tremendous feat of strength, skill and courage. It is at least a dozen years since the last was shifted by this means, but for one day in the year it is possible to see such a spectacle again, when the annual barge-driving race organised by the Transport on Water Association takes place (from Greenwich to Westminster).

Even though racing barges are unladen, each may weigh anything up to 35 tonnes; yet, for the 12 km of the course, they will be propelled forward simply by the strength of two pairs of arms, and two wood paddles 10 m long. Not only is muscle needed but considerable skill, for there are currents and other hazards along the way. Barge-driving may well be one of the slowest races you'll ever watch, but it is also one of the most unusual: unique, in fact.

I had watched the event from the shore previously; this time, I chose to go in a launch. On Greenwich pier, a crowd was gathering. The excitement began to build up, as it does at any race, at least an hour before the first competitor was even to be seen. A television cameraman was positioning his gear; a river-police launch zipped by in a cloud of spray, with blue light flashing; and already there were queues for hot-dogs, commemorative T-shirts, programmes, lavatories. Supporters were decked with rosettes in their favourite's colours, officials with gold braid, and waiting launches with bunting or lines of signal flags.

By 10.45 the first of the barges were being hauled to the starting-line by their respective tugs. Each barge was gaily painted in carnival style, and in some cases their crew wore costumes to match their theme: 'Trafalgar', 'Tottenham Hotspur', 'London Pride' or whatever (and of course, it being the summer of 1981, there was a 'Lady Diana'). The umpire's small hydrofoil busied around, like a very small dog with a flock of very large sheep. The only people ignoring all the goings-on were two beachcombers on the foreshore concentrating on their metal-detectors.

11.0 strikes and it is time to board the catamaran from which we will be following the race — in the select company of a dozen mayors, complete with their gold chains, from all the waterfront boroughs. Some 3,000 spectators are filing onto a fleet of such launches, more will be on the shore along the route.

11.25. The weathervane on the pier is of the fixed opinion that the north wind is here to stay (it will make the going hard) but at any rate the sun suddenly breaks through, and on board there is already a glass in every hand and a cheerful hubbub of people intent on enjoying the day. We and some hovering gulls watch the starter's boat move off: on board is a figure in red tunic with pleated skirt, big silver badge on left arm. This is a Doggett's Coat-and-Badge winner — that is, one who in the past came first in the annual rowing race for Thames watermen, which first started in 1715. The launches are on the move, taking up position (under radio orders).

11.30. A siren blast, and they're off! No burst of speed — it needs *tremendous* heaving on those oars to overcome the initial inertia and get the huge vessels to move forward. Then they pick up speed, the oars develop a rhythm. And almost immediately there's a demonstration of what the oarsmen are up against, as one of the barges is driven sideways by a current and has difficulty in getting on course again.

To drive his long oar through the resisting waters, strong enough to bend (and sometimes break) it, each man in the pair has to take a run from the stern of the barge and up onto the hatch-combing to get sufficient purchase.

12.0. We're passing two great ships from Sweden and, like all others moored along our route, they sound their sirens as the barges go by. Many of the lighter barges, which had been placed to the rear at the start of the race, have by now caught up with the bigger ones. Two barges have almost collided, and there's too little clearance between them for the oars to sweep.

12.30. 'Bowherald' of Cardiff, unloading sand, sounds her great hooter. We pass one waterfront inn after another, their verandahs lined with cheering spectators. The barge 'Chase Me Charlie', which had been in the lead, has now fallen back: her straining crew have stripped to the waist, and the muscles in those tattooed arms are bulging.

12.45. At Wapping Old Stairs, sightseers are sitting on the sea-wall with legs dangling. Along this stretch of the river are silted-up creeks between Dickensian warehouses slowly rotting away. 'St Paul's' is in the lead but can she keep it up? Her crew's faces are crimson, their teeth gritted, shirts clinging with sweat. A mallard on a moored dinghy preens unconcerned, back turned to the struggle.

1.0. Past sailing-barges and under Tower Bridge. Youngsters visiting the Tower of London cheer and wave. There's a renewed chorus of sirens as we pass HMS 'Belfast', a naval frigate and a minesweeper alongside her. Each bridge that we glide under is lined with spectators leaning over and clapping.

1.30. Our launch has moved ahead to the finishing line, to await the arrival of barges. Suddenly, a clamour of hooting from the assembled tugs as the winner shoots forward under Waterloo Bridge: 'St Paul's' is way ahead, her oars still keeping up a fine rhythm. There's leaping up and down, somebody pops a champagne bottle, then one by one the others come in. Nearby, Big Ben strikes two. A gruelling race is over.

The oarsmen in these races are all Freemen of the Watermen's Company, or their apprentices. That means they are qualified and licensed both to convey passengers ('watermen') and to carry goods ('lightermen').

Their unique knowledge of tides and currents has often been handed down through many generations of watermen — not just from fathers to sons but sometimes from father to daughter too: one competitor in this race was a 17-year-old girl, making Thames history. The youngest was 16, the oldest (Ronnie Fagin, a 'living legend') was a ripe 55.

There are two interesting books about the life of the lightermen in the old days: 'Men of the Tideway' by Dick Fagan, and 'Under Oars' by Bob Harris.

Sailing

Other attractive villages or small towns where there is plenty of sailing activity include:

CUMBRIA
Roa Island
Ravenglass*
Haverigg
Harrington

LANCASHIRE
Glasson Dock near **Lancaster**

DEVON
Bideford*
Dartmouth*

HAMPSHIRE
Lymington near **Beaulieu***
Bucklers Hard near **Beaulieu***
Hamble near **Southampton***

ISLE OF WIGHT
Yarmouth*
Bembridge
Wooton Bridge

WEST SUSSEX
Bosham and other villages near **Chichester***

ESSEX
Burnam-on-Crouch near **Southend***

SUFFOLK
Woodbridge
Walberswick near **Lowestoft***

HUMBERSIDE
Bridlington*

Where to find out more

For addresses of marinas and harbours contact the National Yacht Harbours Association. 06284 71361

For lists of sailing schools (including windsurfing) and clubs contact the Royal Yachting Association. 04862 5022

The RYA is also the main source of information on powerboats, hydroplanes and motor cruising, but for information on small hovercraft write to the Hover Association, 4 Collinwood Road, Risinghurst, Oxford.

The Windsurfer Class Association can supply information about windsurfing schools. 01–794 5652. (These organisations can also tell you where races and regattas are to be seen each year.)

Sailing is not, of course, the only maritime sport. Anyone thinking of taking up another sport by, on or in the sea can obtain information about what's involved, training, clubs and the whereabouts of facilities from the organisations listed below; or, if you merely want to be a spectator, where races or other contests are being held each year.

Sand Yachting: British Federation of Sand and Land Yacht Clubs. 0253 725981
Sea Angling: National Federation of Sea Anglers. 0825 3589

Sea Canoeing: British Canoe Union. 97 41341
Sea Rowing: Amateur Rowing Association. 01–748 3632
Sub-Aqua Diving and Snorkelling: British Sub-Aqua Club. 01–584 7163
Surfing: British Surfing Association. 0202 746154
Water-Skiing: British Water-Ski Federation. 01–584 8262
Wildfowling: Wildfowlers' Association. 0244 570881

Where swimming is concerned, there is a variety of events from local round-the-pier races to occasional attempts at cross-Channel records. The latter start at **St Margaret's Bay** near **Dover*** (Kent). The Amateur Swimming Association can supply details, 0509 30431. Swimmers who want the sea with the chill taken off can also find out from the Association where the best sea-water pools are (filled and emptied by each tide). There is, for instance, a huge one at **Cleethorpes*** (Humberside) surrounded by sand and palms, while the one at **Whitley Bay*** (Tyne and Wear) even has artificial waves.

There are naturist beaches, where bathing naked is allowed, at resorts in Cornwall, Kent and Sussex, for example; for information on naturist holidays write to the Central Council for British Naturism, Orpington, Kent or Cornish Leisureworld, Carlyon Bay, St Austell, Cornwall.

15 Boat-trips

It's unthinkable to visit the seaside, and not go to sea! Even the briefest ferry-crossing, or quick trip round the lighthouse, immediately turns auntie with her beach bag and sun-specs into a true descendant of Nelson with telescope and eye-patch. No gangway? Then she will be heaved aboard by weatherbeaten hands that have helped thousands of such aunties, without dropping even one into Davy Jones' locker, intrepid mariners all.

Which trip to choose?

There are harbour cruises — lots to see and especially interesting for ship-spotters. I went round Portsmouth Harbour on the big motor vessel 'Solent Enterprise' spending an hour looking at one vast warship after another, white ensigns flicking bravely in the breeze, and at the busy commercial port, with its cross-Channel ferries coming and going. More sadly, the sight of the creek where there are berthed naval ships waiting to be scrapped or sold. Boys strenuously canoeing by the side of a huge grey fleet auxiliary (a tanker, to supply fuel to warships at sea) looked as small as scurrying mice. We passed little pleasure-boats, white sails taut; and terns bobbing on the waves. There was the boatyard where 'Gipsy Moth IV' and other famous yachts were built and launched. And everyone craned to see the royal yacht 'Britannia'.

Flags interest me, so I asked the significance of the ones 'Britannia' was flying. The familiar white flag with the red cross of St George, with the Union

Jack in an upper quarter, is the flag of the Royal Navy — even I knew that one! But the white-and-red with a red dot in each quarter? 'That means an admiral is aboard', I was told. Some other ships at anchor were flying red-and-yellow flags: the upper one, quartered, stood for the letter 'R'; the lower, diagonally striped, for 'Y'. R and Y are shorthand for the message 'Please pass slowly'. Signal flags are seen less often now that radio messages are used more.

I hung over the taffrail as the cruise ended, appreciating the skill — the delicacy — with which the skipper manoeuvred his boat alongside the great, barnacled-encrusted timbers of the landing-stage. Shrieks of alarm from the switchback and rollercoaster of the fairground by the pier, but down here not the slightest bump to upset auntie.

Then there are the ferries, small and large. I crossed the Mersey on one of the most famous of them all. Its sounds (hoot and clang, clatter of feet, bang of gangplank) are familiar to thousands of commuters who use it like a bus, to get from their homes in the Wirral peninsula across to work in Liverpool. The very first ferry was provided by monks at Birkenhead Priory, but after Henry VIII broke up the monasteries the ferry rights passed to various owners. What was once a very long crossing, of one-and-a-half hours by sail, and dangerous in those tricky currents, is now gobbled up in ten minutes by the powerful 25 h.p. engine; but the captain still needs great skill when there is fog or the seas are rough, for the Mersey is the fastest-flowing river in England, the tide rises 10 m, and it is one of the trickiest of all the world's waterways. Yet the ferry has never missed a crossing. My very first view of Liverpool was as everyone should see it for the first time — from the ferry. It was at dusk, in winter, and the lights had just been turned on. That immense floating quay lay ahead, and beyond it reared the tall Liver and Cunard buildings, bright twinkling streets behind: one of the most famous waterfront views in the world. It is said that the ferry is becoming too expensive to continue (fares are already heavily sub-sidised) and everyone will be forced, one day, to go through the Mersey tunnel instead. That will be a sad day for Liverpool.

Then there are crossings to islands, often with seabirds and seals to be seen. A group was already waiting for 'Glad Tidings' when I arrived at the Seahouses (Northumberland) quay. We stood and watched one of the traditional cobles being launched, to go out for salmon (these east coast boats have high bows, and keels designed for berthing on beaches). The air was sharp with the smell of salt and fish; young fishermen were playing football among the long-idle lime kilns (lime used to be baked here for export), the Trinity House stores and the lifeboat house. The quayside was dotted with bollards, a 'snake's honeymoon' of ropes, stacks of fish boxes and a round, red mine from the Second World War — now a collecting box for the Shipwrecked Mariners' Society.

At last we were aboard and soon out of the harbour for our two-and-a-half-hour trip, leaving behind the terns on the weedy rock pools and the gulls perched on the navigation light at the end of the jetty. The tyres that serve as fenders were hauled in, and the boat began to pitch a little. The shore receded fast: to the north lay sand dunes and a beach still peppered with concrete tank traps from the war, and in the hazy distance, Bamburgh Castle. The spur of rock on which this stands points its finger to the Farne Islands, our destination, part of the same jagged outcrop of whinstone. A dozen gulls hopefully followed 'Glad Tidings': they might have done better to follow the solitary trawler that passed us, laden, on its way into the harbour.

The mate of 'Glad Tidings' chatted to me about his life on this wood boat — though built only ten years ago, she is of traditional construction (larch on an oak frame, built in Arbroath, Scotland). The crews of these pleasure-boats have to make enough money in summer to see them through the winter, eked out with occasional work on farms or lorry driving. Apart from taking out food and water to the wardens on the islands, there is nothing else to do once the holiday-makers have gone.

Suddenly we had arrived at the islands, owned by the National Trust, and the boat paused in the lee of a cliff thronged with guillemots, kittiwakes and shags — the hubbub was deafening. On the top of the Pinnacles (stack rocks, just off-shore) a thousand guillemots — rather like slender penguins — manage to perch. The dark sea reflected the black rocks, white with droppings at the top, encrusted with barnacles below. Out at sea, a great crowd of shags were afloat.

The boat moved on. Three razorbills, stiff and immaculate as head-waiters in a hotel, made off at our approach, but most of the birds were quite unconcerned by the engine noise or the chatter of the passengers. Inland, we could see a throng of tiny puffins (called the parrots of the sea, because of their big, colourful beaks), each standing sentinel at his nest, a burrow in the turf.

Every precious ledge in the cliff, however tiny, was occupied by kittiwakes, preening, gossiping or squabbling. Shags, too, had their nests here — some of them were quite large piles of seaweed. Puffins out at sea dived at our approach, to surface a long distance away. It is difficult for their stubby little bodies to get airborne quickly.

Now we were near Longstone Island (made famous by Grace Darling: see Chapter 28), and surrounded by the gently bobbing heads of seals, big eyes watching us curiously. There is a colony of 5,000 here, some of them 30 years old. A slow curve of the back as one dived. Occasional puffy breaths. A watchful cow, mottled body, rearing up to take a closer look at us. And several with noses only above water — fast asleep, their bodies swinging like pendulums below the surface. Such gentle, inoffensive creatures.

On we went again. Terns flew overhead, beaks laden with small fish (sild or sand-eel) which they were carrying back to their young. On the next island lie the ribs of the last sailing-ship to be wrecked in these islands, in 1916, and the nests of shags — the downy young almost as big as the parents who still take care of them. I saw a solitary oystercatcher with long red beak, and later a rare roseate tern.

There were hundreds more puffins on these cliffs, darting anxious glances at our approach or making away hurriedly, bright orange feet spread wide at take-off. I watched a young shag plunge its head far down its parent's throat to gobble the half-digested food brought up for it. The little terns were vociferous:

The old paddle-steamer 'Waverley' goes from resort to resort every summer with day-trippers on board.

the more vulnerable the bird, the louder its voice; and only the powerful ones, large and saw-billed do not need to shout.

We were helped out of the tossing boat and scrambled up the steep rocks of Staple Island with, for the most part, more attention to safety than to dignity. Even in late summer (when most of the birds will have ended their breeding season and gone back to sea), these islands are worth visiting — a wilderness of fissured rocks and gulleys, colourful with moss or lichen. But earlier in the year it is possible to come within touching distance of the shags, sitting unperturbed on their eggs, and of the miaouing kittiwakes. And so down those slithering rocks again, back to harbour and to a well-earned Craster kipper tea.

(The public are not admitted to the islands during the breeding season which lasts from 15th May to 15th July. Details from National Trust information centre, 0665 720424.)

Boat-trips

Nearly every resort has short boat-trips (coastal or estuary) available, and a number have half-day or full-day ones too. The following resorts are particularly well supplied with boat-trips to a variety of places up and down their coast; many of these bigger boats have dining-saloons and bars:
Minehead* (Somerset)
Plymouth* and **Torquay*** (south Devon)
Falmouth* (Cornwall)
Poole* and **Bournemouth*** (Dorset)
Southampton* (Hampshire)
Portsmouth* and **Southsea** (Hampshire)
Ryde* (Isle of Wight)
Great Yarmouth* (Norfolk)
Bridlington* (Humberside)
Scarborough* (North Yorkshire)

From the ports of Kent and from **Newhaven*** (East Sussex) there are day-trips to France, from Lancashire, to the Isle of Man, from **Felixstowe*** (Suffolk) to Belgium.

Places like **Liverpool***, **Plymouth***, **Southampton*** and **Portsmouth*** have particularly interesting round-the-harbour (or round-the-docks) boat-trips. The Mersey estuary cruises of the 'Royal Iris' are famous, 051 227 5181. For more trips to islands, see Chapter 23. For coastal voyages on historic vessels, see Chapter 6.

In most resorts it is possible for a party to hire their own boat and skipper and go on a route of their own choosing. Some boats are equipped for sea-angling. Tourist Information Centres have details.

Ferries
The following take cars as well as pedestrians across estuaries:
CORNWALL
Fowey* – **Bodinnick** 072687 232
King Harry near **Falmouth*** – **Philleigh**

0872 86231

DEVON (south)
Dartmouth* – **Kingswear** Lower: 080 425 342 Higher: 080 43 3351
Devonport, Plymouth* – **Torpoint** 0752 812233

DORSET
Sandbanks near **Poole*** – **Shell Bay** 092 944 203

ISLE OF WIGHT
Cowes 098 382 293041

For its members, the AA has a free leaflet with times and sailing details of ferries.

Ferries across estuaries for pedestrians only:
LANCASHIRE
Fleetwood* – **Knott End** 03917 71141

MERSEYSIDE
Liverpool* – **Wallasey** and **Birkenhead*** 051 227 5181

AVON
Weston-super-Mare* – **Brean Down**

DEVON (north)
Appledore – **Instow** 0271 860578

CORNWALL
Padstow – **Rock** 08413 239
Helford – **Helford Passage** 0326 250278
Fowey* – **Polruan** and **Bodinnick** 072687 394 or 453
Falmouth* – **Flushing** 0326 318534
Falmouth* – **St Mawes** 0326 318534

DEVON (south)
Portlemouth – **Salcombe*** 054884 2286
Plymouth* – **Torpoint** 0752 812233

Plymouth* – Cremyll 0752 822202
Star Cross – Exmouth* 03952 72009

HAMPSHIRE
Southampton* – Hythe 0703 843203
Portsmouth* – Gosport 07017 24551

WEST SUSSEX
Bosham – West Itchenor 0243 512301

SUFFOLK
Felixstowe* – Harwich* 02555 2004

Felixstowe* – Bawdsey 03942 3469
Walberswick – Southwold 0502 722467

TYNE AND WEAR
North Shields* – South Shields*
0632 566521

Further reading
'River Ferries' by Nancy Martin (Dalton)
describes not only river but also island ferries
and ferrymen, and their history – sometimes
dating back to Roman or even earlier times.

16 Maritime ceremonies

In any month of the year, somewhere around the coast, ancient traditions are being honoured – or new ones taking root. Some of the old ceremonies go back to the Middle Ages and may have their origins in reinforcing ancient laws and rights regulating fishing, for example: necessary public declarations in the days when few fishermen could read legal documents. Others which take the form of an act of Christian worship (on beaches or boats, or in church) may have older, pagan origins – prayers for a good harvest of fish or thanksgiving at the end of the fishing season. ('God keep our nets from snag and break. For every man, a goodly take.') Others keep alive the memory of historic events. And some of the more recent ones are just for fun.

Perhaps the most meaningful are the services of thanksgiving for the 'harvest of the sea'. Often a church is decorated with lobster-pots and fish, and the hymns are ones with a maritime theme or those associated with the lifeboat service. Trafalgar Day is remembered in October with church services from St Paul's in London to Little Madron near Penzance (Cornwall), with much naval ceremonial. Trinity Sunday in June is an occasion when churches in various places (St Mary's, Scilly Isles; Gravesend, Kent; Harwich, Essex) have services for safety at sea, and the work of Trinity House, see Chapter 26. Rogation, the customary period for interceding (May), is when sea blessings often take place. Many civic ceremonies involve processions of admirals, mayors and other colourful dignitaries. And then there are those which are pure carnival – all fancy-dress and fireworks. Take your pick!

Some maritime ceremonies

The following list is not exhaustive. See also other chapters, such as those on the Navy and lighthouses. Where no telephone number is given, phone the nearest Tourist Information Centre for fuller details.
LANCASHIRE
Fleetwood* Blessing the Waters. Early June.
03917 71141

CORNWALL
Bude* Blessing the Sea. August. 0288 2318

DEVON (south)
Plymouth* Seafarers' service at St Andrew's
Church. July.

Brixham* Harvest of the Sea; service at parish church. May. 08045 2861. Re-enactment of William III's landing. July. 0803 26244

DORSET
Poole* Beating the Bounds of the Harbour.
July. 02013 5151

HAMPSHIRE
Portsmouth* Searchlight Tattoo; D-Day and
Seafarers' services in cathedral. September.

ISLE OF WIGHT
Havenstreet to Ryde* Boggit Hunt:

74

participants in fancy dress run or cycle across land and into the sea. Boxing Day. 098397 2809

EAST SUSSEX
Hastings* Blessing the Sea. Lifeboat is used as pulpit. May.

SUSSEX to KENT
Cinque Ports When the court of the Ports meets at one of the Ports there is a special church service with mayors and dignitaries in procession. Summer (dates vary).

KENT
Dymchurch Dr Syn Day (smuggling event, see Chapter 8). August, alternate years. 030382 2708
Hythe Venetian fête (water carnival). August, alternate years. 0303 68234
Broadstairs* Dickens festival. June. 0843 62853
Whitstable* Blessing the Sea. July. 0227 272233
Rochester* Admiral of the Medway's Court, on a barge. June or July. 0634 77890

LONDON
Harvest of the Sea. Service at St Mary-at-Hill, Lovat Lane, EC3. October. 01–626 4184
Dunkirk Commemoration. Service at St Lawrence Jewry by the Guildhall, Gresham Street, EC2. May. 01–600 9478. Trafalgar Day. Service at St Paul's. Very impressive. Also a parade at Trafalgar Square. October. 01–248 5202

ESSEX
Southend* Blessing the Whitebait. September. Whitebait Banquet. September. 0702 710404

Brightlingsea Opening of the oyster season. Mayor goes out in a boat for the ceremony. Late August/September. 0206 76071

HUMBERSIDE
Hull* Admiral's Review, of sailing ships. The Admiral is the Lord Mayor. Mid-May. 0482 223111
Flamborough Harvest of the Sea service at St Oswald's. October. 0262 850336

NORTH YORKSHIRE
Whitby* Blessing the Boats. July. 0947 602674 Planting the Penny Hedge. (A penance for a mediaeval murder – takes place at the sea's edge.) May. 0947 602674

CLEVELAND
Redcar Blessing the Lifeboats. October. 06493 48522

TYNE AND WEAR
Cullercoats near **Tynemouth** Blessing the Nets. May/June. 0632 524494

NORTHUMBERLAND
Norham near **Berwick-upon-Tweed*** Blessing of the Salmon Nets. Takes place at midnight. Mid-February. 0289 7474
Berwick-upon-Tweed* Tweedmouth Feast and crowning of the Salmon Queen. A week-long carnival. Late July. 0289 6332

It is now a tradition among swimmers to take a dip on Christmas or Boxing Day, no matter how freezing the weather. This began at **Brighton*** and now takes place at **Hastings***, **Eastbourne*** and **Bournemouth*** and is spreading to other resorts too.

The shoreline
and its wildlife

17 Sand and shingle beaches to explore

Sandy beaches are popular with everyone on a seaside holiday. There is a tremendous difference between the vast expanse of, say, Weston-super-Mare (where the tide goes so far out you may think it will never come back) and similar resorts — usually complete with donkey-rides and ice-creams, bathing huts and deckchairs — and the intimate little coves of south Devon and Cornwall. These coves are among my favourite beaches — and none is more attractive than South Sands (near Salcombe, Devon). Here is a beach sheltered by high cliffs, and fringed with rocks and rock pools: a perfect spot for collecting shells and seaweeds or looking for tiny crabs hiding in the crevices. Pine trees and sub-tropical flowers sweeten the sea breezes (even palms and banana trees grow in the National Trust gardens at Sharpitor, on the nearby headland), there's a ferry to take you to and from Salcombe, the ruin of a castle out there on a rock, sailing-boats and small trawlers passing by, and perched up on the cliffside the house where Tennyson wrote 'Crossing the Bar' (the bar being just beyond South Sands).

I associate South Sands with the soft plash of waves and the slap of children's bare feet on the sand as they run to search for driftwood or pretty stones; the salty tang in the air; winkles on the rocks, limpets that tighten their vice-like grip if you touch them, and the anemones folded neatly up as the tide leaves them behind. The water-beaten rocks are slippery with bright green sea-moss, and hung about with brown bladderwrack full of blisters for children to pop. In clear pools, pinky weed is delicate as a feather boa; flung up onto the sand, tangleweed is strong as a leather strap.

There are lots of little coves like this, many of which (south-facing) are sun-traps when the weather is not too good elsewhere.

Nothing could be a greater contrast than the sands of Morecambe Bay: it takes four hours to walk right across from one side to the other, something never to be undertaken without a guide, for death in the quicksands is a very real possibility if you do not know the right way to go.

I walked with Cedric Robinson, one of the two fishermen who act in the summer as Queen's Guides. (No payment is required from the walkers, though some, realising he has no salary, make a gift: you simply need to book well ahead by phoning 044 84 2165 and to turn up at whatever time the tides and the guide determine.) Although the walk is at a leisurely pace, it can involve wading knee- or thigh-deep through the channels of rivers flowing down to the sea and it's best to wear wool socks and plimsolls. Shorter walks of two-and-a-half hours are also conducted.

As we set off from Grange-over-Sands (most walks start from the other side) there was a billowing sky which Constable would have appreciated. Stepping across a narrow stretch of limestone 'pavement' we found ourselves in squelching grey mud at first but, after a few minutes of walking, were well out into this great wet desert. The sun flashed silvery on the firm sand, and the vastness all round seemed to have no limit. Little gullies of trickling water and the ripple-marks of the departed waves patterned the sands. Here and there worm-casts or the trails of worms hinted at the crowded life that was teeming just below the seemingly barren surface. 'The bay is one huge mass of food', said Cedric. 'It brings in thousands of birds: dunlin (the 'sea mice') and oystercatchers, during the migratory seasons, and I've seen a thousand shelduck feeding at one time.'

I picked up a lot of hen-pennies' shells: delicate, pink and tiny as one's little-fingernail. These minute bivalves are beloved of flukes, the plaice-like fish which (along with whitebait, shrimps and cockles) provide fishermen with their livelihood from the bay.

As the tide flows in, the flukes come too — hunting for the hen-pennies and baby cockles which live just below the surface. The fluke flops itself into the sand, sinking in to look for its meal. Having chewed out the meaty contents, the fluke then discards the bits of broken shell and it is these telltale leftovers (known as sherlings), and marks left in the sand, which (when the tide is ebbing) give fishermen a clue to the flukes' whereabouts.

Fishing in the bay is not done from boats. Like all the other fishermen, and like his father and grandfather before him, Cedric goes on foot by night or day, in winter as well as summer, to net the fish. The skill lies in knowing where the fluke will be coming in (and in keeping one's feet out of the quicksands). After that it is simply a matter of setting up stakes with nets stretched between and awaiting the next tide — with the hope that there may be a slight breeze to ruffle the water so that the fluke (which, unlike plaice, are not stupid) cannot see and avoid the nets ahead of them.

I looked back towards Grange, almost Mediterranean in the way its little white houses are piled up on the steep sides of the bay. Distance made the hills of the Lake District beyond seem blue. The further we walked, the deeper the gullies. The sand seemed to squeak slightly as it was trodden on, and shadows from the clouds drifted across it. 'On a very clear day', said Cedric, 'you can see Blackpool Tower.' As he occasionally probed the sand ahead of us with his stick, he explained the necessity for guides.

Before the railway came round the Bay in 1857, the journey from one side to the other involved crossing the sands in a cart or coach — and plenty went down in the quicksands, as tombstones in Cartmel tell. (Inland, you can still come across milestones saying: 'To Lancaster. Over the sands, 15 miles'.) Even now deaths occur. The quicksands cannot be marked with warning notices because their position changes with each tide, particularly after bad weather. One winter a swollen river changed the course of its channel into the Bay by several miles: millions of tonnes of sand altered position in just one night. And another hazard is the speed of the tide, which comes in faster than a galloping horse. There are springs, too, which bubble up through the sands.

The coastguards and their helpers (see Chapter 27) have special techniques, involving a mud-sledge and pumps, to help people sucked into the sands. Tug-ging is no good: in an experiment with rope from a helicopter, the helicopter began to be pulled down too. A youngster on a motorbike was a recent fatality: once his cycling boots had gone below the surface and filled with sand, not even the fire-brigade could haul him out before the tide came in over his head. So a guide who understands the changing effects of wind and water is essential, unless you stay on the firm sands around, for instance, Grange.

As a child, Cedric Robinson used to go cockling with his father, and he has told the story of those days and of the Bay today in a fascinating book 'Sand Pilot of Morecambe Bay' (David & Charles), with drawings by his wife Olive. They would harness their horse Daisy to the cart and set off. Sometimes Daisy had to half-swim through deep channels or trot fast when chased by the tide, but warm blankets and a bag of oats were taken along for her while the hunt for cockles was in progress.

Life was tough for the family, housed in a cottage which shared one outdoor tap and earth-closet with five others, in Flookburgh (the church of which appropriately has not a cock but a fluke on its weathervane). Their light was from candles, their cooking and water-heating depended on a coal fire. Young Cedric, despite helping with fishing, net-tarring, boiling shrimps, packing whitebait and looking after Daisy, found time to sing in the choir, and the older Cedric still sings — on the sands when he is alone. In singing mood or not, he has to go out there at dawn or in mist, very often, because tide and fish wait for no man.

The best season to net whitebait is in frosty weather, when there are no shrimp to be had. Whitebait are not a popular catch with Cedric's family who have to tear themselves away from the TV to give a hand with cleaning, removing seaweed or small jellyfish, and packing so that the fish can be despatched to the cities with no delay.

For shrimping and cockling, tractors have replaced horses-and-carts now: nets are trailed behind to gather in the fish. Some salmon, too, are caught as they come down the Kent (the fastest river in Cumbria), with the barefoot fishermen dashing to outrun the swift fish as they flick their way through the shallows, water flying everywhere. But disease has reduced the salmon from 100 on each tide to only one or two a week.

Guides have been officially appointed at least from the time of Henry VIII; and Cedric's advice to anybody who goes without one and gets stuck is given in perhaps the same words and the same Cumbrian voice as his Tudor predecessors might have used: 'When tha feels theself goin' in, sit on thi arse!'

Perhaps there is something to be said for waiting till the tide is in, and joining one of the annual cross-bay swims instead: some 16 km to go, and with a 1914 record of two hours still waiting to be beaten.

Shrimping on the sands is now more often done with tractors than with horse-and-cart.

Shingle beaches, though not so popular as sand, have their own character, and hold some mysteries too. The most famous is, of course, the Chesil Bank — an immense bank of pebbles 28 km long which the tide systematically sorts into graded sizes (from the smallest at the west to stones of over 5 kg at the Portland end: no one understands why). Behind it is the Fleet, a salty lagoon which shelters birds — there is more about this in Chapter 24. 'Chesil' comes from a Saxon word meaning gravel, and 'Fleet' from one meaning inlet.

I visited a rather similar but less famous formation at Slapton Ley (Devon). 'Ley' means lake, and here the waters that have for 3,000 years been trapped behind the shingle beach are now fresh (fed by streams) not brackish and form the centre of a nature reserve run by the Field Studies Council. The wildlife of the ley is not, therefore, maritime; but it was the steep shingle ridge in which I was more interested when, in company with Peter Holden of the Slapton Ley Nature Reserve, I went walking there.

The most dominant feature of the 3 km ridge is in fact modern and man-made: a huge monument recording the fact that the Americans took over the whole area to practice their D-day landings towards the end of the Second World War, and everyone within the seven surrounding parishes had to leave their homes and farms for the six months involved. There are still trenches and the occasional unearthed mine or shell to be found, and some ageing trees nearby are riddled with shrapnel. The monument is now weathered and patterned with lichen which, after damp weather, bursts into colour — then goes dry and dull again.

As with the seemingly infertile sand, so also the shingle beach supports more life than is apparent. Botanists in particular find it worth more than an idle glance. It is surprising that any plant can maintain a foothold here, for storms can shift the coastline overnight. (In fact there are really two coastlines: the shingle ridge and, nearly a kilometre out to sea, a sudden steep drop.)

There are clearly distinguishable bands on the ridge: first comes fine grit, and then the pebbles. When you pick one of these up, you are holding in your hand a million years of history (or many millions). Flint or chalk, flat slate or pretty quartz, some veined red with iron: each prehistoric pebble has its origin in the bedrock of the surrounding land. It may have travelled hundreds of kilo- metres since the time when, during one of the great Ice Ages, it was ground away from its original source . . . then carried by the melting ice down to the sea floor . . . and, in several great cataclysmic storms and as a result of the rising sea-level, later flung up with millions of others to create this astonishing ridge, a sea-wall built by nature.

Shells lie on top of the pebbles, in fairly neat lines which indicate where the edge of the tide has dropped them: bigger shells high up, the smaller ones (which the weakening ebb could still carry) rather lower down.

At each tide, there is a change in the contours of the ridge and in the distribu- tion of the pebbles, large and small. After a storm, seaweed from the depths gets flung up, or the bodies of starfish or crabs. Anglers wait patiently for plaice and flounder, and a whole variety of gulls keep watch too. But it is in winter that the most interesting birds are to be seen: scoter and eider ducks, for in- stance, along with the terns, shags and cormorants. There is an observatory on the reserve.

The unique interest of the site lies, for scientists, in its plants which, until concrete posts were put in, were being mercilessly destroyed by cars that parked along the ridge. At the top of the ridge, fine shingle is colonised by far more pioneering plants than a quick glance takes in, though you may need to get down on your knees to locate some of them.

In just one small area, Peter pointed out to me half-a-dozen interesting plants. There was the yellow horn poppy with its decorative leaves: they are thick, hairy and curly-edged, features ideal for conserving water, which is vital in this place of salt-laden winds; while its long, thin roots help to bind the loose sand. Early scurvy grass was there, though it needed a close scrutiny to find its minute but very pretty mauve flowers. Growing in an elegant rosette of leaves was the sea-radish alongside its companion the sea-carrot, named for the shape of its big tap-root; and nearby were sea campion, scentless mayweed and – of course – the pretty pink thrift that loves sea air. Among the stones there was a mass of insect life too: earwigs, woodlice, crane-fly larvae ('leather jackets') and all kinds of snails which thrive on calcium provided by the seashells.

The reserve has produced a booklet about what is to be found, here and further inland, with a roll-call of other sand flowers including rarities in the wild like sea pea, sea holly and sea kale.

Like other field study centres, Slapton Ley welcomes the public – children as well as adults. You can follow its nature trails on your own or join a guided walk, not just at Slapton but in other nearby spots too. You can choose from a programme that may include plants, birds and seashore life. You can even take a holiday at the centre, in order to study (for instance) natural history or landscape photography. (For details of what's on, charges and how to get there phone 054858 466.)

At the end of Chapter 12 is a list of seaside resorts showing which have good sandy beaches. In addition there are beaches and coves to be found between these, particularly in Devon and Cornwall. The best way to locate them is to buy a map that indicates where sands are to be found: for example, the 'Leisure Maps' of Estate Publications sold by Tourist Information Centres. Penguin publish a 'Good Beach Guide'.

18 Cliffs and rocks: the dramatic coast

'A solitary rock is always attractive. All right-minded people feel an overwhelming desire to scale and sit upon it.'

So wrote Dorothy Sayers in the opening chapter of 'Have his Carcase'. Fortunately for others who scramble down cliff paths among the scabious and sea-pinks intent on such pursuits, these attractive rocks are rarely topped by corpses with slit throats.

Rocks and cliffs attract because they have drama enough of their own – untamed, wild and rugged; immensely ancient; always a little mysterious; often sinister.

Around the English coast their variety is infinite – varying because the geology of the land and the nature of the sea are so different between one stretch of the coast and the next. The famous white cliffs of Dover and of Beachy Head are totally different from the jagged granite teeth around Cornwall; the multi-coloured sandstone of Alum Bay from the all-red headland of St Bees or the white limestone of Portland. Caves, strange arches, massive landslips, ravine-like chines, crumbling rock yielding up fossils, tunnels below and headlands above with ruined towers, seaside cliffs with ancient lifts, seabird nesting colonies, remote coves, chasms and clefts, stories of smugglers and of wrecks:

cliffs are the castles and the cathedrals of the wild. Their headlands have been used for defence; their reefs and outcrops have brought destruction and death.

A great deal of England's coastline is now preserved by Operation Neptune — the National Trust's campaign to save the most beautiful stretches of the shore — and much of the National Trust's concern is for the areas where cliff scenery is at its most spectacular.

The Countryside Commission helps in a different way, by advising land-owners and local authorities on the management of sites of special merit. The Purbeck Heritage Coast (Studland to Weymouth) is a Dorset example, its geology and natural history of national importance. The results of the Commission's care include a lot of improvements for visitors: footpaths cleared and way-marked, small car parks, guided walks available, information boards and leaflets, and general conservation work.

One of the strangest parts of our shore is at Portland.

Portland is really an island, a huge chunk of limestone dropped into the sea by a giant hand, though a substantial causeway links it to the mainland. As I crossed over this, there was a bright, choppy sea to my left; and the end of that extraordinary 11 km mystery — the pebble ridge of Chesil Bank-to the right. Ahead Portland rose steeply in front of me 160 m high, with houses made of its own pale stone. The road climbed sharply up.

Portland is grim, yet has a fascination. So many world-famous buildings—such as Smeaton's Eddystone lighthouse and the United Nations building in New York, had their origins here, built from stone hewn out of this great, inexhaustible lump.

I wandered around one of the many quarries. New-cut slabs of stone shone intensely white. There was a grandeur about the vast hole in the ground — a veritable palace of a hole. Each layer led down to one still deeper and in the clefts were black shadows, making the light-reflecting walls of the hole seem even brighter. Precisely cut stones were piled up like children's bricks; nearby an untidy tumble of rough 'spoil' was already being colonised by grass. Rock-doves circled, perhaps looking for nest-sites. And down below, behind me, the sea was pounding impotently against cliffs of this same rock which, except for granite, is the most durable stone of all. Hard, smooth, white and fine-grained, just right to be chiselled with elegance: a stone that is admirably suited to classical architecture.

For Christopher Wren this was 'the' stone, and immense quantities were needed for the building of his St Paul's. The islanders expected to receive the benefit of a levy (determined by a local jury) on all stone taken from Portland, and disputes arose over this. Wren maintained that the stone was needed for the King's use and thus was free of levy. Said he: "Tis all one to me what your jury do, it shall not alter'. There were demonstrations — stone wagons were overthrown and loading piers destroyed. 'Multitudes of unruly persons', committed 'insolency and disturbances'. And in the end, the Portlanders got their money.

Like most islanders, they were stubborn and independent. There was no causeway until the 19th century, and even the ferry was not greatly used because tricky currents made crossing hazardous. Therefore many old customs survived long after they had died out on the mainland, witchcraft was believed in right up to Victoria's time, and there was much intermarrying among the few families of the island. Strangers were regarded with suspicion: a Tudor writer commented: 'The people be good at slinging stones, and use it for defence of the isle'. They had plenty of such ammunition, but went short of wood (there are still very few trees on this bare, windy island), so they burned cow-dung for fuel — which deprived the soil of its usual fertiliser. As an alternative, 'chamber-lye' (urine) was collected and poured onto the soil before spring came.

Despite its bleakness, Portland has always been inhabited — an Iron Age fort was discovered, with underground chambers for storing corn, and Roman remains. Agriculture — still carried on by the communal strip-farming method of mediaeval times — did not really give way to quarrying until powered machinery made the latter more economic. Up till then, stones of six to seven tonnes were hewn by hand, lifted by primitive cranes and hauled by horses — a vicious strain on these poor animals. The earliest quarries were, for obvious reasons, placed near the shore; and the spoil from them was dumped in great tips by the sea, the 'wears' that are still clearly visible today.

The islanders' isolation ended only when it was decided to build a causeway. This came about as a result of a calamitous storm in November 1824, so devastating that not only were 80 houses and the ferry destroyed but the mighty Chesil Bank itself was reduced from 10 m in height to its present 6 m — in one night. Man moves less decisively than nature so it took 11 years (and a 39-page Act of Parliament) to get the causeway started, but in 1839 it was at last opened with a procession, banners, music and civic banquet.

Portland, no longer completely an island, now had to get used to the arrival of 'kimberlins' (outsiders). In 1847, the government decided to build a naval harbour at Portland: the French, traditional enemy, were fortifying Cherbourg — unpleasantly close — and the British had no equivalent defence anywhere between Portsmouth and Plymouth. The old castle called the Verne was to be strengthened too, to defend the harbour. As labour to build the harbour walls was needed, it seemed a very good idea to bring in prisoners awaiting trans-portation to Australia (see Chapter 7) and so a model prison was built — it even had underfloor heating. This is now a Borstal, while the Verne has become a training prison.

I can think of no place in England so dominated by its geology as Portland. Cliffs, houses, castle, prisons, churches — all are of the same stone, and the dust from the quarries colours even road surfaces. And yet the grey uniformity is impressive. As to the rugged coastline, this stands comparison with Cornwall's wilder shores. The tidal race whirls round the tip, Portland Bill; big waves foam over rocks glistening with seawrack; gulls glide far below you among the fissured cliffs; there is a ceaseless, surging roar from the sea; and the sound of gusty wind, carrying the tang of salt high up into the air, is rarely stilled. A dramatic place to visit.

Quite near, yet totally different: the cliffs of Lulworth Cove. Here much of the rock is not invincible limestone, but softer material, prey to sea-waves, wind, frost and storm. Over the millennia the cliffs have been worn away — a great round mouthful has gradually been bitten out of the south coast, creating the most famous of English coves, so beautiful that even bank holiday crowds and the huge car park beside the approach road cannot entirely destroy its charm.

I clambered up a steep path from the beach to one of the clifftops. The water that spread below showed clear and greenish, pale stones glimmering through it, seaweed swaying lightly in the pattern of ripples made by small pleasure-boats and by two black-clad scuba divers wading out.

The headland opposite had multicoloured stripes running diagonally. To the left, chalk cliffs rose sheer and white except where painted green by the grass which drapes itself wherever it can manage to take root. Below my feet was a sandy landslip, and on the gritty beach beneath this, children were searching for pebbles and exploring rock pools, their voices floating up clearly.

Out across the beach runs a stream; just above, there used to be a watermill

Where hard and soft rock alternate, the sea can carve out arches and caves as at Durdle Door, (Dorset).

on its banks and the millpond is still there, clear and still, with clumps of watercress in the water and yellow wallflowers hanging from its walls, reflected in the shining water.

A little further west is Durdle Door, a great outcrop of white limestone which the sea has fashioned into an immense arch.

This short piece of coast, which draws so many visitors, is attractive simply because there is such a great variety of rock and cliff formations, colours and shapes, within so small a space: quite the opposite of Portland's uniformity.

The reason why the sea has been able to sculpt Lulworth Cove like this is the geological mixture. Once, the shore must have presented a fairly straight, unbroken, but thin cliff of limestone to the sea. But with time the sea wore through a chink in this armour-plating and got at the soft clay behind. Bit by bit, a lot of this was washed out and so a cavity grew behind the limestone wall, with the gap in the limestone steadily enlarging too. At the back of the clay belt is rather harder chalk, and at this point the sea's penetration has had to halt.

Few of the visitors who pour into Lulworth Cove are much concerned with its origins, however: it is enough simply to enjoy the beauty that is a consequence of the sea's destructive capacity.

Where to find cliff scenery

CUMBRIA
St Bees Red sandstone; seabird colonies.
Humphrey Head Point and **Arnside**
Limestone cliffs facing **Morecambe Bay***.

LANCASHIRE
Heysham·Promontory with Saxon chapel ruins.

AVON
Portishead Headland; Battery Point.
Clevedon Clifftop walks.
Weston-super-Mare* Wooded headland; Iron Age earthworks.

SOMERSET
Burnham-on-Sea* Promontory; Iron Age earthworks.

DEVON (north)
Lynmouth* Cliff railway.
Watermouth Caves.
Ilfracombe* Tunnels through cliffs to beaches. Torrs clifftop walks; caves.
Morte Point Clifftop walks.
Clovelly Village is on cliff face.
Hartland Point Dramatic views.

CORNWALL
Bude* Small caves in cliffs.

Bedruthan Steps Clifftop walk, jagged rocks below.
Holywell Bay Cave.
Gwithian to **Portreath** near **Redruth** Cliffs with seals below.
Land's End Dramatic rocks; clifftop walks to **Treen** with fine scenery.
Kynance Cove Weird rocks; caves.
Mullion Cove Caves and tunnel.
Lizard Unique stone (serpentine); clifftop walks.
Porthscatho Clifftop walks.
Polperro to **Looe*** Clifftop walks.

DEVON (south)
Salcombe* and **Hope Cove** Clifftop walks.
Paignton* Goodrington Cliff; gardens and paths.
Torquay* Numerous clifftop walks.
Babbacombe Cliff railway.
Shaldon Tunnel through cliff to cove.
Seaton* Clifftop walks.

DORSET
Lyme Regis* Dowland Cliffs: chasm caused by landslip.
Charmouth Cliffs with fossils.
Golden Cap 200m of golden sandstone; clifftop walk.
Burton Bradstock Clifftop with masses of wildflowers.
Portland See text.
Lulworth Cove See text.
Kimmeridge Bay Crumbling cliffs with fossils.
Swanage* Clifftop walks; seabird colonies.
Poole* Disused limestone cliff workings with bats at **Seacombe** and **Winspit**.
Bournemouth* Cliffs with chines (ravines); Hengistbury Head. Canford Cliffs; Compton Acres gardens.

ISLE OF WIGHT
Alum Bay Multicoloured cliffs with chairlift. View of the Needles – chalk stacks in the sea.
Blackgang Chine (with pleasure garden).
Luccombe Chine.
Shanklin* Cliff with electric lift. Chine with waterfall.
Sandown* Clifftop walks.
Ventnor* Clifftop walks to **St Catherine's.**

EAST SUSSEX
Seaford* 100-m headland; Iron Age earthworks.
Eastbourne* 160-m **Beachy Head**; clifftop walk to **Birling Gap.**
Hastings* Cliff with remains of Norman castle; lift; labyrinth of caves; coastal country park with cliffs.

KENT
Folkestone* Cliff with old water-driven lift; Leas (gardens) on top; Landslip – The Warren.
Dover* Castle on top of cliffs; cliff walks.
Margate* Caves at **Lower Cliftonville**.
Minnis Bay Chalk cliffs to east.

ESSEX
Walton-on-the-Naze* The Naze is a low cliff with tower.

SUFFOLK
Dunwich Dramatic erosion of cliffs.

NORFOLK
Cromer* Cliffs with fossils; clifftop walks and gardens.
Hunstanton* Red-and-white (carr and chalk) cliffs; clifftop walks (chapel and old lighthouse).

HUMBERSIDE
Flamborough Head 50-m chalk cliffs; seabird colony; stack rocks; caves.
Bempton Cliffs 130m with seabirds.

NORTH YORKSHIRE
Speeton Cliffs with seabirds.
Cayton Bay High cliffs.
Scarborough* Clifftop gardens; lifts; castle on headland; spectacular cliffs all the way to **Saltburn.**
Robin Hood's Bay Village on cliff face; fossils. **Ravenscar** cliffs are 200m.
Whitby* Cook monument on cliff.
Runswick Bay Two rocky headlands.
Staithes Boulby Cliff, 230m; fossils.

CLEVELAND
Saltburn 100-m cliff with Victorian tramway; Cleveland Way footpath to **Staithes.**

TYNE AND WEAR
South Shields* Marsden grotto in cliffs and Marsden Rock.
Tynemouth Headland with castle and priory ruins.

NORTHUMBERLAND
Bamburgh Red sandstone outcrop with castle.

Two coastal museums which explain local geology and fossil finds are at **Penzance*** (Cornwall) and **Sandown*** (Isle of Wight). Many small local museums have some relevant exhibits, often including mementos of wrecks.

Further reading
A good small book about rocks in the landscape is 'Britain Before Man' (Stationery Office).

19 Beachcombing among rocks and pools

'Break, break, break', wrote Tennyson in sombre mood, 'On thy cold grey stones, O Sea!' (But in reality the stones on the shore are of every imaginable colour.) 'Break, break, break, At the foot of thy crags, O Sea!' And the stones had a similarly mournful effect on Matthew Arnold:

> Listen! You hear the grating roar
> Of pebbles which the waves draw back, and fling,
> At their return, up the high strand,
> Begin and cease, and then again begin,
> With tremulous cadence slow; and bring
> The eternal note of sadness in.

So much for poets. When I pick up a pebble on the beach my thoughts are very different, as I hold in my hand something which it has taken nature millions of years to colour and to shape — each pebble unique as any human being, and with a secret history that is far, far older.

Most will have travelled hundreds of miles to the sea, starting life perhaps in a distant mountain far inland. During each of the Ice Ages, the underlying rocks of England, in all their diversity, were split, ground up, shifted, over-laid then re-exposed, all the time being moved along when the glaciers began to melt and make their way to the sea, carrying boulders with them. Down on the sea bed, endlessly pounded and shifted, rubbing smooth against one an-other, the pebbles were formed — to be flung this way and that by the tides and ultimately thrust up onto the beaches. The process continues, and in the course of a short holiday — particularly if the seas are rough — you can see for yourself how the contours of a pebbly beach can change almost daily, and the distribu-tion of the shingle alter. Some beaches that were once sandy are now covered with stones, and sometimes the reverse occurs.

Why do some beaches yield a far greater variety of interesting pebbles than others? I asked a local expert after I had gone beachcombing on the Cumbrian shore. Haverigg and, even more, Fleswick Bay (near St Bees) are a pebble-collector's paradise. At Fleswick, cornelians, obsidian and porphyry are to be found, amongst many other decorative stones. He explained: 'Some of the Lake District's mountains are extinct volcanoes which, millions of years ago, flung up a variety of rocks which have since been subject to erosion and carried to the sea. There are the ancient granites, for instance, and above them the more recent sandstones. The latter, as the name suggests, were once silt laid down when the whole area later disappeared under the sea.'

He identified some of the prettier pebbles for me. A mottled pink one was a conglomerate: bits of granite with particles of other rock, which must have got mixed as sediment before they solidified together. A stripy one had been created when layer upon layer of sediment, each a different colour, had been laid down, one on top of another, as waters rose and then receded again, perhaps a fresh layer accumulating every six months or so — millions of years ago. To look at such a pebble is rather like looking at a slice from an old tree, each year's growth clearly indicated by a new ring round the tree-trunk.

In many coastal towns, there are shops selling rocks and gemstones, local as well as exotic ones (you can discover them in, for instance, Whitehaven, Croyde, Truro, Southampton and Brighton). When in Poole (Dorset), I found Mr Allen's shop in an old grain warehouse particularly interesting. Part of it is a (free) museum of rocks and fossils. He told me the story behind some of the more intriguing exhibits, like, for instance, a chunk of local coral agate. Once, when Dorset was deep under a semi-tropical sea, there were coral reefs where cows now graze. As agate formed around the coral, it encapsulated it for all time in a highly decorative stone. Who can resist buying in a treasure-house like this? I came away with not only agate but a slice of Whitby jet — in its polished black surface the spiral of a big fossilised ammonite is exposed. And I bought a copy of Edward Fletcher's excellent book 'Pebble Polishing' (Blandford Press) which, whether or not you want to invest about £30 in a pebble-polishing machine, is an excellent guide to the best beaches, and identifying the stones. Another good one for this purpose is the Penguin Natural History Guide called 'Rocks and Pebbles'. Since Edward Fletcher's book not only advises on what kind of machine to buy but spells out the limitations (some of the mottled and striped stones I find most interesting cannot be ground smooth without breaking up), it is a good idea to read it *before* embarking on this fascinating hobby. If you get really hooked, there is a monthly magazine, 'Gems', which takes one into the subject really deeply, contains details of field study centres etc. which run short holiday courses, and has news of lapidary clubs. For membership of the Geologists' Association, see Chapter 20; it has a junior division too.

The best coastal hunting-grounds are around west Cornwall, east Yorkshire, Norfolk and Suffolk — but good pebbles can be found on almost any shore, and there is continual change. The 'longshore drift' of the sea carries stones southwards down the east coast, but northwards up the west coast. It carries them from west to east along the south coast. Shells, too.

Poets seem to have found shells more inspiring than pebbles. Geoffrey Scott wrote of one:

> *I sing to myself all day*
> *In a husky voice quite low,*
> *Things the great fishes say*
> *And you most need to know;*
> *All night I sing just so.*

My own collection of seashells sings neither by day nor by night, but looks decorative in a glass bowl of water, luminous and pearly-sheened. The current assortment came from just a few km of unpromising-looking, barren beach behind Henry VIII's castle at Yarmouth (Isle of Wight). There are limpets and topshells, periwinkles and whelks, cowries and spire shells, cockles and piddocks, slippers and razors, water-worn pieces of green bottle and red brick, too. Where buffeting has broken the whelks open, one can see the intricate architecture inside that has twirled and twisted to such decorative effect.

Why do some beaches yield so great a crop of empty shells, while others have none at all? It's a matter of sea currents. And why do most snail-like species all curve in the same direction (to the right)? No one knows. But if you find a left-curving shell of a species that normally curves to the right, you've got something as valuable as a rare stamp — so keep looking! In some places (for instance, East Wittering, West Sussex) you may find fossil shells, millions of years old.

Fascinating though the lifeless shells are, they cannot compete with the interest of the living shore, the creatures of the rocks and the rock pools left when the tide goes out. The seaweeds are revealed growing in distinct zones: brown channel wrack at the top of the shore, living a life that is alternately dry and brittle or wet and slithery; bladderwrack next, with little balloons to pop; and down where the water is deep at high tide, the long, giant straps of oar-

Rock pools provide an endless source of interest for children and adults alike (Constantine, Cornwall).

weed which need many metres of water in which to grow. In the rock pools are the more delicate seaweeds — in pretty pinks, reds and greens. It is possible to dry and press such seaweeds by floating them in water and then sliding a postcard underneath. Joyce Pope of the British Museum (Natural History) told me that she presses the weed by putting a piece of old tights over it and then newspapers until, under her mattress, the seaweed is flat and has stuck itself to the card. (The tights keep the newspaper from sticking to the seaweed.) She sends the postcards to her friends, a much more original idea than buying picture-postcards. Joyce has written a book called 'Beachcombing and Beach-craft' (Hamlyn) with more good ideas in it.

Among the pools lurk all kinds of small creatures, even tiny crabs: look, but leave them where they can go back to the cover they need. On the rocks may be sea anemones with evocative names like beadlet or dahlia (their tentacles close once the sea has receded), barnacles and limpets clinging tight. Snakelocks anemones stay under the water: the tiny creatures living inside them give them their green colour, really vivid if sunlight reaches them.

Beachcombing

Many local museums in coastal towns (see Chapter 11) like **Croyde** (north Devon), **Plymouth*** (south Devon), **Portland** (Dorset), **Portsmouth*** (Hampshire), **Brighton*** (East Sussex) and **Scarborough*** (North Yorkshire) have collections and curators who are happy to discuss your finds with you. There are several shell museums — for instance: **Buckfastleigh** (south Devon) 03644 3452 and **Holt** (Norfolk) 0263 740349. These display not only shells but also things made from or with shells. Houses or grottos elaborately decorated with shells can be seen at: **Exmouth*** (south Devon) and **Margate*** (Kent).

Most resorts have shops selling local seashells, sea urchins, books on shell crafts and so on. (*Don't* buy their tropical shells, which may have involved the ruthless slaughter of live creatures, some now becoming rare.) Shell decorating (on boxes and so forth) is a Victorian craft enjoying a revival; and in some places (such as **Poole's*** Craft Centre) you may see shell decorators at work.

Other beachcombing activities include hunting for driftwood and for shrimps, cockles, winkles, or mussels to cook at home or on the beach.

Good beaches for shells can be found at: **Drigg** (Cumbria), **Porthcurno** (Cornwall), **St Anthony** (Cornwall), the **Scilly Isles**, **Torbay** (south Devon), **Studland** (Dorset), **Sandwich** and **Whitstable*** (Kent), **Leigh On Sea** (Essex), **Brancaster** (Norfolk), **Skegness*** (Lincolnshire), **Scarborough***, **Robin Hood's Bay** and **Whitby*** (North Yorkshire).

In **Plymouth*** (south Devon), a new beachcombing scheme is starting. Children meet a leader on the beach (a young marine biologist) who will help them find specimens and also keep them from any destructive disturbance of marine life. After a snack lunch, finds will be examined under a microscope. Contact Plymouth Tourist Information Centre for details.

Further reading

There is no shortage of good, simple books explaining the life on the seashore. The one in the 'How and Why' series (Transworld) is excellent for children. Barrett and Yonge's 'Guide to the Sea Shore' and Angel's 'Seashore Life' (Jarrold) are excellent, as is Ingle's 'Guide to the Seashore' (Hamlyn paperback). These books do a great deal more than identify what is to be seen — they explain how sea creatures feed, reproduce and move about, and how the shore 'works': the shaping of the coast, the tides, the life below the sands, and much else. For a book to make identification simple there is 'The Hamlyn Guide to the Sea Shore and Shallow Seas'.

A good introduction to shell collecting is 'Discovering Sea Shells' by B. Charles (Shire). A book on turning driftwood into sculpture is Jean Thornber's 'Driftwood Sculpture' (Celestial Arts). Tony Soper's 'Shell Book of Beachcombing' (David & Charles) is full of useful information and has sensible warnings about avoiding shellfish from waters polluted by the outfall from towns. Another book published by David & Charles, 'Collecting Natural Objects' by J. Rendell, has information on things to make from driftwood, shells, pebbles, rocks, fossils and even sand. Finally, a pack obtainable from the Council for Environmental Education, 'The Coast and You', contains a number of illustrated pamphlets about the shore: how to enjoy its natural history and geography, and how to preserve its beauty and wildlife. 0734 85234 ext 218

20 Fossils for the finding

I bent down and scraped away a centimetre or two of loose sand. There on the beach where a group of children were playing while their parents relaxed in deckchairs, there beneath my hand was the fossilised footprint of a dinosaur: an iguanodon that had passed this way about 120 million years ago. The footprint was three-toed, and about a metre long.

On my own, I would not have recognised what it was; but I was walking with Stephen Hutt, conservation assistant of the Isle of Wight Geology Museum at nearby Sandown. Mr Hutt, once a London policeman but a fossil enthusiast from boyhood, used to explore these beaches in his spare time, and made such spectacular discoveries that when a post at the museum became vacant he got the job. It was he who found a bone from the 29 metre diplodocus – the longest land animal that ever lived, previously believed to have roamed only in America.

Some 5,000 iguanodon footprints have been charted on various beaches of the Isle of Wight, so he was, I think, somewhat amused by my excitement at touching this, the very first one I had ever seen.

Since footprints are concave, how was it that this fossilised one – rock-hard and deep red – stood up slightly above the level of the surrounding ground? Stephen explained. When herds of iguanodons roamed the land, they grazed in what was then sub-tropical vegetation and came down to rivers to drink. What is now seashore was then river-bank, and prints were occasionally left in the nearby mud, gradually drying hard. When the river flooded, red sandy silt settled in the great footprints. After the waters receded, this deposit was left behind and, in its turn, became rock-hard. The softer surrounding rock wore away, leaving footprint casts behind. Perhaps it was a one-in-a-million chance when this kind of thing happened, which proves that (since so many such footprints have survived) iguanodons must once have been as common as rabbits – long, long before rabbits (or men) evolved.

Buried hundreds of metres below the present surface of England there must be millions of other fossilised remains that will never see the light of day. The reason why this particular coast is a fossil-hunter's paradise is not only that prehistoric life flourished here but that the cliffs are of clay, chalk and soft sandstone which the sea and weather steadily erode – exposing fresh layers of fossils (after every rainstorm, in particular). There are more dinosaur fossils here than in any other place in Europe: you would have to go to China, America or the Gobi desert to find anything comparable.

Museum staff regularly look for fossils. Taking fossils from a beach is, except in a few places, legal but it is very desirable to let the museum know what you have found (and precisely where) so that they may make a record of any significant discoveries. The telephone number is 0983 404344. In fact, for most people, an hour or two at the museum is the best starting-point, because otherwise it is very easy to stare right at a fossil and not recognise it.

How many people realise, when crossing the beach right by the car park, that they are standing on one of the oldest fossil-beds in the island? Looking back beyond the pier, one can see clearly the different strata in the striped cliffs where they are exposed to view. Those same strata continue over to the car park side. The land was once wrinkled up into a great fold. As time and weather eroded the top of the fold away, its central core, the oldest rock, was exposed and it is on this that one is standing. Walk further east and one moves onto the other strata, one by one. And as the nature of the rocks change, so also do the fossils revealed in them.

The very old red sandstone and grey marls are the dinosaurs' level. Their bones have been turning up regularly for the last 200 years or more, and it is quite possible to find a vertebra lying on the beach after a storm. As well as bits from the 10-m iguanodons, bones of 20-m brachiosaurs have turned up too (odd creatures, with fore-arms longer than their back legs). Two years ago museum staff found an almost complete iguanodon (they're not telling where!) which is now being re-assembled in a back room at the museum.

After the marls come shale. We are now past the dinosaur stratum, and looking at material laid down in lagoons by the sea much later, overlaying the dinosaur beds. In the shale are to be found fossils of prehistoric sea creatures.

Next are the greensands (which are not green), where iron has left strange patterns. On some of the boulders here, you can see ripples. On what was once soft material, water movements left their mark on the sea bed, for the last time; and more sand was laid on top which hardened for ever in the shape the sea had impressed upon it. Other boulders were patterned all over with the fossilised shapes of tiny shellfish from 100 million years ago. One clearly showed the shapes of oysters on its underside. And Stephen pointed out tiny jet-black traces in other rocks: the spines or jawbones of small fishes. I came away with a brachiopod, a bivalve that had lived 80 million years before. These used to be called lamp-shells because they look a bit like 'Aladdin'-type lamps. The other trophy on my desk as I write is a chunk of fusain, fossilised wood from the dinosaur beds, even older: the black bark streaked with red from iron traces that had leached into it.

The museum does not disdain amateurs and, despite the cost, the museum sometimes offers to make and give resin casts of their finds in order to retain the originals. (Since the cast of a one-and-a-half-metre skull weighs about 9 kg whereas the original weighs two-and-a-half tonnes, this is a fairly persuasive inducement!)

Where to look for fossils

CUMBRIA
Cockermouth

AVON
Weston-super-Mare*

SOMERSET
Watchet

DEVON (south)
Torquay* Hope's Nose.
Seaton* East of River Axe.

DORSET
Lyme Regis* Eype Mouth to Pinhay Bay.
The Fleet
Weymouth* to Ringstead Cliffs.
Portland

HAMPSHIRE
Barton near Bournemouth*

ISLE OF WIGHT
Whitecliff Bay
Redcliffe
Shanklin* to Sandown*
Luccombe Chine to Bonchurch

Ventnor* to St Catharine's
Alum Bay to Yarmouth*

WEST SUSSEX
Bracklesham
Selsey

KENT
Folkestone* The Warren.
Minster On the Isle of Sheppey.

ESSEX
Walton-on-the-Naze*

NORFOLK
Trimingham near Cromer*
Cromer*

NORTH YORKSHIRE
Cayton Bay near Scarborough*
Scarborough* White Nab headland, Gristhorpe Bay.
Robin Hood's Bay
Whitby* to Staithes

A precise indication of these localities can be found in the field guide of the Geologists'

Association. This is an interesting organisation to join. It welcomes amateurs, has a journal, and arranges day-trips and holidays to places with interesting rocks and fossils. Its address is c/o Geology Department, University College, London WC1E 6BT. 01-387 7050 Unless you intend to confine yourself to picking up fossils found loose on the beach, you should at least send for their free 'Code for Geological Field Work'. Amongst other things, it stresses the importance of leaving plants, animals and the cliffs undisturbed, and to beware of unstable cliffs or swiftly rising tides. It is worth buying a timetable of the tides from local shops. In some areas (not those listed above) so much damage has been done by fossil-collectors that it is now illegal to take anything without a licence.

There are coastal museums with good collections of fossils at: **Lyme Regis*** and **Charmouth** (Dorset); **Bognor Regis*** (West Sussex), **Brighton*** (East Sussex); **Scarborough*** and **Whitby*** (North Yorkshire). Many of these towns, and others, have fossil shops: these, and Tourist Information Centres, may give you suggestions for fossil-hunting routes to walk.

Further reading
A good book for beginners is 'Finding Fossils' by Hamilton and Insole (Penguin).

21 Coastal walks with a view

A walk along the coast can be as gruelling or as easy as you care to make it. Not long ago, David Leighton set off on a year-long sponsored walk for charity all round the coast of Britain: 11,200 km, averaging some 32 km a day. An exhausting marathon that few will wish to copy. But a walk of even a kilometre along the coast can take you well away from roads and people if you know where to go.

There's no difficulty about this. Tourist Information Centres and local shops have Ordnance Survey maps (the 'Pathfinder' series shows footpaths), plenty of leaflets and small books about walks in their area. Individual enthusiasts for walking often compile these, but in addition the organisations mentioned below put out a mass of such things, so there is no need to fear getting lost or stuck half-way.

The 'long-distance footpaths' of the Countryside Commission sound daunting but no one is obliged to go all the way. There is, for instance, a coastal path right round the south-west peninsula starting at Minehead in Somerset and continuing for 800 km to Studland in Dorset. You can pick it up (and put it down) wherever you choose.

Some of the other long-distance paths that go across-country end up by running along a coast. The Cleveland Way includes a coastal stretch, from Saltburn in Cleveland to Filey in North Yorkshire. From Filey Brigg, the Wolds Way takes over, starting along spectacular cliffs. The South Downs Way has a final stretch following the cliffs round Beachy Head (East Sussex), while the last lap of the North Downs Way lies between Folkestone and Dover (Kent). Each of these Ways is clearly marked at every turn, and is described briefly in one or more free leaflets from the Countryside Commission (0242 21381); and, in considerably greater detail, in their series of paperbacks – beautifully produced and with large-scale Ordnance Survey maps incorporated. These books are so good that they would be useful to non-walkers too, who want to find byways down to the shore.

The Commission is also responsible for footpaths going nearly all the way round the Isle of Wight, described in leaflets obtainable from County Hall, Newport, Isle of Wight. They also have a very good, free booklet of 'Recreational Paths' in England and Wales, a few of which are coastal.

Then there are the country parks – areas of countryside (some on the coast) which provide shorter paths to walk. Although they are kept in a natural state, provision is made for car-parking and toilets. Many have information centres, wardens to advise visitors or lead guided walks, refreshments, picnic tables and recreations like swimming, sailing, riding or fishing. A few charge an entrance fee; a few close during the winter. Some located on the coast are listed at end of chapter.

The country parks are far smaller than the great national parks, of which only a few have any coastline — though even inland parks sometimes conduct walks outside their own perimeter. For example, naturalists from the Northumberland National Park regularly take people to the coast south of Berwick for easy-going walks of one to three hours, perhaps studying the creatures of the rocky shore or watching the arrival of the autumn migrants. The Countryside Commission can send free leaflets about national parks that have a shoreline offering opportunities for walks along the coast of Cumbria, Somerset and north Devon (Exmoor), or the North York Moors.

There are also well-signposted nature trails, mostly inland but with some following a shoreline. They tend to be in nature reserves or, occasionally, on National Trust estates. Leaflets are obtainable locally from nature reserves (see Chapter 24) and Tourist Information Centres. The English Tourist Board (see page 9) can send you a list — among other information, it indicates which are suitable for wheelchairs.

In addition to all these footpaths conserved by official bodies of one kind or another, there are innumerable rights-of-way over private property, common lands and so forth — usually but not always signposted. The Ordnance Survey's 'Pathfinder' maps show them clearly. In addition local councils, wildlife societies and footpath preservation groups put out leaflets or describe them in bulletins and newsletters. A modest membership fee entitles anyone to join.

Another source of leaflets on walks is sometimes the local bus company (see next chapter). These invariably say where buses connect with footpaths to take the weary walker home.

Hundreds of kilometres have been officially designated by the Countryside Commission as 'heritage coast', meaning a particularly beautiful stretch, now protected from despoliation (see maps on pages 10, 11 and 12), and these are very good areas for walking in.

The National Trust owns much of our coastline — roughly speaking, all the best bits. Their beautifully illustrated report, 'Enterprise Neptune' ends with a map and a complete list of the land they own on the coast, a good guide to where to go. (The Trust's phone number is 01-222 9251.)

The Kent Rights of Way Council has produced a list of maps, guides and, for those who like company or the presence of a leader, walking groups in its area. It also has details of yet another long-distance footpath, not so far taken under the wing of the Countryside Commission: the Saxon Shore Way, along 224 km of the Kent coast. (The Council's address is Lion Yard, Lewson Street, Teynham, Sittingbourne, Kent.)

Last but not least, the Ramblers' Association and its local branches. This is not just for those who go out in a group, big of boot and heavy with haversack: the Association also welcomes families who want nothing more than a gentle stroll on their own. It is a bizarre fact that the majority of people never walk further than a few metres from their parked car; so you don't have to stagger far to get away from the crowd, and enjoy a footpath all to yourself. The Association is out to encourage even such modest endeavours as this. Its monthly magazine has 24 pages packed with good things — ideas about where to walk or where to holiday, burning issues to do with the conservation of coast and countryside, book reviews, conducted walks and so on. Details obtainable from the Association (01-582 6878).

Much of this chapter has been about footpaths in areas well known for their scenic beauty; but, starting from even the most unpromising spots, there are also good walks to be found. I cannot improve on this description of one which begins near Cumbria's biggest chemical works (at Whitehaven). It was written for a Tourist Information Centre leaflet by a local member of the Ramblers' Association, who described the route as one of the most delightful coastal walks in England:

> The path crosses a stile and continues along the cliff edge, sometimes almost over it, with wonderful views of the coastline and a glorious feeling of isolation, with the sea on one side and the Cumbrian mountains in the distance on the other — no houses, no people, until you reach the light-house . . . Continue by the cliff edge past the third largest colony of sea-birds in England, until the path drops into a small valley . . . Fleswick is a delightful, hidden bay, the beach made of pebbles and semi-precious stones, circled by the great slabs of sandstone and orchestrated by the sound of sea-birds and of pebbles shifting on the sandstone bed as the waves slide them to and fro . . . Turn right on coming out of Fleswick. Along this path on a warm, sunny day the scent of the gorse and other flowers can be almost overpowering — the up-draught from the high cliffs causes the air to be almost completely still, keeping the perfume round you as you walk. It may be for this reason that there always seem to be so many moths and butterflies in this area. The path finally drops down to the attractive resort of St Bees.

That's what coastal walking is all about!

Shore walks are doubly interesting with a naturalist as a guide (Scilly Isles).

Country parks around the coast

Leaflets giving further details of the walks below can be obtained from the Countryside Commission, 0242 21381.

CUMBRIA
Bardsea near **Ulverston** Shingle beach, nature trail.

CHESHIRE
Wirral Dee estuary (see Chapter 24).

CORNWALL
Mount Edgcumbe near **Plymouth***
Coastal parkland.

DEVON (south)
Berry Head near **Brixham*** Beautiful headland, fort, nature trail.

DORSET
Durlston near **Swanage*** Cliffs and caves.
Upton Park near **Poole*** Alongside Poole Harbour.

HAMPSHIRE
Lepe to **Calshot** near **Hythe** Cliffs and shore.

ISLE OF WIGHT
Fort Victoria near **Yarmouth*** Beach and fort.

EAST SUSSEX
Seven Sisters near **Seaford*** Beautiful marshes, nature trail.
Hastings* Cliffs and beach, nature trail.

22 The coast by bus

One of the best ways to view the coast of England if you are not a long-distance walker is to take a bus or a series of them (only a few British Rail trains run for any distance along scenic shores, for example the Exeter to Newton Abbot and the Lancaster to Barrow lines). In some places there are even open-top doubledeckers that run during summer. A variety of cheap tickets is on offer (particularly for families, pensioners, children etc.) and these often make bussing far cheaper than car-driving. Bussing is free of the hassles involved in map-reading, parking and so forth. You travel slowly enough to see everything, through high windows above the level of hedges.

I asked bus companies to suggest some of the most interesting coastal sites outside the main towns but accessible by bus, and they came up with so many first-rate recommendations that it was impossible to do justice to them all within a few pages of this book. So I ended up by writing an entire pamphlet on the subject which you can obtain free, from the National Bus Company (01-583 9177). The pamphlet is called 'To the Sea by Bus' and it describes the most scenic coastal bus journeys that are available around the shores of both England and Wales, with a map and with the phone numbers to ring for the timetables of each area.

Bus services

The phone numbers for details of bus services around the coast of England are:
North-west coast 0946 63222 and 0772 54754
Cheshire coast 0244 315400
Avon 0272 558211
West Country 0392 74191
East Dorset-Hants 0202 23371
Isle of Wight 0983 522456
West and East Sussex 0273 606711
Kent 0227 66151
Essex 0245 56151
Suffolk and Norfolk 0603 60421
Lincolnshire 0522 22255

Yorkshire 0482 27142
Northumberland 0325 65252

For details of express coaches to, or along, the coast, phone 01–730 0202 or ask a travel agent or coach depot.

Further reading
In my book 'England by Bus' (Hamlyn), I have described in detail many one to three-day journeys by bus, including the Cinque Ports (Kent and Sussex shore), the South Hams (coast of south Devon), an East Anglian journey (Essex and Suffolk shores), the Isle of

Wight, St Mary's (Scilly Isles), Exmoor's coastline (Somerset and north Devon), Penwith peninsula (Cornwall), a Dickens trail that includes the north Kent shore and a Norman trail that includes the Sussex coast.

The pleasures of seeing the coast in an open-topped bus at Broadsands near Torbay (Devon).

23 Islands accessible from the shore

It takes only a few metres of sea to make one feel like a voyager; and to step onto an island only ten minutes away from the mainland is like arriving in foreign parts.

This is not entirely an illusion. Islanders do live rather different lives from those on the mainland; and often old habits and attitudes take at least a century to change after they have vanished from the mainland. There is apt to be more peace (even on the Isle of Wight, largest of them all, traffic is so moderate that in the whole island there are only eight sets of traffic-lights; and on some inhabited islands there are no cars at all). Forms of wildlife long vanished from the mainland may survive on islands. And above all there is the proximity of the sea, encircling all — in winter storms, perhaps cutting off access to the mainland completely for many days at a time.

An island, say the geography books, is a piece of land surrounded by water. Nature and man have played havoc with that definition. Some so-called islands are now part of the mainland because the sea or rivers have piled sand and silt into what were once navigable channels. The Sussex towns of Rye and Pevensey ('ey' means island) used to be perched on islands: now they rear up in the middle of flat grazing land where the sea used to be. Kent's Isle of Grain ('grain' meaning sand not wheat) is no longer separated because farmers on it deliberately filled in part of the Yantlet Creek, to the annoyance of seamen and despite litigation. But its neighbour, the Isle of Sheppey ('shepp' for sheep, and 'ey' for island), is still cut off by the Swale channel though this now has an elevator bridge across – its centre part goes up like a lift when a tall boat wants to pass underneath. Wallasey Island is similarly connected, by swing-bridge, to Barrow-in-Furness (Cumbria).

Many islands are accessible on foot at low tide – St Michael's Mount at Penzance (Cornwall) is an example; and Holy Island (Northumberland) can even be reached by bus, probably the only bus in England with a timetable determined by the tides and not the clock.

Others have had a causeway built up above sea-level (for instance, Portland) which technically may deprive them of their status as islands, yet once on them you feel their insularity all the same.

There are tiny islands in harbours (like those at Ilfracombe, Devon, and St Ives, Cornwall) which support minute fishermen's chapels and lights, intended as landmarks for returning seamen. At the other extreme are big islands far out of sight, with communities that in many ways run their affairs independently of England (so independently, in the case of the Isle of Man, that it is not in fact part of England at all, and still has its own law-making processes).

To many islands, large ferries or small launches go to and fro regularly. Alternatively, you may arrive at some by helicopter, and see below you the island laid out like a map on a sea-blue background before you land. This is the way I arrived at St Mary's, largest of the Scilly Isles. Looking down, I was struck by the number of lighthouses visible at the same time. The isles include hundreds which are mere rocks, with plenty more such hidden beneath the sea – so blue, so pretty and sometimes so deadly. We flew in low over the islets, and on towards St Mary's – every cove, granite outcrop and stone-walled field laid out beneath our feet, no places kept secret from helicopter sightseers.

But a helicopter journey is over too quickly for my taste: only a sea-trip distances the mainland really thoroughly, and makes its cutting-off palpable. Helicopters cock a snook at tides, rough seas and tricky currents; they take all effort out of departure and arrival, and once in the air are about as exciting as a car. But on a boat . . . !

Even the waiting to cast off is full of interest. At Portsmouth (Hampshire), I boarded a ferry to go to the Isle of Wight, with time to look about. There was plenty of action here in the harbour mouth, tugs going to and fro and some towing a naval frigate out to sea. The signal-flags flying from the rigging of HMS 'Victory' were visible in the distance. 'Free Enterprise III' (a cross-Channel ferry) came in. Our own ferry, 'Brading', was flying the white-above-red flag which meant that her skipper is a pilot, qualified to navigate in the harbour and out into the Solent.

We passed the old quarter of Portsmouth on the left (port side), with an ancient inn called 'The Coal Exchange', weatherboarded buildings and stone bastions; and then were soon out in the Solent. The ferry rolled very slightly in the stiff wind and, sitting on a pile of slatted life-rafts, I could feel the throb of

In spring, even the smallest cliff ledge may be used for nesting by kittiwakes.

The sea sculpts rocks into strange formations, like Marsden Rock (Tyne and Wear) which is a bird sanctuary.

the engines below. In the green sea our wake made patterns of foam; the red ensign flapped wildly at the stern and a wisp of smoke pulsed from the funnel. From the upper deck I could see down into a lifeboat hanging in its derricks — inside were ropes neatly coiled, oars, buckets (for bailing, presumably) and a rope ladder: potent reminders that, although no Isle of Wight ferry has ever needed to use its lifeboats within memory, the sea is still powerful. Perhaps three times a year it exerts its authority with waves mountainous enough to keep the ferries in harbour, and the islanders cut off. And then Ryde came into sight, a tumble of Regency and Victorian houses clinging to the steep hill that descends to the shore. After the bustle of Portsmouth, it was like stepping back in time.

The island has this feeling throughout. The beauty of its scenery — particularly at the west end and around the shore — stands comparison with those tourist high-spots, the West Country and the Lake District. Yet, despite its greater proximity to the Channel ports and to London, it is not so overwhelmed by visitors as these are, during the peak periods. The reason can only be that strip of sea. Easy though it is to go across (with or without a car: the island is well supplied with buses) the channel is sufficient to reduce the number of visitors, to slow down so-called progress, and to keep the island relatively unspoilt.

Wight is an entire county in itself. My next island was tiny by comparison — Brownsea, in the middle of Poole Harbour, only two-and-a-half km long. The boat passed dense green woods, darker even than the deep green sea, and a tiny cluster of cottages came into sight, a clock tower, and two white turrets by the wooden jetty. The cottages, too, were castellated — it was as if a child had said, 'Let's play castles'. And indeed there is a make-believe castle behind, a Victorian folly built on the remains of a Tudor fort. But the white flag with acorns is a welcoming one, signifying the National Trust's ownership of the whole island.

I landed under the eye of a stone St Christopher bearing the Christ child across the waves, and walked up past lobster-pots to a path leading to the nature reserve. From the hide I watched cormorants, black-headed gulls and oystercatchers in a lagoon which attracts ducks and redshanks too when winter approaches. Fluffy young shelduck trotted across with their parents. There were butterflies about.

Further along, the little church is still used regularly (not only by the 23 inhabitants but also by the Scouts who camp on the island), and is lighted by candles as there is no electricity. The owner of the island at the beginning of the century (a Dutch cigar merchant, whose splendid effigy lies in the church) had a fireplace put in the church for his comfort.

The islanders provide their own water and sewage services, but get electricity by cable from the mainland. Children go to school by boat. People have lived on this tiny island at least since Roman times; and the Vikings found it worth pillaging. There were cottage industries in Victorian times. The attractions of island life still exert a strong pull, even though the mainland is so near that occasionally deer swim across.

I walked across the meadow where the open-air theatre was being erected ready for summer's performances. The only players were strutting peacocks (there are 200 of them living wild on Brownsea); under the legs of a peahen were two half-grown young, reducing her progress to a waddle. The island also shelters that rarity, red squirrels. It has nearly 400 species of moth, 120 different wildflowers. In each of the months that it is open to visitors it has something different to show — in April, daffodils; in May, rhododendrons (and this is when the peacocks do most of their displaying); June is the time to see the various chicks; July is for butterflies, for waterlilies on a pool in the woods, and for the dragonflies; August is when gorse and heather make a blaze of colour; September brings migrants on their way south, and it is then that the red squirrels, coming down to hunt for beech mast (the seeds), are easier to spot.

I sat on the edge of a sandy cliff, at a respectful distance from the ledge where two gull chicks waited to be fed. Evidently the distance was not respectful enough for a parent gull began to 'dive-bomb' me, with a wicked gleam in his eye and a formidable beak yelling abuse. Time to get the boat back, I decided.

And then I went north and, by contrast with busy little Brownsea, stepped far back into another time with a different set of values.

Lindisfarne — even the ancient Celtic name is made of poetry and mystery, an echo of surf on an untamed shore. This is the Holy Island of Northumbria, a centre of early Christianity, of mysticism and of beautiful things. Here monks illuminated the Lindisfarne gospels (AD 700), made mead from honey and built the soaring arches of a priory (1093) which, even in ruins, is one of the greatest of Norman relics among many in the wild places of Northumberland. Sir Walter Scott wrote:

> Dry shod, oe'r sands, twice every day,
> The pilgrims to the shrine find way.
> Twice every day the waves efface
> Of staves and sandalled feet the trace.

Now the pilgrims come in unholy coachloads across the causeway at low tide to this small island, and it is best to arrive early, before the throng, if one is to recapture something of the spirit of this ancient place.

Further on from the priory — a steep climb — is Lindisfarne Castle, perched on top of a rock, dominating Holy Island. This was one of many Tudor defences against the marauding Scots, and is the cosiest of any castles I have visited in England: a 17th-century visitor called it 'a pretty fort', and so it is. Small and snug, it was turned from a ruin into a home in 1903, by Sir Edwin Lutyens, who had a genius for designing in stone — here, as elsewhere, achieving a monumental effect that is in no way overwhelming. I could live at ease in this castle,

Islands like Lindisfarne (Northumberland) provided good sites for castles and for monasteries too.

while the North Sea did its worst round the foot of the rock. Lutyens never produced mock-mediaeval effects, and yet the way he used stone and iron and *space* is in harmony with then and with now, too. The lines of the simple 17th-century furniture and the good colours of the textiles are all in character with their surroundings, strength and serenity combined.

Out beyond Holy Island itself is yet another islet, with a cross, accessible at low tide. Here St Cuthbert lived as a hermit and kept a lamp burning in a tiny chapel to guide mariners. After storms 'St Cuthbert's beads' are still flung up on its shore (in fact, they are fossilised remains of small sea creatures called crinoids). The monks who first brought Christianity to the north came from that other holy isle, Iona. St Aidan was their first bishop — Cuthbert, a Scottish shepherd-boy, became briefly (AD 685–7) the most famous. His body now lies within Durham Cathedral. Monks and islands (or headlands) seem to go together — fish and seabirds provided them with food, and the sea a means of transport.

More islands that are easily accessible

CUMBRIA
Isle of Walney near **Barrow*** Bridge. Nature reserve, gliding club, sandy beach.
Piel Island near **Barrow*** Ferry (summer weekends). Castle. Inn. The usurper Lambert Simnel landed here. It is by Roa Island, sailing centre, which is now connected by road-causeway to the mainland.

MERSEYSIDE
Hilbre Island near **Hoylake** Accessible on foot at low tide. Fossils, cliffs, old cottages, canoe club, considerable wildlife interest (birds and seals). Permit needed, obtainable locally. 051 625 9441

AVON
Steep Holm near **Weston-super-Mare*** Boat — by arrangement. High cliffs, remains of priory and fortifications, considerable wildlife interest (including 60-cm slow-worms), self-catering accommodation.

DEVON (north)
Lundy near **Ilfracombe*** Boat or helicopter. High cliffs, seabirds, a few old buildings and cottages, hotel, inn, lighthouse, seals, etc.

CORNWALL
St Michael's Mount near **Penzance*** Boat or, at low tide, causeway. Steep island with castle on top. Owned by the National Trust.

SCILLY ISLES
Ship, plane or helicopter. The largest island is **St Mary's***. Others with inhabitants are: **St Martin's** (fine beaches), **St Agnes** (pretty coves), **Gugh** (Bronze Age remains), **Tresco** (sub-tropical gardens and collection of figureheads), **Bryher** (almost wild). Mildest climate in England; considerable wildlife interest; a few historical buildings.

DEVON (south)
Drake's Island near **Plymouth*** Boat. Owned by National Trust. Fort, adventure holiday centre for youngsters, museum, audio-visual show. Little Drake's Island (with beach) accessible from it at low tide.
Burgh Island near **Bigbury** Access by tractor, or walk across sands at low tide. Smugglers' inn, holiday flats.

HAMPSHIRE
Hayling Island near **Portsmouth*** Bridge (on north side) and ferry (on west). Sands, hotels, creeks, sailing-boats.

KENT
Isle of Sheppey near **Sittingbourne** Bridge. Port of **Sheerness***, abbey, fossils, beaches, wildlife reserve, historic villages. **Harty** and **Elmley Islands** are virtually part of Sheppey.

ESSEX
Canvey Island near **Southend*** Bridge. Dutch Cottage Museum (the marshes of Canvey were drained and cultivated by 17th-century Dutch), marshes with wildfowl, boats.
Wallasea Island near **Burnham-on-Crouch** Causeway. Frequented by wildfowl.
Mersea Island near **Brightlingsea** Causeway (road). Roman burial chamber, cottages, fishing, seaside amenities.

NORTHUMBERLAND
Farne Islands near **Seahouses*** (See Chapter 15.)

Further reading
An exceptionally well written and designed guidebook is 'The Shell Book of the Islands of Britain' by Booth and Perrott (Guideway).

24 Birds of beach and cliff

Although keen birdwatchers tend to make for bird reserves, there are plenty of other places around the coast which have birds to watch, and common species are no less interesting in their habits than the rare visitors. Even during summer, when there is less bird activity to watch, the places they frequent are often a pleasure in themselves. Take, for instance, the Dee estuary: a great place for birds and one of the most beautiful stretches of shoreline. Along the Cheshire side of this is the Wirral Country Park. A railway used to run here and the disused track (all 19 km of it) is now a carefully preserved country walk, full of wildlife; and beyond it there is access to the estuary, where flocks of birds arrive as if from nowhere to spend the winter. But even in summer there are others to watch — for example the shelduck, which breed in rabbit-holes.

I started off from the small interpretation centre at Thurstaston and with Rob Andrews, one of the Country Park's rangers, walked to the top of the cliff of boulder-clay, laid down in the last Ice Age. Here paths wound down to the broad estuary. It was low tide, with golden sand and grey silt exposed for kilometres: cocklers were out with their tractors, a disturbance that tends to frighten off the birds, which also want to find the cockles. Redshanks, oyster-catchers and black-headed gulls all breed nearby; but further along a change in the ecology has driven them away — the food-rich mud has been taken over by large expanses of sea-marsh. An imported weed, sea cord grass (spartina), is spreading like a disease here and in Southampton Water.

We sat on a clifftop bench, and watched the distant birds, while Rob pointed out how the estuary is changing year by year. The deep water channel of the Dee (once navigable right up to Chester, but no longer) has swung over to the Welsh coast, which is being eroded while silt builds up on the southern coast. I could barely distinguish the silvery ribbon of the Dee it was so distant, winding close to the soft blue haze that enveloped the shore of Wales. These changes mean changes in the bird population, too.

One can walk for hours along the clifftops and then further still along the tideline, right to the conservation village of Parkgate. This is the place to be at the extra high tides, over 10 m deep, of the spring and autumn equinoxes: as the seas sweep over the grassy saltmarshes, the bird population (foxes and small mammals, too) is forced inland, and flocks of thousands come right up to the village street: a fantastic sight. Even the very secretive water rails appear in their dozens and can be photographed with ease.

As at reserves and field centres, it is often possible in a country park to go on a guided walk with an ornithologist like Rob; and there are explanatory slide or film shows from time to time as well. The Wirral Country Park is one that even provides for campers and caravanners who want to spend a whole holiday enjoying the shore and its wildlife.

Many other places are, of course, not 'managed' like a country park or reserve, but are simply wild places left to nature — or sometimes used for grazing, wildfowling and other country purposes. For example, at Grune Point, overlooking the Solway Firth (near Silloth, Cumbria), I walked alone in a wilderness of marsh and winding creeks early in the year. The ground was waterlogged (though the tide was out) and the early morning sun gave the distant mud a silver sheen; but under the wiry turf it sucked at my feet. There was the sweet smell of gorse; bluebells and lady's smock grew beside a ditch; and the trill or peep of unseen birds was in the air. I followed a track leading to where the waders were feeding busily before the return of the tide, the mud marked with

Oystercatchers have long red beaks with which to probe the food-rich shore.

their footprints. Ducks flew in overhead — there were already a lot of shelduck feeding by the creeks. A passing farmer — a stint-holder — gave me good-morning and stopped to chat. The stint-holders are local people who have grazing rights on the marshes (each stint entitles its owner to graze one maiden heifer), a system devised back in the 16th century to limit the number of cattle and prevent over-grazing. Stints, which can be inherited or bought, are super-vised by a committee of the stint-holders themselves.

The marshes increased dramatically (by thousands of acres) during the 18th century when heavy storms shifted the course of rivers and the position of silt in the Solway. Some parts are not yet stable, and heifers have been known to dis-appear in quicksands, the farmer told me. He pointed to a bay, a distant hangar and the remains of machine-gun posts, relics of the days when this area was used as a training airfield during the Second World War. Now the only fliers here are the ducks and waders.

This little-frequented spot of the north-west has some features in common with the north Kent marshes in the south-east, even though the two are so far apart. There are innumerable footpaths to follow (you need a large-scale Ord-nance Survey map), from which birds can be watched. Last Boxing Day's count along the Yantlet Creek included shelduck, turnstones, redshanks, curlews, dunlin, brent geese, mute swans and reed buntings. It was a fine, clear morning despite the piercing wind. The walk (of about 30 people) was being led by the North Kent Wildlife Society — typical of similar societies in most counties, well worth paying the modest subscription to join, because of the conservation work they do and in order to get invitations to join in walks such as these, with ornithologists and botanists as informed guides. Yantlet Creek, once a seaway, is one of my favourite walks. Still salty, it attracts a great variety of ducks and waders which winter there before their return to feeding-grounds in the far north. Others nest along the banks — safe island sites have been pro-vided for them by the county's Wildfowlers' Association, which manages this reserve. Wildfowlers shoot duck on the sea marshes, but not indiscriminately, and they do conservation work in an area which they have designated to be free of shooting.

The swannery at Abbotsbury (Dorset) is part of a very different nature reserve. The mute swans are not wild: they have been 'farmed' ever since the Middle Ages, when they were a staple part of the diet at the abbey which used to be here. They are the only colony of managed swans in the world. Another unusual feature is that though swans are really fresh-water birds, this herd lives on the salt water of the Fleet — the stretch of sea that lies behind the long Chesil Bank. Like other waterbirds they have a gland to desalinate the water they consume.

I walked through thickets of bamboo and flowering shrubs, beside a brook that runs noisily along the path. It leads to a meadow where a hundred swans' nests are dotted about, loosely built from the nearby reeds: it is very unusual for swans to nest in a colony like this. Earlier each nest would have held one or more huge eggs, with one parent sitting and the other patrolling: foxes are the main enemy, and the swans do not fear people (though the public are not admitted until laying is over, about May). Now the white swans were accompanied by their fluffy, grey young, which followed in flotillas wherever they led. The breeze ruffled their soft feathers and rippled the water, brilliant against the sombre background of the pebble bank. The loudest sounds were the contented clatter of beaks in water, or the slap of big feet on muddy bank and an angry hiss as one cob suddenly chased another off. The swans, so stately on the water or in flight, stumble and lurch in ungainly fashion when they try to move fast on land.

John Fair, the swan-herd, tossed a bucket of corn into the water and immediately all necks plunged as one, three of them tangling together as they grabbed. A latecomer flew in honking and crash-landed, feet first, to join the feast.

The protected water and the food supply attract wild birds, too: coot were about in large numbers when I was there, and at one time or another every kind of English waterfowl shows up. Terns nest here, and in early summer there are godwits, dunlin and other migrants passing through. Herons and cormorants regularly fish in the Fleet.

Increasingly, exotic species (escapes from zoos) take up residence here — and in many bird reserves: there were flamingoes among the swans and an ibis flew over. (For opening times, phone 093583 222.)

Birds often favour the places most holiday-makers avoid — such as muddy estuaries, and their adjoining saltmarshes. They can be at their most interesting outside the peak holiday seasons: when nesting in spring, or when arriving from the icy north during the autumn migration (some staying but many merely pausing before flying on much further south). In the spring, these migrants put in another appearance — breaking their return flight to the northern waters which, with warmer weather, will again become a rich food source for them. At these seasons, while the estuaries come alive with travelling waders, watchers on the headlands may see throngs of other migrants such as swallows and martins.

Most estuaries have a variety of habitats (sand, shingle, mud, saltmarsh, rocks) which attract a variety of wading birds. These are fascinating to watch because they are both larger and more exposed to view than perching birds, difficult to observe in woodlands. At low tide the birds can be watched (at a distance, using 8×40 binoculars or even a small telescope) while they feed; at high tide, look for them roosting together in a crowd somewhere nearby.

After estuaries and some sandy beaches, the next best place to go bird-watching on the coast is likely to be a rocky shore or island. There are some cliffs which for centuries have housed spectacular seabird colonies roosting and nesting on ledges, among boulders or (where there are grassy slopes) even in burrows. It is off such coasts that you will see birds diving for fish. You are most likely to see the birds on the cliffs at nesting time; later they may range over miles of sea, hunting for fish and resting on rocks or on the sea itself, where they are safe from predators.

Finally, even such unlovely places as wastelands and rubbish dumps near coastal cities if they are a source of food, may be full of birdlife, especially scavenging gulls.

Watching birds is doubly interesting if you are able to identify them and to understand their behaviour a little. Apart from books, there are plenty of sources of information. Increasingly, coastal walks and reserves are being equipped with interpretation centres, informative notices along footpaths, and leaflets explaining what is to be seen. One can take walks with naturalists, see what they are doing at observatories around the coast, and book for birdwatching holidays. More details are given in the list at the end of this chapter. Finally, there is a rare opportunity to see seabirds at close range, in Mousehole (Cornwall) where the Yglesias Bird Sanctuary (073673 386) often has some in pens while tending their injuries before releasing them into the wild again.

Herring gulls flock wherever food may be found – in the wake of trawlers or even on the rubbish-tips of coastal towns.

Where to see seabirds, wildfowl and waders

The following list names some cliffs, beaches, estuaries, sand-dunes and other habitats where birds congregate. Most of these sites are protected reserves. Where admission to a reserve is by permit only, this has been stated. In the case of migrant birds, these can be seen only in winter (or, if flocks are merely pausing in England on their way to and from hotter places, only in autumn and spring). Most seabirds are seen inshore only at breeding time (spring and early summer), and spend other months out at sea. For fuller details, including any explanatory leaflets or permits, phone the responsible authority (indicated in the list by initials or name): phone numbers are given at the end of the list.

CUMBRIA
Solway Marshes Estuary marshes. Waders and wildfowl. (NT)
St Bee's Head Sandstone cliffs. Seabird colonies. (RSPB)
Ravenglass* (permit) Sand-dunes. Terns, black-headed gulls. (Cumbria County Council)
Walney Island (permit) Marsh and dunes. Gulls, wintering wildfowl. (Cumbria Trust for Nature Conservation)
Bardsea (country park) Beach. Waders. (Cumbria County Council)

LANCASHIRE
Leighton Moss Mere. Ducks and waders,

resident and migrant. (RSPB)
Morecambe Bay* Estuary, sand and
mudflats. Migrant wildfowl and waders.
(RSPB)
Ribble Marshes Saltmarsh and mudflats.
Waders and wildfowl. (National)

MERSEYSIDE
Formby Dunes Sand-dunes and beach.
Migrant seabirds. (NT)
Hilbre Island Mudflats. Waders. Observatory.
(Wirral Borough Council)
Wirral Way See text.

AVON
Middle Hope Beaches. Gulls and migrant
waders. (NT)

SOMERSET
Brean Down near **Weston-super-Mare***
Cliffs. Seabirds. (NT)

DEVON (north)
The Great Hangman Cliffs. Fulmars and
auks. (NT)
Lundy Island Cliffs. Seabirds (resident and
migrant). Observatory. (NT)

CORNWALL
Pencarrow Head Cliffs and beaches.
Seabirds. (NT)
Pentire Head, Portquin Bay Cliffs and
beach. Auks, house martins, seals. (NT)
Cubert Common Cliffs and sand-dunes.
Seabirds. (NT)
Chapel Porth Cliffs. Razorbills and other
seabirds. Nature trail. (NT)
Penberth Cove, Treen Cliff Cliffs. Sea-
birds. (NT)
Helford River Cliffs and estuary. Wildfowl
and waders. (NT)
St Anthony in Roseland Beaches, cliffs,
estuary. Winter wildfowl. (NT)
The Dodman Beaches. Gulls and migrants.
(NT)
Whitsand Bay Cliffs and shore. Seabirds,
migrants. (NT)

DEVON (south)
Salcombe* Cliffs and beaches. Gulls. (NT)
Slapton Ley See Chapter 17.
Exe Estuary Estuary mudflats. Migrant
wildfowl and waders. (National)

DORSET
Golden Cap Cliffs and beaches. Shags,
fulmars, gulls etc. (NT)
Abbotsbury See text.
Ferrybridge Wyke Regis Sand and shingle.
Gulls, terns, waders (resident and migrant),
wildfowl. (Strangways Estate)
Portland Bill Cliffs. Seabirds. Observatory.

(Dorset Naturalists' Trust)
Radipole Lake Sea lake. Migrant waterfowl,
waders, terns. (Weymouth Corporation)
Durlston (country park) Cliffs and beach.
Gulls, fulmars, shags etc. (Dorset County
Council)
Arne (permit) Estuary mudflats. Migrant
ducks and waders. (RSPB)
Brownsea Island Marshes and lagoons.
Herons, terns, waders, waterfowl. (NT)

HAMPSHIRE
Stanpit Marshes Sandbanks and salt-
marshes. Ducks (resident and migrant).
(Hampshire Naturalists' Trust)
Keyhaven Marshes Saltmarshes, mudflats.
Gulls, terns, migrant waders. (Hampshire
Naturalists' Trust)
Farlington Marshes Saltmarshes. Migrant
waterfowl and waders. (Hampshire
Naturalists' Trust)

ISLE OF WIGHT
Newtown Harbour Mudflats and estuary
marshes. Migrant wildfowl and waders. (NT)
St Catherine's Point Cliffs. Seabirds and
migrants. (NT)
Bembridge Cliffs. Seabirds. (NT)

WEST SUSSEX
Chichester Harbour* Mudflats. Wildfowl
and waders. (Various private owners)
East Head, West Wittering Sand-dunes,
saltmarshes, mudflats, beaches. Wildfowl and
waders. (NT)
Pagham Harbour Mudflats, saltmarsh.
Waders and wildfowl. Interpretation Centre.
(Southern Water Authority and others)

EAST SUSSEX
Seaford Cliffs Cliffs, saltmarshes. Gulls.
(Seaford District Council)
Seven Sisters and **Cuckmere Haven** Cliffs
and estuary marshes. Wildfowl and waders.
(East Sussex County Council)
Crowlink Cliffs. Gulls. (NT)
Beachy Head Cliffs. Gulls, migrants.
(Eastbourne Borough Council)
Rye Harbour* Shingle, saltmarsh, mudflats.
Wildfowl, waders, terns. Interpretation Centre
and hides. (Southern Water Authority and
others)

KENT
Dungeness Shingle and lagoons. Wildfowl,
waders, gulls, terns. Hides, observatory.
(RSPB and others)
Bockhill and **St Margaret's Bay** Cliffs and
beach. Gulls, fulmars etc. (NT)
Sandwich Bay Sand-dunes, saltmarsh,
mudflats. Waders and wildfowl. (Kent Trust
for Nature Conservation, NT and RSPB)

South Swale Mudflats. Wildfowl and waders. (Kent County Council)

ESSEX
Leigh On Sea, Two Tree Island Mudflats, saltmarsh. Wildfowl and waders. (National)
Fingringhoe Wick Saltings. Wildfowl. Interpretation Centre, hides, trail. (Essex Naturalists' Trust)

SUFFOLK
Havergate Island (permit) Marshes, lagoons. Waders, gulls, terns, etc. Hides. (RSPB)
Minsmere Marshes, lagoons, sand-dunes. Waterfowl and waders, resident and migrant. Interpretation Centre, hides. (RSPB)

NORFOLK
Horsey Marshes, sand-dunes. Seabirds. (NT)
Cley near **Sheringham*** Marshes. Migrant waders and waterfowl. Observatory. (Norfolk Naturalists' Trust)
Blakeney Point Mudflats, sand-dunes, saltmarsh. Terns, waders, wildfowl. (NT)
Holkham Marshes, sand-dunes. Waders and wildfowl. (National)
Scolt Head Island Sand-dunes, marshes. Terns, waders and wildfowl. (National)
Brancaster Beach, sand-dunes, saltmarsh. Waders, wildfowl, little terns. (NT)
Titchwell Saltmarsh, beach. Terns, wildfowl and waders (resident and migrant). (RSPB)
Holme Dunes Sand-dunes, saltmarsh, beach. Waders and wildfowl (resident and migrant). Observatory. (Norfolk Naturalists' Trust)
Snettisham Mudflats, saltmarsh, beach. Terns, wildfowl, waders (resident and migrant). Hides. (RSPB)

LINCOLNSHIRE
Gibraltar Point Sand-dunes, marshes. Migrant and other seabirds, seals. Observatory, Interpretation Centre, trail. (Lincolnshire Trust for Nature Conservation)
Saltfleet by Theddlethorpe Dunes Sand-dunes, marshes. Migrant waders and wildfowl. (Lincolnshire Trust for Nature Conservation)
Tetney Saltmarsh, sand-dunes, beach. Terns, migrant waders and wildfowl. (RSPB)

HUMBERSIDE
Blacktoft Sands Saltmarsh. Shelduck etc. Hide. (RSPB)
Spurn Head Mudflats and beach. Waterfowl and waders. Observatory. (Yorkshire Naturalists' Trust)
Bempton Cliffs Chalk cliffs. Gannets, fulmars, auks etc. Information Centre. (RSPB)

CLEVELAND
Seal Sands Mudflats. Waterfowl, waders. (Tees and Hartlepool Port Authority)

TYNE AND WEAR
Marsden Cliffs and stacks. Kittiwakes, fulmars, cormorants.

NORTHUMBERLAND
Embleton Bay and **Dunstanburgh** Sand-dunes, cliffs and beach. Seabirds, waders, eider duck. (NT)

Telephone numbers for further information about access and the best months for visiting are:
National nature reserves – Nature Conservancy Council: 01–235 3241
National Trust: 0285 61818
RSPB (Royal Society for the Protection of Birds): 0767 80551
County Naturalists' Trusts:
Cumbria 09663 2476
Devon 0392 79244
Dorset 0202 24241
Hampshire and **Isle of Wight** 0794 513786
Essex 020628 678
Norfolk 0603 25540
Lincolnshire 05212 3468
Yorkshire 0904 59570
The Norfolk Trust issues a 'Guide to Nature Reserves on the North Norfolk Coast' with a map.
There are far more reserves than these, not open to all the public but anyone who joins a conservation society (such as the RSPB or a county naturalists' trust) will find that their membership card will usually enable them to obtain a permit to visit.

Conducted walks with ornithologists are available not only at some bird reserves but also from other sources, such as Field Studies Centres and National Parks (see Chapters 17 and 21). In the Scilly Isles, David Hunt takes groups out walking or by boat, 0720 22740; and Wildwatch do nature excursions along the north Yorkshire coast, 0947 840884. Nature trails or walks are included in two free leaflets: 'Trails and Rambles' (English Tourist Board, 01–730 3400) and 'Nature Walks' (National Trust, 01–222 9251). Such trails have explanatory noticeboards along the way or leaflets.

Further reading
'Birdwatching on estuaries, coast and sea' by Clare Lloyd (Severn House) is an exceptionally good book because it not only identifies all the coastal birds and explains their habits but also has sections describing what you can expect to see on different types of shore. It tells you how to join birdwatching groups, lists periodicals and books to read, and so on.

25 Fish from English waters

In the year that Jules Verne's 'Twenty Thousand Leagues under the Sea' was published (1869), Brighton's aquarium opened: one of the first in England. It was a sensation, visited by European monarchs and oriental potentates.

Its architectural splendours have been carefully preserved: the homely haddock and the modest mussel find themselves living within cloister-like arcades grand enough for any archbishop. Ornate columns of cast-iron support a fan-vaulted ceiling, with a brilliant colour scheme of terracotta, white and aquamarine, discreetly spotlighted. At opening time, the fish gliding silent behind the glass walls of their tanks add to the feeling of monastic calm — until the hubbub of families and school-parties takes over. This is not one of England's most outstanding aquaria (those at Skegness and Plymouth are much bigger) but it has great charm, and a number of new developments are now being carried out.

Although the aquarium includes tropical fish, sea-lions and a dolphinarium, it was our own native fish (and seals) which most interested me: eyeball-to-eyeball encounters with what I more often meet in the form of a fishfinger or scampi-in-the-basket, perhaps.

Steve Savage proved better than the guidebook or the uninformative labels when it came to explaining what was what, and together we wandered from one tank to another. Steve is the young aquarist responsible for the feeding and cleaning of all the inmates (except the dolphins) and he is a self-taught biologist with an immense knowledge of fish. As a boy he had a passion for them, spending all his spare time on and around the sea and all his spare money on books, a microscope, and painting and photographic gear to record what he saw.

When he left school he took a job in the building trade, then tried for a place at an art college but, just as he was offered one three years ago, the vacancy for an aquarist came up and he seized the chance. 'All sea life fascinates me,' he says. 'I can sit and just stare for hours. It calms you . . .' His greatest ambition is to go off and study sea-lions in the wild.

When he first joined the aquarium, he didn't like to see the sea-lions in captivity, but he has a different opinion now. One of his tasks is to feed them in front of a public audience delighted by their antics as they plunge after the fish. Steve now believes the sea-lions are well content in their pool which, seemingly small, goes down over 6 m: in the wild, sea-lions enjoy diving far more than swimming any distance.

In another pool, the slight slap of fin or tail through water is the only sound you hear from a seal as it turns, slowly rolls, glides sensuously round and round. Perhaps a quiet sigh occasionally but no barking, and none of the juggling tricks of sea-lions. All the motive power and the steering which those great bodies need comes from the flexible tail-fins: seals have no flippers to stand on as do sea-lions.

Seals find the small estuaries of Sussex rivers attractive, or sometimes get washed up on a beach after being injured. A baby turned up in the High Street of Lewes once — quite a distance inland. Several of the Aquarium's seals were foundlings of this sort.

Steve chatted to me about the local fish, too, as we watched them in the underwater glooms of their tanks, light flickering on the water as it pulsed steadily among the rocks, seaweeds and gravel.

A sinister-looking blue-black lobster peered from a cranny, long red feelers vibrating in the water. Waiting in ambush, ready to pounce? Not so, said Steve. The lobster, despite its armour-plating, fears for its life and is in hiding from its deadly enemy, the octopus, which has tentacles able to crush even that ironclad body. In any case, the lobster outgrows and loses its shell once or twice a year and then has to keep well out of sight from all predators until its new one hardens. A lobster can live to be 50, but few escape the lobster-pot long enough for that. Lobsters in fact are not a menace to the living but are scavengers, living on whatever leftovers other fish let fall to the sea-bed; and anything they don't clear up their companion sticklebacks do.

In the next tank was the unlovely lumpsucker (producer of lumpfish roe, the poor man's caviar). With the sucker on its underside, it was firmly stuck to the glass of its tank, eyes protuberant, mouth huge, skin horny. No beauty — except perhaps in the eyes of another lumpsucker. When mating time approaches, the underside of the male becomes brilliantly coloured, and lumpsuckers breed uninhibitedly in the Aquarium.

Some fish are more intelligent than others, Steve said, and pointed out the trigger fish — pursed lips, big rolling eyes and a brain equal to the task of reasoning out the best way to prise a mussel open. It gets its name from its ability to use a fin as a locking device, fixing itself onto any handy crevice so immovably that even a large predator cannot pull it away. Trigger fish are almost unique in being able to swim backwards.

Other fish use different methods to avoid trouble. Flat fish (plaice, sole, turbot and the like) lie motionless on the sea-bed. We spotted with difficulty a dab, camouflaged to be indistinguishable from the gravel it was lying on, except for watchful eyes standing up as if on stalks.

There were silver-black mullet, gliding like airships, apparently idle but in fact continuously feeding on the invisible plankton that turns the sea into nourishing soup. They are equipped with teeth particularly suited to scraping the green algae off rocks. But for Steve, I would have overlooked the tiny tube-worms sharing the tank. The tubes (of white calcium) are very small; and the worms inside are almost invisible unless you bend down and spot minute black threads waving from the ends. And on the rocks nearby, sea anemones: not plants, but creatures with hungry appetites. A little puff of soft grey tentacles forever swaying in the current — searching, searching. When satisfied, the anemone shuts up shop, folding the tentacles away inside and resting on the rock, just a pale green blob. Sea anemones can move about, but only very slowly.

There is no end to the variety of shapes a fish can take: Steve's fascination is understandable. One of the most elegant of our native species is perhaps the semi-transparent pipe-fish, a 50 cm relative of the little seahorse. It seemed to be treading water, tail trailing on the floor of the tank, head floating high above, only the eyes active — swivelling this way and that in their big sockets, always vigilant.

Down there in the subdued light and the near silence of this watery world, eyes never close and mouths are always ready to snap open. There are only the watchers and the watched; those who eat and those who get eaten.

And yet . . . 'cold-blooded', is how we describe unfeeling humans. Or 'a cold fish'. But some weeks after my visit, I came across an account (by a Russian anarchist who in 1902 wrote a book on 'Mutual Aid') of how he had, in Brighton Aquarium, watched for two hours the rescue by its fellows of a crab accidentally trapped under an iron bar. How ignorant we are of what cold fish may really feel.

Aquaria

For opening hours, feeding times and any further information, phone the numbers given.

LANCASHIRE
Morecambe* 0524 414110
Blackpool* 0253 21623

MERSEYSIDE
Southport 0704 32553

AVON
Weston-super-Mare* 0934 413040

CORNWALL
Newquay*
Looe* 050 36 2423

DEVON (south)
Plymouth* 0752 21761
Brixham* 08045 2204
Paignton* 0803 56927
Torquay* 0803 24439
Teignmouth* 062 67 3383

DORSET
Lyme Regis* 029 74 2309
Weymouth* 03057 79626
Poole* 020 13 86712

HAMPSHIRE
Hythe 0703 843011

Southsea 0705 732654

EAST SUSSEX
Brighton* 0273 604233
Eastbourne* 0323 25252 ext 7

LINCOLNSHIRE
Skegness* 0754 4345

HUMBERSIDE
Bridlington* 0262 70148

NORTH YORKSHIRE
Scarborough* 0723 64401

There is a seal sanctuary at **Gweek, Helston** 032622 361
Seals can often be seen at **Blakeney Point** (Norfolk) as well as around islands.

Further reading
'The Sea Shore' by C. M. Yonge (Fontana) describes inshore fish. 'Fishes of the Sea' by J. & G. Lythgoe (Blandford) is useful for identifying them. For children, the 'Observer Book of Sea and Seashore Life' is a good choice.

The working coast

26 Lighthouses: beacons of the night

It stood at the end of a winding track among springy turf and wildflowers sturdy enough to survive the salty winds: a stone tower painted sparkling white, with its big lantern facing out to the sea beyond Dorset.

Anvil Point lighthouse is almost exactly a century old. It is not one of the tallest lighthouses — being on a cliff 50 m above sea-level, it does not itself require great height — and it needs only one flight of stairs to get up to the top. In charge when I called was young Terry Buckland, a supernumerary (the Trinity House term for a trainee) whose enthusiasm for lighthouse work spilled over in his evident pleasure in showing visitors round.

Like all lighthouses, Anvil Point is immaculately kept — all shining paintwork and winking brass, the great window cleaned every week and its exterior hosed down.

Terry led me up inside the lantern, where blinds were drawn to keep the sunshine off the huge, louvred prisms and lenses of pure optical glass that enclose the 1,000 w lamp itself. The lenses magnify the beam, the prisms concentrate its direction, sending out a ray of light powerful enough to be seen nearly 30 km away. The lamp is, of course, electric now: a century ago, it was only paraffin. 'There are two lamps, and two motors to revolve them', Terry explained, 'so if one fails the other automatically takes over.'

In fact, when I called, the whole operation of the lighthouse was being adapted to automatic working. When this is completed, there will no longer be a team of lighthouse keepers sharing the watches and responsible for turning on the light manually, but just one, to see to maintenance.

Terry clearly felt himself lucky to have got into the lighthouse service, because opportunities are fewer now that automation is occurring in so many places. A Londoner, he became fascinated by lighthouses when, as a schoolboy, his class was taken on a visit to one. He thought that keepers would be expected to have some kind of nautical background, and so he took a building job. But, when he was visiting another lighthouse while on holiday, the keeper encouraged him to apply, and he was accepted.

'It was really weird at first! Getting used to the watches. And not knowing where you'll be going next.' (Supernumeraries are moved about, spending a month or so at one lighthouse and later going to others.) 'It's surprising how quickly a month passes, even when you're out on a rock — landed at the lighthouse by helicopter. You look after the engine, read, go on watch, sleep. I love it!'

Up in the lantern, Terry explained how and why the lights flash (at Anvil Point, the rhythm is six flashes per minute). Out at sea, a ship may have four lighthouses in view. Each therefore has a different pattern of flashes, to avoid any confusion.

There was a superb panorama from this vantage-point: Terry sometimes brings binoculars up to watch the seabirds, and we had a good view of Durlston Castle and the entrance to the old Tilly Whim caves where stone used to be quarried. But before the sun broke through that morning, there had been thick fog: Terry had turned on the fog signal outside for a couple of hours — its blast is used whenever visibility is bad.

It was time to take weather measurements (at fixed hours the local meteorological station phones for a report). I walked with Terry to the weather-box outside where every three hours temperatures are recorded. Humidity, air pressure and rainfall have to be noted too, and the wind measured. (Force 3,

Most onshore lighthouses are open to visitors who can climb right up into the lantern from which prismatic lenses direct the powerful beam.

he said — a stiff breeze.)

By now, Terry will have moved on to another lighthouse — and another — until, training complete, he is fully qualified to be a lighthouse keeper, a boyhood ambition achieved.

Lighthouses have an ancient history: within the grounds of Dover Castle (Kent) are the remains of a Roman one: simply a tower at the top of which a brazier was lit at night. But it was only in Stuart times that they began to be put up in any number: about a dozen were built at notorious danger spots along the south coast to the chagrin of the wreckers.

The most famous and impressive are on rocks out at sea and can be viewed only from a distance, perhaps on boat-trips; but some others on the shore open their doors to visitors (free) and a lighthouse keeper will show you round: these are listed below.

Perhaps the most famous of all is the Eddystone Lighthouse standing in the sea 20 km off Plymouth. A ship-owner built the first one, in 1698, which was followed by others — each disappearing through storm or fire. The famous Eddystone of Smeaton (a clockmaker by trade) was built of stone in 1759. This survived the waves' onslaught but the reef on which it stood cracked: when the new lighthouse was built on other rocks, this one was re-erected on Plymouth Hoe, where it can be visited. Its light consisted of 24 candles and was visible for 8 km. Today's Eddystone has a 570,000 candela (candlepower) light, visible for 38 km, which flashes twice every ten seconds. This is not one of the most powerful lights around England: the one at St Catherine's has $5\frac{1}{4}$ million candela.

Just as each lighthouse has its own distinctive pattern of flashes so that it cannot be confused with another, it has also its own pattern of foghorn blasts, used whenever visibility is so bad that the light might not be seen. Even the tallest and strongest lighthouse is sometimes beset by waves that reach the lantern and make the walls shiver, but fog is now the only thing that can render a lighthouse invisible. No lighthouse has been destroyed by storm for centuries; and lights powered by diesel cannot be dowsed.

Most lighthouses of England and Wales are, along with other aids to safe navigation such as buoys and lightships, under the control of Trinity House — from which background information, including maps showing the position of lighthouses and lightships, can be obtained free (01-480 6601).

Here is how Trinity House began. In the Middle Ages there was established a religious guild of seamen which had a number of benevolent objects. Concerned by the dangerous ignorance of self-styled pilots who earned a living by navigating big ships into port, and also alarmed that foreign pilots were learning the secrets of how to navigate in England's estuaries, they later persuaded Henry VIII to issue a charter under which they, the 'Fraternitie of the most glorious and blessed Trinitie', were given the responsibility for safe navigation. They acquired a coat-of-arms with four galleons, which is still used: the Trinity House flag is like the merchant navy's red ensign but with the galleons in its fly (the bottom right quarter). It was, however, a long time before Trinity House also got control of virtually all lighthouses, many of which were in private ownership up to Victoria's reign.

The men (no women, even though Henry VIII's charter specifically referred to members being 'as well men as women') who run Trinity House are known as Elder Brethren. Over the centuries their functions have varied but their responsibilities today cover (apart from charitable donations to needy seamen) the licensing of pilots and the maintenance of nearly 100 lighthouses, about 20 lightships and 700 buoys. (Other buoys maintained by local harbour authorities

A familiar landmark: the lighthouse at Beachy Head (East Sussex). A 'trip round the lighthouse' is always popular.

are subject to Trinity House inspection.)

At Harwich or Cowes Trinity House tenders, small motor vessels, go out to service the buoys, or to take out supplies to offshore lighthouses and lightships — though these days supplies are often delivered by helicopter instead. Round the coast are depots for such supplies, and to these buoys weighing three to 12 tonnes are taken for overhaul. Though, strictly speaking, the depots are not open to the public, one *may* be allowed to have a look — as I was, when I wandered around the Penzance depot in the company of one of the officers who explained how the dintinguishing lights, bells and whistles of the buoys work, and the significance of the odd names painted on each one — Knight Errant, Udder, Montamopus and so on. Some buoys depend on simple but ingenious devices for their signals; others carry very sophisticated electronic gear. There are similar depots at East Cowes (Isle of Wight), Blackwall (London), Harwich (Essex) and Great Yarmouth (Norfolk).

What are buoys for? They are the signposts of the sea — indicating what direction a ship should take in order to avoid shallows, rocks or other under-water hazards. For example, in a wide estuary the only deep-water channel may be not only narrow and winding but also apt to change position from time to time. A ship wanting to follow it will keep within the area marked by buoys: red to one side, green to the other. To make the distinction even clearer, red buoys are always squarish and green ones more pointed. The responsible authority has to keep checking the sea-bed and the moorings and, if necessary, adjusting the position of the buoys.

To indicate isolated danger-points (such as a single rock below water), more slender buoys — black with red stripes — are used, and these have a light with a double flash at night. Red-and-white vertical stripes are used on buoys designed to draw boats *towards* safe water, with their own particular pattern of flashes at night. Yellow-and-black (in various combinations) tells the navigator where to expect a bend in a channel, where shallows are about to end, and so on; after dark, these are distinguished by rapid flashes in different patterns.

All the time research goes on (at the Dungeness research station) into improved techniques. Lightships have been replaced with special buoys known as Lanbys that carry automatic radio signalling devices or, in two cases, by towers standing on the sea-bed. Some older lighthouses carry lenses of ultra-pure optical glass weighing five tonnes: now it is possible to get as strong a beam with much smaller units similar to car headlamps.

But, despite all these navigational aids, there are still areas around the coast and up estuaries where only local knowledge and skill will keep a ship safe.

That is why the skipper who is competent to take his ship all round the world is more than willing to hand over to a local pilot when he is approaching a port — not least because, as already explained, underwater hazards are not static and only a local pilot will know what changes yesterday's storm may have brought about.

Most pilots are self-employed; but they have to be licensed annually by Trinity House after passing various tests of fitness and competence. Of some 650 pilots, at least 450 operate in and around the Thames estuary. You can see (but not enter) pilot stations at many harbours and other places round the coast, and watch pilot launches taking the pilots out from them to the big ships. Some of these launches are owned by Trinity House and will be flying its flag. Other flags indicating a pilot's presence are white-and-red: left-half white and right-half red means, on a large ship, 'I have a pilot on board'; top-half white and bottom-half red means 'I am a pilot boat'. Much you might want to know about the subject is in the book 'Sea and River Pilots' by Nancy Martin (Dalton).

Every June you can watch the Brethren in procession (led by their Master, the Duke of Edinburgh) as they go from their annual court to a service at St Olave's, Hart Street, in the City of London. For information, phone the Corporation of Trinity House (01-480 7662). The work of the men who keep watch in lonely and isolated places is often forgotten. But before every Christmas there are people who *do* remember, contributing to Christmas parcels that are delivered (weather permitting) by lifeboat, or RAF cadets in helicopters, or fishing-boats. Some volunteers go to sing carols. There is also a penfriends scheme which is run (worldwide) by Gabriel Rolo, 13127 Old West Avenue, San Diego, California, for people who would like to correspond with lighthouse keepers.

Lighthouses open to the public

Lighthouses are normally open every afternoon except Sunday or during fog, but telephone to check just before you go. Dates quoted below are dates of origin — all have been rebuilt subsequently. 'Cand.' is approximate candela (candlepower). Height is that of the tower, excluding the rock or cliff on which it stands.

CUMBRIA
St Bees Lighthouse near **Whitehaven*** 1718, 150,000 cand., 17 m. 0946 2635

DEVON (north)
Foreland Lighthouse **Lynmouth*** 1900, 1 million cand., 15 m. 05987 226
Lundy South Lighthouse near **Ilfracombe*** 1879, 600,000 cand., 16 m. 02373 455
Bull Point Lighthouse near **Woolacombe*** 1879, 800,000 cand., 17 m. 0271 870535
Hartland Point Lighthouse near **Bideford*** 1874, $1\frac{1}{4}$ million cand., 18 m. 02374 328

CORNWALL
Trevose Lighthouse near **Padstow** 1847, 800,000 cand., 27 m. 0841 520494
Pendeen Lighthouse near **St Ives*** 1900, 2 million cand., 17 m. 0736 788418
Lizard Lighthouse near **Helston** 1751, 4 million cand., 19 m. 0326 290431

DEVON (south)
Penlee Fog-Signal Station near **Torpoint** 1902. 0752 822460
Start Point Lighthouse near **Kingsbridge*** 1836, 800,000 cand., 28 m. 0548 580225

DORSET
Portland Bill Lighthouse on **Portland** 1906, $3\frac{1}{4}$ million cand., 41 m. 0305 820495
(Previous Victorian lighthouses can still be seen nearby — now private houses.)
Anvil Point Lighthouse near **Swanage*** 1881, 500,000 cand., 12 m. 092 92 2146

ISLE OF WIGHT
St Catherine's Lighthouse near **Ventnor*** 1840, $5\frac{1}{4}$ million cand., 26 m. 0983 730284

KENT
North Foreland Lighthouse near **Broadstairs*** 1790, 200,000 cand., 26 m. 0843 61869

NORFOLK
Cromer Lighthouse **Cromer*** 1719, 100,000 cand., 18 m. 0263 512123

HUMBERSIDE
Flamborough Lighthouse near **Bridlington*** 1806, $3\frac{1}{2}$ million cand., 27 m. 0262 850345

NORTH YORKSHIRE
Whitby Lighthouse **Whitby*** 1858, 400,000 cand., 7 m. 0947 602296

TYNE AND WEAR
Souter Lighthouse near **Sunderland** 1871, $1\frac{1}{2}$ million cand., 23 m. 0783 293161

NORTHUMBERLAND
Longstone Lighthouse near **Seahouses*** 1826, $3\frac{1}{4}$ million cand., 26 m. 02555 2377

Other lighthouses though not open, are accessible. These include some at the ends of piers: the one at **South Shields*** (Tyne and Wear), for instance, which attracts sightseers who look for the doll which was pressed into the still-soft concrete when the lighthouse was built in 1895 and which is still there. Museums with sections on the work of Trinity House include those at **Exeter*** (south Devon), **Bembridge** (Isle of Wight) and **Harwich*** (Essex), and the National Maritime Museum, **London**. See also Chapter 11.

There are independent Trinity Houses at **Hull*** (Humberside), and **Newcastle*** (Tyne and Wear) where it is planned to open a maritime centre with exhibits on the work of Trinity House.

Further reading
Of many books about lighthouses, the following are good: 'A History of Lighthouses' by P. Beaver (Davies) and 'Lighthouses' by Hague and Christier (Gomer Press).

27 Life-saving: coastguards and volunteers

The breakers were right beneath her bows,
She drifted a dreary wreck,
And a whooping billow swept the crew
Like icicles from her deck.

She struck where the white and fleecy waves
Looked soft as carded wool.
But the cruel rocks, they gored her side
Like the horns of an angry bull.

No prizes for remembering from which famous poem* those verses come!

The same disasters still continue to happen: storms, fast currents and human miscalculation regularly drive ships onto England's rocky shores, and if seamen then escape death it is often due to the vigilance and courage of coastguards aided by trained volunteers. Many of the techniques for life-saving when ships are wrecked on the coast have changed little over the years: old methods continue to be the best.

But life-saving was a hit-and-miss business up to 24th November 1864. That wintry night proved to be a turning-point.

The previous evening, the steamship 'Stanley' had left Aberdeen carrying 30 passengers, 26 crew, about 50 cattle and sheep, and a mixed cargo. She was heading for London but when, a day later, a storm blew up, Captain Howling decided to make for shelter in the Tyne estuary.

Rain was sheeting down and the tide was rising. The seas rapidly grew heavier, and the force of the waves drove the 'Stanley' off course and straight onto the savage rocks that you can see at Tynemouth.

Wrecks here are no novelty and the coastguards of Tynemouth had a few rockets bearing rescue-lines (a device invented by a friend of Nelson, incidentally) which they could fire to ships in distress, with breeches buoys to follow, with which people could be hauled to safety. But it was dark, and gale-force winds were blowing from the east. All was confusion and panic, the lines got tangled and damaged beyond all possibility of use. As hour succeeded hour, more people were washed overboard and drowned while the watchers on the shore stood helpless, listening to their screams above the howl of the gale. Just after midnight, the 'Stanley' broke in two: everyone in the stern was drowned. All told 27 people died. And that same night more lives were lost from two other ships that ran onto nearby rocks, and from the lifeboat that in vain attempted to get alongside the ships. Such bodies as were later found on the beaches lie in a mass grave (still tended) in North Shields.

Appalled at this multiple tragedy, some local people got together to ensure that the muddle and lack of equipment through which so many people had been left to die should never happen again. The Tynemouth Volunteer Life Brigade was formed.

I walked up to the headland where the Victorian white-and-blue weather-boarded Watch House now stands — headquarters and museum of the Brigade. Here a battery of guns once stood ready to repulse the Spanish Armada. In one direction is a 30 m cliff with gaunt ruins of an ancient priory where two Northumbrian kings are reputedly buried; in the other rises the colossal column on which stands the figure of Lord Collingwood, the Tynesider who (as every good

---

* Baffled? Longfellow's 'Wreck of the Hesperus'.

Tynesider is still quick to point out) was the admiral who actually won the Battle of Trafalgar, Nelson himself having been killed earlier on. This clifftop is a perfect place from which to watch the great ships heading for the port of Newcastle — on a fine day, that is. In stormy weather, it is the Life Brigade who will be on the lookout.

The first volunteers (over 170 of them, from fish-quay 'humpers' to solicitors) undertook to keep themselves up to the mark at regular training sessions and to be on call at any hour of night or day when a rescue might be needed. This is still their way of working: during one Christmas Day recently, they were called to three wrecks. Similar Life Brigades have now been established all over the world, but Tyneside was the first and its volunteers still wear a version of the original uniform.

Despite electronic navigational aids, despite the latest lifeboats and helicopters, breeches buoys remain essential for saving lives. The breeches buoy (invented in 1820 by an Isle of Wight man) got its name from the fact that it comprised a lifebuoy with canvas breeches attached so that the person being carried would not get washed out of the buoy by heavy waves while being conveyed by ropes and pulley from ship to shore. A simple device, yet one capable of lifting a man ashore in a mere four minutes. The museum contains a demonstration breeches buoy, as well as an absorbing collection of historical material — innumerable photographs of wrecks together with figureheads and other parts brought ashore after wrecks. They have models of ships and a lighthouse, Bobby Shaftoe's soup tureen, an old bellows once used for giving the 'kiss of life' and a mortar which fired a cannon-ball carrying a chain out to stranded ships. There are sad relics — the ship's bell from the 'Stanley', some silver from her captain's cabin and clay pipes of her crew; and the rum-barrels on which some seamen managed to float ashore.

Many parts of the English coast are treacherous but none more so than the mouth of the Tyne where the deep-water channel is so very narrow, the tides so fast and, always waiting for prey, those aptly named rocks, the Black Middens ('midden' means a rubbish heap), particularly sinister when hidden in fog or sea-spray.

Honorary Captain Lawrence is delighted to show interested visitors round (phone 0632 572059), and it was he who vividly described to me some of the rescues his 20 colleagues have accomplished along the 8 km of coast for which they take responsibility.

'In bad visibility it can take longer to locate the ship than it does to get the men off it. Fortunately today's vessels don't break up quickly like the old wood ones. But you have to make swift decisions, all the same — for instance, assessing the right size of hawser in relation to the ship; and when the deck is rising and falling some 10 m in high seas, you've got to tauten and slacken accordingly. There have been two occasions when as many as 30 ships have been driven onto the shore in one storm.

'These days there are fewer wrecks, but we have other rescues to do — like saving people who have fallen over a cliff. Some of our volunteers have trained as rock climbers and can abseil down to get them.'

Together we clambered up into the lookout tower where a searchlight is housed. From here there is a superb view of the river and the buoys marking the only navigable channel along it, two old lighthouses, and the piers, over a kilometre in length, that were built at the turn of the century to provide some shelter for the mouth of the Tyne. Repairing them is a never-ending task: every winter the sea sweeps away some of the 40-tonne granite blocks from which they are made.

As I sit writing this at home, thunder and lightning are slicing through the evening and a gale is tossing the trees in my garden. The weather forecast is bad. Back there at Tynemouth, volunteers will have turned out to keep vigil at the Watch House tonight.

In total some 8,000 volunteer life-savers around our shore act as auxiliaries to the 560 professional coastguards. The auxiliaries work in teams but do not wear uniform — simply a distinctive sweater and badge: you may come across them engaged in training practice.

The Coastguard service, founded in 1822, was originally set up to deal with smuggling but after 1923 the coastguards were given the task of life-saving. Basically, they are now co-ordinators of rescue services such as the lifeboats, naval or RAF helicopters and shore-to-ship radio stations. They may call on local boat owners for help, and they summon the auxiliaries (usually by radio-paging devices rather than the old maroon signal which used to go echoing out). If you see a boat or swimmer in trouble, or someone in difficulty on a cliff, you should dial 999 and ask for the nearest coastguard. Coastguards also give free advice on sailing hazards, tides and weather.

Most of the 7,000 people rescued every year are not on ships: a third are amateurs in small craft (including even toy inflatables), and the majority of others are people cut off by the tide on beaches or cliffs. Almost invariably they have run into bad weather unprepared, and the coastguards would like everyone venturing onto the sea or taking long beach walks to listen to weather forecasts by any of the following means: local radio reports; Radio 4 at 6.25 a.m., 1.55 p.m., 5.50 p.m. or shortly after midnight; Radio 3 at 6.55 a.m. (or 7.55 a.m. at the weekend); or phone the local coastguard for advice. Many coastguards now work from modern centres with sophisticated communications. Others still keep a lookout from coastguard cottages around the coast, some of them in remote spots.

Finally, the beach lifeguards who patrol where tricky currents or underwater hazards sometimes get swimmers into trouble. Their principal role is prevention rather than rescue, and to see them around in their distinctive cap and swimming trunks is usually warning enough, I was told by schoolteacher Stewart Bursey, a leader of the Bournemouth lifeguards. Most but not all are volunteers who patrol on a rota throughout the summer. Even 14-year-olds can be recruited as cadets. Training and practice are provided during the winter through clubs that operate under the auspices of the Royal Life Saving Society (or, in Cornwall where conditions are different, under the Surf Life-Saving Association). Life-guards are equipped with VHF radio, these days; and inflatable power-boats.

At summer maritime festivals, the local lifeguards often put on a demonstra-tion. 'Ours at Bournemouth is one of the most spectacular', Stewart said, 'with 16 clubs parading.' There are swimming and rowing races, and reel-and-line contests — in these, a man swims out with a line attached to his belt (as if to get a casualty) and is then reeled back in by a team of five others. Later an incident is set up with a number of casualties to be recovered and given first aid.

Anyone wanting to volunteer can get details from the Royal Life Saving Society (052785 3943).

Where lifeguards are patrolling, you may notice a pair of red-and-yellow flags flying above the sea: this means you are safe to swim within the area marked by the flags. An all-red flag means 'danger — no swimming'.

Two other signal flags are: black-and-white — 'leave this part clear for surf-boarders'; blue-and-white — 'aqualung divers are below'.

You can avoid any necessity for rescue by the lifeguards if you use common-sense about currents, the sea-bed and tides, and ask local people for advice.

Currents: Look at the surface of the sea — where a submerged rock or bank is setting up a strong current below, the surface is likely to be disturbed. Dangerous currents occur round headlands, and in narrow passages like estuaries.

Sea-bed: If you do not want to get out of your depth, keep testing. Some beaches have extensive hollows under water; or suddenly shelve steeply. Others have underwater sandbanks where you may feel safe but where you could get cut off by an incoming tide. It is wise to swim parallel with the beach and not head out to sea.

Tides: Ask the times of tides. There are, in most places, six-and-a-quarter hours between low and high tide; but on some beaches the tide comes in as fast as galloping horses, and you can see how swift it is if you look at its movement past, for instance, buoys or moored boats.

How deep the water usually is at high tide may be indicated by seaweed growth on breakwaters or cliffs. Tides come extra-high twice a month, when the moon is either new or full (these are called spring tides): just how high may be indicated by the row of seaweed and shells left at the top of the beach by the last spring tide.

Where to find out more about life-saving

At various resorts each summer, life-saving demonstrations take place, often as part of regattas or marine festivals. At **Ilfracombe***(north Devon) even naval and air services join in as well as the lifeboats and coastguards. On **Wearside**, the three volunteer brigades, including the Tynemouth one described above, compete for a shield.

Local museums often have interesting exhibits from their town's life-saving organisations. The one at **Helston** (Cornwall) does, for instance; and at **Swanage*** (Dorset) there is a detailed model showing how coastguards organise cliff rescues. At **Brixham*** (south Devon) there is an important coastguard section in the museum.

Further reading

'Search and Rescue', a leaflet obtainable free from Room 503, Department of Trade, 29 Great Peter Street, London SW1P 3LW. 'Coastguard!' by W. Webb (Stationery Office).

28 Lifeboats and lifeboatmen

You see lifeboats on the beach or at their moorings, on slipways or in boathouses. Few people who gaze at them realise that it is (with a few exceptions) unpaid volunteers who man them whenever a call for help goes out. Since 1824, over 100,000 lives have been saved by these volunteers — even now, over three people a day are rescued.

Sir Winston Churchill summed it all up when he said of a lifeboat: 'It drives on with a mercy which does not quail in the presence of death; it drives on as a proof that valour and virtue have not perished in the British race.' From the outset of the lifeboat service, all sorts of people have volunteered: not just seamen but teachers and shopkeepers, for instance (including women). In the past, hundreds have died while trying to save others, though this happens infrequently now, thanks to the vast improvements in lifeboat design.

What impels these volunteers to help in often appalling conditions? A lifeboatman interviewed in 1902 gave an answer which, 80 years later, still stands: 'I don't know myself. There was the wreck; all the people from the village stood on the beach, and all said it would be foolish to go out. We never should work through the surf. Then, all of a sudden through the storm, it seemed to us as if we heard their cries — they had a boy with them. We could not stand that any longer. All at once we said, "We must go!"'

The Royal National Lifeboat Institution has its roots in the late 18th century when for the first time life-saving groups began to organise themselves here and there. In Bamburgh Castle (Northumberland) is a document of 1771 outlining a system to be followed in storms: mounted patrols were to keep constant watch along the coast, using a speaking trumpet to communicate with wrecked ships. An 'unsinkable' boat had been invented by a coachbuilder (his tombstone at Hythe, Kent, was inscribed 'Lionel Lukin, the first who built a lifeboat'), an adaptation of an ordinary fishing-boat, and one of these was ordered. (Bam-

At the Grace Darling Museum at Bamburgh (Northumberland), the huge boat rowed by this tiny girl is still preserved.

burgh's second claim to fame occurred in 1838 when Grace Darling and her father saved nine men at dawn from a wrecked paddle-steamer. There is now a fascinating Grace Darling Museum at Bamburgh (06684 310) which, along with much else, has some of the innumerable silk shawls and other presents with which she was inundated afterwards, and the heavy great coble which this girl of only 1·55 m rowed through the storm.)

The first purpose-built lifeboat was designed in 1789, by the parish clerk of South Shields on Tyneside (his tin model is in the museum there and one of the early lifeboats stands in the street) and, with improvements, it was made by a local boat-builder, Greathead who got most of the glory and rewards. It depended upon oars — sails came later, steam in 1890, and petrol in 1904.

By 1824 there were 39 lifeboats around British shores, all privately owned (most belonged to Lloyds, the marine insurance corporation). By then a group of men (including William Wilberforce) had initiated the idea of the first national lifeboat organisation.

Today's lifeboats have diesel engines, and the most advanced are equipped not only with radio but direction-finding equipment, radar and echo-sounders. They differ in design because some have to work among rocks and others among sandbanks, for example. With small boat sailing now so popular, many casualties occur close inshore, and to deal with these, small inflatables with outboard engines are used. Although some rescues are left to naval or RAF helicopters, the lifeboats are still vital — they can stay at sea for many hours (even days if refuelled), can tow boats in, are usable even when visibility is minimal, and can take a lot of survivors on board.

When a call for help is received at a lifeboat station (usually from a coast-guard, see Chapter 27), the volunteers are summoned by phone, radio-bleeper or siren and come running. Unless the boat is already moored, launchers help to get it down a slipway or haul it by tractor across a beach.

I visited one of the many lifeboat stations that opens its doors to visitors, at Bembridge (Isle of Wight). Here there are two buildings: one, above the beach, houses the inflatable inshore lifeboat — used to rescue people in trouble near or on the shores — and the other, at the end of a 200-m jetty, houses the big lifeboat. A board announces when the next of the six-weekly practice launchings will take place: spectators gather to watch the splash as, with a loud siren-hoot, the boat with a crew of seven rushes down its slipway into the deep sea at the jetty's end.

The first of the two buildings dates from 1867. It had a harness room (horses were borrowed from farms to haul the lifeboat ashore after every trip) and under the floor is a remnant of the railway up and down which the lifeboat was pulled, back in the days of oars and sail.

Things are different now — and more colourful, too. Inside, yellow oilskins and red lifejackets hang on a blue-painted wall; the big inflatable with outboard motor is bright orange. The past year's achievements had been typical: a small yacht had lost its mast in rough weather (three people were rescued); an empty and drifting dinghy was retrieved for its owner; a mother and children were taken ashore from a sailing-boat aground on a ledge, while father stayed to right the boat at the next high tide; and, a grim service, the body of a man who had fallen over a 100-m cliff was brought back for burial. There were other call-outs, too: a vain search for a missing aircraft, a hoax SOS and so on.

I walked along the jetty with Coxswain Peter Smith, one-time skipper of a motor yacht in the south of France, but a lifeboat coxswain for many years. Alongside the jetty were visible some of the knife-like ledges of rock which can cause such havoc on this part of the coast; and cormorants, perched on the beacons marking a sewage outlet, kept watch for fish.

Inside the big boathouse is a smell of tar from the woodwork, and of oil. The huge lifeboat looms high overhead, its great brass twin-screws highly polished (a staircase has been put in, so visitors can get a deck-level view too). Built about ten years ago, the boat will ultimately be of historic interest for it was the last one to be designed on traditional lines, with the white, blue and red hull that is so familiar from the RNLI's collecting-boxes. Later, I visited Yarmouth, also on the Isle of Wight, where one of the most up-to-date lifeboats looks totally different, designed for far greater speed. The boathouse also includes the winding-engine needed to haul the lifeboat up the slipway again at the end of a task.

Hung on a wall of the boathouse was a neat row of orange oilskins, each named for a crew member. The last in the line was labelled 'doctor': the local GP goes out with the crew to give any medical aid that may be needed.

The very earliest lifeboats were adapted from fishing-boats with the addition of cork for extra buoyancy. Today's boats have nothing in common with these primitive predecessors. Once I had climbed up to deck-level, Coxswain Smith explained to me how it is that his great boat — able to take 100 survivors on board — can right itself in four seconds if waves overturn it. Each part of it, except the wheelhouse, is sealed off from the next by watertight doors. This makes it a cluster of watertight compartments and unsinkable. And it has a high superstructure, which contributes to its self-righting capacity.

The boathouse contains models of old lifeboats, a map of local wrecks, and boards listing rescues carried out from Bembridge lifeboat station. All told, 687 lives had been saved by the date when I was there, with no loss of lifeboatmen —

The Padstow lifeboat sets out on another mission. At many lifeboat stations, launches and other demonstrations can be seen regularly.

the most dramatic operation being the saving of 110 men from a transport ship that was wrecked during the First World War. The most recent action was listed as: 'Landed a sick man from Nab Tower'.

Visitors are sometimes shown around by a member of the crew, but more often by someone from the local lifeboat guild, a body of volunteers who support their local lifeboat by fund-raising and so on. Wherever there is a lifeboat, such helpers are welcomed.

Lifeboat museums and display centres

CUMBRIA
Maryport* Maryport Museum has one gallery of lifeboat history. (See Chapter 11.) 090081 3738

LANCASHIRE
Lytham St Anne's* Lifeboat House at **Lytham**. 0253 736316 On Lifeboat Sunday (June) there is an open-air service. 0253 725610
Blackpool* Lifeboat House. 0253 21623

AVON
Bristol* National Lifeboat Museum. 0272 291939

DEVON (north)
Clovelly Lifeboat House. 02373 381

DEVON (south)
Exmouth* Lifeboat House. 03952 5092

DORSET
Poole* RNLI Head Office: models and paintings. 02013 71133 Old Lifeboat House: old lifeboat. 0202 695443

WEST SUSSEX
Shoreham Lifeboat House. 0273 592339

EAST SUSSEX
Eastbourne* Lifeboat Museum. 0323 30717

KENT
Hythe Tomb of Lukin, inventor of lifeboat.
Walmer Lifeboat House. 030 45 4386

ESSEX
Harwich* Old Light Tower. 02555 3108

SUFFOLK
Southwold Old Water Tower. 0502 722422

NORFOLK
Caister-on-Sea 'Never Turn Back Inn' has relics of 1901 lifeboat disaster.
Cromer* Old Lifeboat House. Has coastguard and other life-saving exhibits too. 0263 512503

NORTH YORKSHIRE
Whitby* Old Lifeboat House. Includes the last oared lifeboat. 0947 602001

CLEVELAND
Redcar Zetland Museum. Oldest surviving lifeboat is here, plus other sea-rescue exhibits. More exhibits in the Lifeboat House. Occasional lantern-slide shows. 06493 485332

TYNE AND WEAR
South Shields* South Shields Museum. Model of first lifeboat from 1789 and another model of it is in the church. 0642 568740

NORTHUMBERLAND
Bamburgh Grace Darling Museum. 06684 310

In the chapters on museums and historic ship collections are noted others that have lifeboat exhibits. The Town Docks Museum at **Hull*** (Humberside) has some (see Chapter 11); and so does the Helena Thompson Museum at **Workington*** (Cumbria). There are lifeboat monuments at **Southport*** and **Lytham St Anne's*** (Lancashire), **Margate*** (Kent) and **Bridlington*** (Humberside). The parish church of **South Shields*** (Tyne and Wear) has lifeboat windows.

How to find out about lifeboats and to help the RNLI

Round the coast of the British Isles there are stationed 135 lifeboats (supplemented by 30 or more in reserve and 120 small craft for work close inshore). The list below gives the numbers to phone if you want to find out when you can go and see a lifeboat station. Most are open to the public, though at somewhat unpredictable hours — it all depends when volunteers are available.

At the RNLI's headquarters in **Poole*** (Dorset) there are open days each summer when the works depot can be toured and demonstrations are laid on. 02013 71133

The RNLI depends entirely on donations from the public to continue its work, and these days a large lifeboat may cost a quarter of a million pounds. There are several ways in which you can help. You can go to events such as the fêtes held to raise money at almost every coastal resort that has a lifeboat, or put a donation in an RNLI collecting box whenever you see one. If you join 'Shoreline', a national membership scheme, in return for an annual subscription you will receive a magazine, can wear RNLI ties and brooches and can help to run their fund-raising events, particularly on Lifeboat Day (in August) when lifeboats often put to sea for special displays, or when annual lifeboat blessings or thanksgiving services are held.

To find out when a lifeboat station is open to the public, or when practice launchings are going to take place, phone the Coxswain.

CUMBRIA
Silloth* 0946 830691
Workington* 0990 2301
St Bees 0946 4821
Barrow* 0229 22310

LANCASHIRE
Morecambe* 0524 414115
Fleetwood* 03917 3939
Blackpool* 0253 46646
Lytham St Anne's* 0253 735528

MERSEYSIDE
New Brighton* 06578 4961
Hoylake 051632 2103
West Kirby 051632 1354

AVON
Weston-super-Mare* 0934 20369 or 26369

SOMERSET
Minehead* 0643 2257

DEVON (north)
Ilfracombe* 0271 63460
Appledore 02372 4006
Clovelly 02373 232

CORNWALL
Bude* 0288 2003
Port Isaac 020 888 383
Padstow 0841 532421
Newquay* 063 73 2874
St Agnes 087 255 2307 or 2149
St Ives* 073670 5540

SCILLY ISLES
St Mary's* 0720 22445

CORNWALL
Sennen Cove 073 687 231
Penlee 073 673 242
The Lizard-Cadgwith 032639 430

Coverack 0326 250715
Falmouth* 0326 312215
Fowey* 072 683 3595

DEVON (south)
Plymouth* 0752 67492
Salcombe* 054 884 2333
Torbay 0803 559257 and 4899
Exmouth* 03952 4036

DORSET
Lyme Regis* 02974 3284
Weymouth* 0305 786280
Swanage* 092 92 2015
Poole* 0202 741295
Mudeford 04252 72162

HAMPSHIRE
Lymington 0590 76188
Calshot 0703 819293

ISLE OF WIGHT
Yarmouth* 0983 760243
Bembridge 098 387 2858

HAMPSHIRE
Portsmouth* (Langstone Harbour)
0705 722351 extns 6291/2/5
Hayling Island 07016 3572

WEST SUSSEX
Selsey 024361 5255
Littlehampton* 09064 3922
Shoreham Harbour 0273 592461

EAST SUSSEX
Brighton* 0273 680492
Newhaven* 07912 4067
Eastbourne* 0323 30836
Hastings* 0424 423438
Rye Harbour* 07973 2419

KENT
Dungeness 0679 20647
Littlestone-on-Sea 06793 3211
Dover* 0304 202620
Walmer 03045 4069
Ramsgate* 0843 55486/57462
Margate* 0843 24065
Whitstable* 0227 51755
Sheerness* 0795 873731

ESSEX
Southend* 0702 67421
Burnham-on-Crouch 0621 782296
West Mersea* 020634 220
Clacton* 0255 25122
Walton-on-the-Naze* and Frinton
02556 5985
Harwich* 025 55 2259

SUFFOLK
Aldeburgh 072885 2130
Southwold 0502 723292
Lowestoft* 0502 65272

NORFOLK
Great Yarmouth* and **Gorleston-on-Sea**
0493 68372
Happisburgh 06925 474
Cromer* 0263 512727
Sheringham* 0263 823206
Wells-next-the-Sea 0328 710271

LINCOLNSHIRE
Skegness* 0754 3430
Mablethorpe* 05213 3327

HUMBERSIDE
Humber Mouth (Cleethorpes*) 0472 55727
Humber 09646 228
Withernsea* Burton Pidsea 479
Bridlington* 0262 79967
Flamborough 0262 850226

NORTH YORKSHIRE
Filey* 0723 512044
Scarborough* 0723 75520
Whitby* 0947 3645

CLEVELAND
Staithes and **Runswick** 0947 840315
Redcar 064 93 471897
Teesmouth 064 93 4587
Hartlepool* 0429 66938

DURHAM
Crimdon Dene 0783 270501
Seaham 0783 75502

TYNE AND WEAR
Sunderland 0783 56912
Tynemouth 0632 573864
Cullercoats 0632 572248

NORTHUMBERLAND
Blyth 06706 3440
Newbiggin-by-the-Sea 0670 817778
Amble 0665 710277
Craster 066576 286407
North Sunderland 0665 720222
Berwick-upon-Tweed* 0289 6209

Further reading
Many lifeboat stations sell informative booklets and wallcharts about the service and its history. The following can be ordered free (but please send a donation) from the RNLI at 202 Lambeth Road, London SE1. Some are particularly suitable for children: 'History and Work of the Lifeboat Service' (picture-strip book); chart of lifeboat stations; and three colourful wallcharts – a pair on 'How the Lifeboat Service Works' and one on 'Lifeboats of the RNLI' (the types of boat). There are three 'General Information' booklets, one of which deals with the inshore lifeboats bought with money raised by 'Blue Peter', the children's TV programme. There is also a list of books and other items which can be ordered by post. 'Amazing Grace' (by Joanna Dessau) is the most recent, and accurate, of many novels based on the story of Grace Darling. Perhaps the best publication for a quick overall view is the large wallchart (folded) which Bartholomews publish and the RNLI sells. In the centre is a map showing the location of all the lifeboat stations. There are 40 colour pictures illustrating every type of lifeboat in use (and some historic ones), memorable rescues, the gallantry medals that are awarded, and much else.

29 The Navy on view

There are now only three naval ports round England's shores (plus a training base at Portland), ultimately to be reduced to two. The Navy no longer builds its own ships, only services and refits them. There used to be one more naval base, Sheerness, but this is now a commercial port.

The public normally has only limited access to the ports (for details, see list at end of chapter) but once a year Navy Days are held, and people swarm in by their thousands. Not only are the dockyards then open to view, but ships and sometimes even submarines can be boarded.

It was one of those days when the weather plays fast-and-loose, brilliant sunshine one moment and a downpour the next, when I went to Chatham. The stupendous size of the place is what first strikes you, for the high walls fronting the road give no conception of what lies beyond: nearly 500 acres of buildings, docks, a railway system and colossal 'basins', each capable of holding some 20 or so warships of one kind or another. As our car edged its way along, the bows of just one of these – a mere frigate, nothing special – loomed overhead like a great cliff.

During Navy Days, the serious business of the port comes temporarily to a standstill. The ships are dressed overall – their signal flags fluttering from stem to stern, like an unusually colourful line of washing; and each one flying the white ensign, the Navy's own flag. Children throng the place, their attention equally divided between the ships and the stalls selling popcorn and candyfloss.

A troop of Sea Scouts marched by, a young Marine in impeccable white helmet and belt stood smartly to attention at the foot of a gangplank, a naval charity's shop was doing a brisk trade in souvenirs, from clay pipes to T-shirts.

Sloping up to each grey hull was a gangplank, and at each gangplank was a queue. Everyone going on board had to leave their bags behind, or have them searched. Once aboard, the sightseers slowly shuffled round – impressed by, but mostly uncomprehending, the electronic gadgetry of the modern Navy, and more inclined to linger over the domestic details of shipboard life: the crew's comfortable cabin spaces, the food displayed in the galleys.

Inevitably it is the nuclear submarines that attract most sightseers, though the aircraft carriers with helicopters on deck come a close second. A whole day is not enough to see everything. There were boat-trips down the estuary; demonstrations of rope-climbing, and of WRNS doing p.t. exercises; the French navy had sent an anti-submarine destroyer to take part (the Belgians, Danes and Dutch had come as well), and the French sailors, conspicuous with red pompoms on their caps, showed visitors around. Plenty of on-shore exhibits, too – even a tank like an outsize aquarium with Naval frogmen in it. (Small boys behaved just as they do at any aquarium – tapping and pressing their noses on the glass, and getting in return a distinctly fishy look through the frogmen's goggles.) Sea and Marine cadets competed in field-gun contests.

The high spot of each day is the display with helicopters and, later, the formidable Sea Harrier – built to take off in a second from the deck of HMS 'Invincible', for reconnaissance or attack: a deafening shriek and the Sea Harrier is up and away.

The helicopters took part in demonstrations of search-and-rescue techniques, a mock underwater attack on HMS 'Triumph' and anti-submarine warfare. But suddenly the skies opened and a deluge of rain sent all the spectators running to the nearest undercover exhibit. I found myself in a hut surrounded by objects which sounded like candidates for a word quiz programme: boat-gripes, block tufnols, bollard-strops and other mysteries, all to do with rope work. The 'biggest bell-rope in the world' was on display, along with examples of knots of fiendish complexity. In the company of a macramé enthusiast, I pored over carrick bends and monkey's fists, square sennits and ossel hitches, cockscombing and the pineapple knot.

It is really only after getting home and studying the pictorial brochure produced on these occasions that the significance of what one has been seeing begins to sink in. Although there are to be cutbacks (Chatham dockyard is to be closed down in a few years' time), Britain has the biggest Navy in the world after America and Russia: some 200 ships, with 70,000 officers and men – not including 3,000 WRNS. Many of the ships are very different from those which were used in the Second World War and include: nuclear missile submarines; guided missile destroyers; nuclear-propelled submarines; frigates, high-speed ships armed with guns and missiles; patrol submarines; minesweepers and mine hunters; and patrol ships – offshore protection ships. The Royal Marines' commandos are carried in specialised ships for assault action or to undertake amphibious operations. Finally there are about 40 ships used for making charts, carrying stores and so forth.

One of the most striking ships open to the public during the Navy Days is the huge (175-m) missile destroyer, HMS 'London'. What is the purpose of such a great vessel?

She carries an Admiral, to command groups of other ships in action. Her main function is air defence and she is equipped to launch missiles. But she can also hunt submarines with her torpedo-carrying helicopter. She has a detachment of Royal Marines, for commando work. The ship's company is trained for a variety of other tasks, too: boarding ships, riot control, salvage — and even disaster relief such as helping communities struck by an earthquake: the Navy's role is not confined to warfare.

HMS 'Endurance' was in complete contrast: her bright red hull surprised me until I realised that to be conspicuous is essential to her work. She operates in the icy wastes of the Antarctic, helping to survey uncharted waters and assisting scientists who work there.

Chatham Dockyard employs over 8,000 people (7,000 of them civilians). Two thousand naval personnel live in HMS 'Pembroke', Chatham's barracks or, in modern parlance, 'accommodation centre'. The dockyard of today bears no resemblance to its beginnings. In Tudor and Stuart times, ships were merely moored in the Medway estuary, with ship-building or repairing carried out on the banks. The vast basins were not built until the 1850s. They took the place of a muddy creek (with oyster beds) which separated the mainland from a marshy island.

As long ago as 1663, Pepys was taken, as Clerk of the Navy, to the Dockyard (which still occupied only a relatively small area at Chatham) to look at the possibilities: 'By barge to St Mary's Creek, where Commissioner Pett do design a wett docke at no great charge and yet no little one. He thinks towards ten thousand pounds. And the place is likely to be a very fit place when the

During Navy Days, there are spectacular displays to watch in the naval ports.

king hath money to do it with.' But Charles II had no money to spare. During the early 18th century, a number of buildings went up, which can be seen on the daily guided tours. But it was not until 1854 that the idea of building docks in place of the creek was revived.

It was decided to use convicts (there were 1,200 in the dockyard prison) to do the work. They were guarded by warders with rifles standing on high wood towers, and clothed in garments marked with the 'broad arrow' that labelled them as prisoners. Their first task was to make an embankment round the island to keep the high spring tides out. Then the convicts began making bricks, partly from the clay on the island itself: 110 million were made in about eight years. As they dug, they found hundreds of bones: the remains of earlier French prisoners-of-war who had died on the infamous hulks which used to be moored nearby. The bones were reburied and one of the convicts, a mason, carved a memorial to the prisoners; both memorial and bones were later moved to the Naval barracks and are still there.

Newly invented Portland cement (made with local chalk and the mud of the Medway creeks, to a formula discovered by a Gravesend man called Aspdin) went into the foundations of the new structures. The three basins that were created lie where the creek used to flow, and when they were being excavated the remains of one of the men-of-war sunk in the Dutch raid of 1667 were unearthed. The level of the island was artificially raised two-and-a-half m. All this great undertaking was designed and organised by the Royal Engineers over a period of 20 years.

The basins can be seen only on Navy Days. During the rest of the year, it is only the older part of the dockyard round which visitors are shown: the classical church (with a model of the 'Golden Hind'), the Admiral's fine house – exterior only; the ropery – at nearly half a kilometre, it is the longest brick building in England; the sail-loft – where 'Victory's' sails were made; and much more of interest.

After visiting Chatham's dockyard, I made my way up to the top of the hills behind it, where – in common with Plymouth and Portsmouth – a colossal memorial stands, commemorating the men of the Royal Navy who died in the two World Wars.

The spot where Chatham's memorial was erected is of special interest. Known as the Great Lines, it is an area of fortifications started in the 18th century to protect the dockyard below. In a tangle of undergrowth, one can still follow paths that lead to old fortifications zigzagging about the hilltop, moats frequented by wildfowl now, and ruined forts which volunteers have been excavating in the hope that they may be opened to the public in due course.

Right up on the top of the hill are wide fields where horses graze and the wind blows hard. The memorial rears up high, a huge needle surmounted by a bluish copper globe that is supported on ships' prows. At its foot is a garden of lawn and roses enclosed by a wall made from white Portland stone. The names of every single man who died while serving in the Navy or Marines during the two wars are inscribed here in bronze. Four more-than-lifesize stone seamen keep vigil, booted and in duffle coats, one holding binoculars. 'All these were honoured in their generations and were the glory of their times', says the inscription above the blue iron gates. The names of heroic occasions are written there, too: Jutland and Dardanelles, Dunkirk and the North Russian Convoys. Down below all is tranquil – the shopping centre of Chatham, boats sailing in the Medway, ancient Rochester slumbering. And past the memorial to men who have no grave but the sea saunter others, peacefully treading the Saxon Shore Footpath which goes close by.

Other places of naval interest

DEVON (south)

Plymouth* Devonport Dockyard (400 acres). Navy Days, usually around August Bank Holiday. Drake Fair, June. Field gun displays etc, June. Harbour cruises. HMS 'Raleigh' (training establishment): open days in July. Memorial — see text. 0752 53777 ext 220

Dartmouth* Britannia Royal Naval College has open day in June. Cadets participate in local maritime events.

DORSET

Portland Training base. There is a ship open to the public free at weekends during the summer, guided tours and the base has open days during July. Harbour cruises are available. Navy Days take place in July. 0305 820311 ext 2379

HAMPSHIRE

Portsmouth* Dockyard (300 acres). Navy Days, usually around August Bank Holiday. HMS 'Victory' is in the dockyard and open to the public. Harbour cruises. Portsmouth is the home base of the royal yacht 'Britannia'. In June/July there are dramatic gun-crew displays (as at the Royal Tournament), a searchlight tattoo and the founder's day parade of 2,000 cadets with 30 bands. The massed bands of the Royal Marines 'beat the retreat' by floodlight. Memorial — see text. 0705 22351 ext 23737

Southsea Memorial on seafront.

KENT

St Margaret's Bay near **Dover*** Memorial to the Dover Patrol which defended the Channel in World War One.

Chatham Dockyard — see text. Navy Days, usually around the late May Bank Holiday. Guided tours of the old part on weekdays. Memorial — see text. 0634 44422 ext 3480

LONDON

Greenwich Royal Naval College. Historic building, especially the great hall, open to the public. 01–858 2154.

Royal Marines: memorial under Admiralty Arch and chapel in St Lawrence Jewry, EC1.

Naval museums

HAMPSHIRE

Gosport Royal Naval Armaments Museum, Priddy's Hard. Permit needed. Submarine Museum, with submarine HMS 'Alliance'. 0705 22351

Portsmouth* Royal Naval Museum, Naval Base. The Museum has travelling exhibitions which are often shown at resorts during the summer. 0705 22351

Eastney Royal Marines' Museum: exception-ally good for a small museum. 0705 22351

KENT

Walmer The home of the Royal Marines is here and there is a history room. 030 95 62121

SUFFOLK

Lowestoft* Memorial to the wartime coastal patrol service, and their museum is in the depot used by the men of the minesweepers. 0502 86250

Churches

Each of the dockyards has its own church open to the public, with naval memorials. St Thomas's Church, **Portsmouth*** has a 'Navy aisle' with memorials to naval heroes. The Royal Marines have corps churches at **Plymouth*** (Stonehouse), **Eastney** (Hampshire) and **Deal*** (Kent).

Civilians, both men and women, who get interested in the activities of the Royal Navy, can participate, on a spare-time basis, by joining one of the following:

Royal Naval Reserve — operations and communications work: 0705 822351 ext 23985

Royal Marines Reserve — skiiing, parachuting, cliff-climbing, diving both in Britain and overseas: 01–237 4331

Naval Auxiliary Service — training is given to volunteers either on ships (seamen, engineers) or on shore (operations, communications) all round the coast: 0705 822351 ext 872304

Youngsters can join:

Sea Cadets, Marine Cadets or Girls' Nautical Training Corps: 01–540 8222

Sea Scouts: 01–584 7030

British and foreign naval ships visit ports all round the coast from time to time, and are often open to visitors. Local newspapers usually contain announcements about forthcoming arrivals and Tourist Information Centres should also know. Most ships visiting **London** moor alongside HMS 'Belfast' opposite the Tower of London. The famous Royal Marines' band is usually to be seen and heard during summer at resorts and ports.

Trafalgar Day on 21st October is the occasion for ceremonial marches and other events in naval ports — particularly at **Portsmouth*** where HMS 'Victory' is dressed overall for the day. The Navy also takes part in the November Remembrance Day Services. The striking of midnight on New Year's Eve is traditionally celebrated in naval ports by the sounding of all the ships' hooters and searchlights playing across the sky. October is the time to enquire about tickets for the spectacular 'Beating the Retreat' in London by the Royal Marines. 01–218 2861

Sandcastles come in all shapes and sizes. Competitions are run at many resorts each summer.

Some fishermen sell their catch straight from the boat.

30 Commercial ports at work

There's a magnetism about ports, however big or small; and even the most workaday ones attract sightseers. Lean over the old swing-bridge at Barrow (which is dominated by Vickers' shipbuilding yards) and you may perhaps spot a nuclear submarine in a floating-dock, the last of the Manx nobbies (a type of fishing-boat), prawners, a Baltic trader, some pilot-boats now converted into yachts and, further along, the bones of an old schooner slowly rotting away. At Hull, although the main docks are behind high walls, from the vantage-point of the great new surge-barrier, you can see into the old harbour where barges wait with their loads of sand, gravel or bricks to go up the Trent or Ouse and thence inland by the canals; opposite may be lightships and buoys coming in for overhaul. Goole is used mostly by smallish coasters, but you might spot a huge car-transporter bringing in a load of cars from Germany. Outside Tilbury (the public are never allowed inside), the Soviet cruise-liner 'Alexander Pushkin', named after the famous Russian poet, is a frequent visitor, which is why some of British Rail's notices nearby are in Russian – and I have come across the Russian crew eagerly buying cheap towels, clothes and even wigs from a mobile shop that comes to Tilbury whenever the 'Pushkin' is due in. It is from Southampton that our own big P & O cruise liners go out; while from Weymouth and many other south and east ports, the cross-channel ferries and hovercraft operate: many taking day-trippers to and from France. The variety is endless; no two ports present the same scene.

John Masefield knew the fascination of even the most ordinary of ships:

> Dirty British coaster with a salt-caked smoke stack
> Butting through the Channel in the mad March days,
> With a cargo of Tyne coal,
> Road-rail, pig-lead,
> Firewood, iron-ware and cheap tin trays.

The bigger the port, the more difficult it is to get in as a mere spectator. You will usually find it is the small ones that are most interesting because you may be able to wander without any restriction along the quays and jetties, to watch the ships loading or unloading.

I visited Whitehaven (Cumbria) which, until overtaken by Liverpool and other ports, was the third biggest port in England. Now it is of minor importance.

Whitehaven's story really begins in Norman times when the monks from a great priory at St Bees used the uninhabited haven for landing fish or shipping goods. After Henry VIII closed the priory, its lands eventually came into the possession of the Lowther family who set about mining the rich seams of coal; and it was then that Whitehaven was built up as a port, for the only way to transport the coal at that date was by sea.

From nothing Whitehaven suddenly became a town: miners, shipbuilders and seamen were wanted in large numbers; they needed houses, shops, inns and churches. Where once there had been only six fishermen's cottages there grew up in the 17th century a population of 2,000 – not haphazardly, but in one of the very earliest examples of town-planning. It is said that Sir John Lowther was inspired by Wren's plans (which were never executed) for the rebuilding of London after the Great Fire. He laid out the streets in a grid pattern, and on a spacious scale (though later the Victorians crammed in more dwellings and the original spaciousness has been lost). The port flourished, exporting coal to Ireland and importing tobacco, sugar and rum from the New World. Coal still goes out from the one surviving mine (out of 70) at Whitehaven;

some others have been preserved and you can visit the old pit-head structures. Up till 1842, women were used like beasts to drag the loads of coal down in the mines.

In the age of iron and steam, the face of Whitehaven again changed dramatically. As well as coal, iron is plentiful in Cumbria and this gave Whitehaven all that was needed for building steamships — until the coal began to run out, other shipyards began to build ships too huge for the tidal harbours at Whitehaven, and railways started to take some of the trade once carried by ships. By the 1930s, the town was at its lowest ebb, with many of its men out of work and its fine buildings decaying.

Fortunately, modern times have seen a reversal of this trend, and new industries have brought fresh activity to the port. For instance, large cargo ships with phosphates from Africa are regular callers: the chemicals are needed for an Albright & Wilson detergent factory not far away. One of the world's last steam-powered dredgers 'Clearway', can be seen puffing away at its never-ending task of keeping channels open for the bigger vessels. The elegant Georgian and Victorian houses have been restored. Whitehaven has a great many listed Georgian buildings in the centre and, architecturally, is one of England's outstanding towns. Leaflets with town trails and a harbour trail are obtainable at the Tourist Information Centre (0946 5678; ask also for their information sheets on the harbour and south beach).

I walked down to the harbour, its quays and jetties busy with the needs of modern industry (the port still handles half a million tonnes of goods a year) yet retaining much 18th-century charm. Through an overhead elevator the yellow phosphate was being conveyed from a ship to great silos nearby — the ground was yellow, and a gusty breeze sometimes whirled a cloud of yellow dust about. Along a railway line set in the cobbled Strand trucks were rumbling in — with a

A great port in its early days: Hull (Humberside). By the triple-towered docks offices, now a maritime museum, was a huge monument to Wilberforce who led the campaign against the slave trade.

hoot, squeak and rattle — hauling coal from the single pit that is still working; up on a distant brow of the green hills surrounding Whitehaven, the black stockpile of coal could just be seen.

Occasionally, a submarine or minesweeper calls on an official visit, and in summer the pleasure-boats crowd into the outer harbour. But it was the cargo boats that I found most interesting. I stood watching 'Ballyrush', a collier from Ireland with an iron hull as black as the coal spilling around her hatches. The enormous ship, low in the water, occupied the whole of one quayside yet she was manoeuvring as delicately as a swan. 'Ay, ay — OK', called the voice from the bridge, and a hawser was slipped from a bollard to splash into the dark water. 'Ballyrush' slowly swung round, missing 'Odin' of Barrow by what seemed like centimetres.

I wandered on, to the Old Quay where the bright red bollards are not bollards at all but cannon from ships involved in the John Paul Jones raid (Chapter 11), and waited to watch another collier, 'Topaz' of Glasgow, make her way out of the dock and to the sea. On the green hills above, the remains of the disused mine buildings looked like castle ruins. The old lamp room, where miners used to collect their lamps before being lowered into the pits, still stands and is now a café lit by pit-lamps, with an interpretation centre. The 'candlestick' chimney nearby, a superb industrial monument, once supplied ventilation to the pit beneath it.

The red, white and blue flag of the Danish Consulate fluttered below: the Consulate, little more than a travel office, dates from the days when timber was imported from the Baltic for pit-props and for ship-building. A number of Whitehaven folk are of Danish origin.

Meantime, 'Topaz' was finding it a tight squeeze to get through the narrow harbour entrance. Slow and stately, she eased her way out, men on the quayside hauling one way then another on her orange hawser, which was then pulled aboard by a clacking winch. A shout from the deck echoed off the stone walls, there were a few throaty puffs of smoke from the squat black funnel, the radar scanner began its steady revolutions and then the rhythmic pulsing of the engine began.

'Topaz' passed close by me, her deck gear tightly protected by green tarpaulins, overalled seamen lowering her loading-derricks to deck-level as she went by, to the sound of her own metallic throb and the swish of water eddying behind her. She still had to be gently manoeuvred this way and that, her first mate up on the bridge directing operations through a loud-hailer: the complexity of harbour entrances at Whitehaven calls for skilled navigation. And at last she was out and away on her voyage home to Scotland, with her 'red duster' (the ensign of the merchant navy) flapping vigorously at her stern.

It is in the outer harbour (the oldest part) that the fishing fleet congregates. It was nearly high tide, so there was no activity on the little boats — waiting to go out on the ebb. The registration letters painted on their hulls showed that only a few were Whitehaven (WA) boats, the rest coming from Barrow (B), Workington (WO), Ballantrae in Ireland (BA) or Castletown in the Isle of Man (CT). There is much less local fish to be caught now (some plaice in the summer and herring from around the Isle of Man, and cod or whiting in winter). West of the harbour, scampi are caught during the summer by digging down into the mud with specially weighted nets.

You can now see just how the old harbour looked early in the century. When I was there a group of youngsters were putting the last touches to a 14-m mural showing how it used to be. They collectively researched the subject, sorting through faded old photographs in the local museum's collection — and have executed the mural in similar sepia colours that blend happily with the surrounding stone walls and cobbles. Long-vanished wine vaults and provision shops have been painted, together with some of the seamen and housewives who appeared in the original photographs. Old inhabitants have recognised once familiar buildings and people as they gradually emerged in the painting. The group told me that, when their painting work is over, they are going to tape-record the old people's recollections and incorporate them in an explanatory pamphlet about the mural.

The further you walk, the further back in time you go — the Old Pier dates from 1633 and has on it the remains of the earliest watch-tower and the fort which was raided by John Paul Jones. Where a railway used to come down from the mines above, carrying coal to the port, is a paved garden with the old railway arches carefully preserved and a 4-m winding wheel. One of the jetties seen from here used to be called the Sugar Tongue, because that was where sugar from Barbados used to be landed, but now it has ice-plants on it, to freeze the fishing catch. You can walk even further along the beach to Salton Pit, the first English coal mine to extend beneath the sea, where you can see the engine house — before steam-power, horses worked the winding-gear which hauled coal (and men) to the surface. And if you want comfort in which to watch the ships come and go, you can sit inside a glassed-in verandah up on the hillside — with panoramic views higher up, of the coastline and of spectacular sunsets.

That would be a good spot in which to read some of the excellent little publications sold in the Tourist Information Centre — particularly, Nancy Eaglesham's brief history of Whitehaven's tobacco trade, back in the time of Sir John Lowther. You can picture the sailing-ships coming in with their valuable cargo. Whitehaven's ships, built sturdily to carry coal, were well suited to transatlantic voyaging. Out they would go to the colonists, carrying such varied necessities as clothing, harness for the horses, cooking-pots, nails, grindstones, gunpowder — even lute-strings, tombstones and powder for the men's wigs — collected together over a period of months. The tobacco shipped back to Whitehaven was then distributed as far afield as France — until wars with France made trade difficult. It was tobacco that gave Whitehaven its original prosperity, though none comes in through it now.

Some great ports had their origin centuries ago — even back in Roman times — but many of the biggest, such as Liverpool, were largely the product of the Industrial Revolution. And then, of course, there are the ports which were great in their time but are now no more. A common cause is the changed outline of the English coast.

At Dunwich (Suffolk) you can see the remains of a port that is still crumbling away as each winter the sea consumes a bit more of the vulnerable coastline. In other places, nature has played a very different trick and what were once ports are now far inland because, year by year, the sea has piled vast quantities of silt up on the shore until a kilometre or more of new coast has been built up. The story of the rise and fall of the famous Cinque Ports is a classic example. These five (later seven) ports along the south coast were powerful and wealthy in the Middle Ages. In return for providing the king with ships in times of war, they were granted valuable trading privileges. Only Dover is still a port now. What happened to the others?

Sandwich (Kent) is now inland. Then comes Dover, still bustling with activity. Hythe's beach is now some distance from the town. New Romney's change of fortune was perhaps the most dramatic of all: there had been a Romney in Saxon times, but its harbour became silted up and a new port was built on the estuary of the River Rother. One night in 1287, a great storm shifted the course of the river completely and New Romney was left high and dry. The hill on which Rye stands was once almost an island, with sea round three sides: now cattle graze where the tides used to come and go. The 1287 storm buried the original Winchelsea under sand and its remains are far out beneath the waves. The 13th-century town you now see flourished for a while as a port (wines from Bordeaux were shipped in, which is why so many of the houses have huge cellars) but winter after winter, heavy seas piled up silt on the shore so that the sea departed further and further away and Winchelsea is now far inland. The last of the Cinque Ports is Hastings (East Sussex), still by the sea but its harbour silted up long ago and so its fishing-boats have to be drawn up on the pebbly beach: it is difficult to believe that this cheerful holiday resort — rebuilt three times after inundations by the sea — was, up to a century ago, the most important of the Cinque Ports.

All of the Cinque ports are worth visiting for their historic buildings, lanes and local museums but only Dover, Hythe and Hastings are by the sea. There is now a Cinque Ports Trail with an explanatory colour leaflet (free from the South-East England Tourist Board, see list on page 9). The museums at Hastings and Winchelsea have Cinque Ports displays.

A number of other one-time ports well deserve a visit even though they now lie inland or are on an estuary that is not deep enough for the vessels of today. Many still have their old quays and warehouses, and usually small sailing-boats frequent their harbours or creeks. Examples are Christchurch (Dorset), Wareham (Dorset), Faversham (Kent), Morwellham (Devon), Topsham (Devon), Exeter (Devon) and Maldon (Essex).

There are other river ports still able to receive seagoing vessels even though they lie quite a long way inland: for example, Ipswich (Suffolk), Bridport (Dorset), Rochester (Kent), Colchester (Essex), and Boston (Lincolnshire). The cities of Newcastle (Tyne and Wear) and Bristol (Avon) have their great ports some distance downstream, but their own museums and older buildings have considerable maritime interest and are well worth visiting.

No two ports are alike. The topography of the coast, and the natural resources of the land behind, originally determined where a port grew up. The very first ports tended simply to be natural harbours — estuaries or sheltered coves where ships could lie safe from the worst that storms or currents could do. They were usually near an area that had something to trade which needed to be carried by ship (before road and then rail transport offered any serious competition): metals, coal, wool and similar goods. Some are quite a long way upriver and not on the coast at all. Only in the 17th century did the idea of building artificial basins, with gates, take off; and most docks are in fact later than this. Sometimes harbour walls were built out into the sea; sometimes a basin was dug out of the land beside an estuary.

A gate is essential wherever there is a big drop in water when the tide goes out — and that applies to almost every part of the English coast (Southampton is a major exception). The ships then remain afloat behind the closed gate, and cannot move out until the tide is fully in again.

Some docks have two sets of gates with a lock in between (as on canals) so that a ship may move in or out even when the water-level in the dock is higher than that of the sea outside. Locks built long ago are sometimes too small for modern ships; at the modern port of Tilbury, which gets some of the world's biggest container-ships, the lock is 330 m long. These days, lock gates (which, though made of hollow steel, may weigh 300 tonnes or so) are operated electrically or hydraulically — some slide back into the walls or fold down onto the floor of the lock.

A big modern dock may have huge gantry cranes to lift the 40-tonne containers that are now commonplace. A really big ship could have 2,000 of these to be unloaded, at the rate of one every three minutes. The cranes are moved about on railway tracks by the dockside, which is likely to be lined with huge transit sheds, grain silos, timber yards or whatever is needed for the particular cargoes handled at that port. Ferry ports, mostly on the east or south coasts, are designed to accommodate the 'roll-on-roll-off' vessels known as ro-ro's, through the stern of which cars and lorries are driven into the hold.

Todays' cargoes are immensely varied: tractors being exported from Grimsby (Humberside) to Scandinavia at the 'ro-ro' terminal.

Oil tankers usually need jetties that reach out into very deep water because some of the tankers are colossal (the largest is nearly 500,000 tonnes and 400 m long). A few even moor out at sea and discharge the oil via a long pipeline to the shore. Oil refineries are now a major feature on some coasts. An eyesore, perhaps, but impressive too and in one case (at Grain, north Kent) you can drive right through the middle of the refinery and then find a good viewing-point to look out for passing tankers. But not for much longer: the refinery is threatened with closure.

Then there are the dry docks, used for ship repairs. Each basin is designed to hold just one ship. Once it is in, the gate is closed and the water pumped out, so that the ship's hull can be worked on. Draining is a tricky business, done very slowly, for specially shaped blocks have to be manoeuvred into position to support the ship as the water vanishes.

As to the ships that use these docks today, the most numerous (after the tankers which carry oil, chemicals and so on), are the 'tramps' which go from port to port, loading a variety of goods on and off. Cargo ships (some carrying bulk loads of a single raw material, such as timber) and cruise liners account for the rest. Multi-purpose ships are steadily being superseded by those de-signed for one particular cargo (such as oil, ore and vehicles). The British merchant fleet is the third largest in the world (only the Japanese and Greek fleets are bigger), with modern vessels, and with more container-ships than any other nation. Though the great ports that cater for these are not usually open to sightseers, there is often a vantage point somewhere nearby where (armed perhaps with binoculars, a picnic and a ship-identification book) you can have an enjoyable day out watching the comings-and-goings.

There is so much of interest in the animation of a port that is still thriving today — so much to see: the great cranes for heavy loads like coal or steel, grain being sucked up into silos or oil being piped ashore, hoppers of sea gravel (used for making concrete), wharf railways, a dredger discharging its mud, buoys or a lightship being brought in for repair, ship-building and repair yards (or ship-breaking). Anything may be arriving, from any part of the world — frozen meat from Australia, giraffes from Africa for a zoo. At some distance from the

At King's Lynn (Norfolk) ships from northern Europe can be seen coming and going.

quay, a great ship will be met by the launch bringing a pilot to navigate her in. She may need a tug or two to help her berth. There will be customs and health officers to check her before the stevedores (dockers) can swing into action — at top speed, for time is money and the sooner the ship can be on her way again the better her owners will be pleased. The burly dockers usually come from families which have done much the same work for generations, though their fathers and grandfathers had few of today's mechanical aids to muscle. The marine section of the Police go about in fast launches (or flat-bottomed dories suited to the shallow waters of some harbours), possibly looking for anything from illegal immigrants to oyster poachers or drowned corpses. Waterguards, uniformed customs officers with the right to board and 'rummage' in any vessel, often arrive in small pinnaces to board ships flying the yellow flag that means they are waiting for customs clearance. In some places, there are gas or oil survey ships, and supply ships serving the oil rigs out at sea. Most ports have fire-fighting tugs. In some ports, such as Rochester, ships cannot berth but have to moor where there is deep water, their cargoes being taken ashore by lighters. Always there is something to be seen — the latest development is the return of sails, but sails electronically released and retracted whenever there is enough wind to save the consumption of expensive fuel. Barges, too, are making a comeback: for instance, a 27-m motor barge is now operating upstream from Tilbury, transporting the equivalent of three juggernaut lorries.

Some coastal ports accessible to the public

CUMBRIA
Maryport* See text.
Whitehaven* See text.
Barrow-in-Furness*Nuclear waste, ro-ro*, ship repairs etc. Unrestricted access to large areas. Shipbuilding yards not open.

LANCASHIRE
Heysham Ferries to Belfast etc.
Glasson Dock See Chapter 31.
Fleetwood* Grain, scrap-metal, ro-ro. For pass, phone 039 17 2323.

MERSEYSIDE
Liverpool* Ferries, container-ships etc. Waterbus tours inside grain and container-ship bases. 051 933 0476
Birkenhead* Large cargo ships etc.

AVON
Avonmouth General cargo, ship repairs etc. No access but good view of the most modern dock (Royal Portbury) from March Lane at **Easton in Gordano**.

SOMERSET
Bridgewater Tankers, ro-ro.
Watchet Imports timber, exports paper. Unrestricted access.

DEVON (north)
Appledore Coasting vessels, ship repair yards. Similar small harbours at, for example, **Barnstaple** and **Ilfracombe***.
Bideford* General cargo. Unrestricted

access.

CORNWALL
Bude* Small harbour.
Newquay* Exports clay and minerals.
Newlyn Granite and fish exports. Public access.
Penzance* Ferry to **Scilly Isles**. Coal etc. Accessible.
Falmouth* General cargo. Ship repairs. Oil exploration base. Accessible to public.
Truro Coastal vessels.
Charlestown near **St Austell** Historic port. Exports china clay.
Par and **Fowey*** Cargo ships, china clay. Guided tours. 072681 2281

DEVON (south)
Plymouth* General cargo. Continental ferries. Ro-ro, tankers etc.
Dartmouth* General cargo.
Teignmouth* Ro-ro etc. Exports clay.
Exmouth* Coastal freighters etc.

DORSET
Bridport* (West Bay) Timber, gravel exports, fertiliser imports.
Weymouth* Continental ferries, cargo ships, ro-ro etc. Most parts accessible.
Poole* Bulk cargo, containers, ro-ro. Grain imports. Largely accessible.

---

* Ro-ro means roll-on-roll-off ships which carry laden lorries.

HAMPSHIRE
Fawley Oil. Harbour cruises and guided City Bus tours around docks in summer.
Southampton* Liners, hydrofoils, continental ferries. Oil, general cargo. Dry docks etc.
Hythe pier is a good viewing point. **Itchen Bridge** provides panoramic views.
Portsmouth* Ro-ro. General cargo. Most parts accessible.

ISLE OF WIGHT
Newport Ferries. General cargo. Public access.
Yarmouth* Ferries etc.

WEST SUSSEX
Littlehampton* Cargo ships.
Shoreham-by-Sea Cargo ships, ro-ro. Good views from roads.

EAST SUSSEX
Newhaven* Cargo ships, continental ferries, boat building. Observation platform at ferry terminal.

KENT
Folkestone* Continental ferries.
Dover* Hoverport, continental ferries, cargo ships. No public access but good views from seafront and castle.
Sandwich Hoverport, coastal vessels.
Ramsgate* Cars imported. Hoverport. Continental ferries.
Rochester* Wood pulp for Kent papermills. Boat-trips from Ship Pier give a good view of the waterfront. The rambling Medway estuary has four landing-piers from which to watch the ships as well as quays, steps and jetties from **Hoo** and **Upnor**, through **Rochester*** and **Chatham** and westwards to **Gillingham, Faversham*** and the channel of **Swale** (with **Sheerness*** dock at one end and little **Harty** at the other).

ESSEX
Colchester General cargo. A public road goes through the port.
Brightlingsea Coasters etc.
Mistley Grain etc.

SUFFOLK
Ipswich* General cargo, ro-ro, container-ships. Guided tours. 0473 56011
Felixstowe* Container-ships, continental ferries, ro-ro etc.
Lowestoft* Grain, timber etc.

NORFOLK
Great Yarmouth* Cargo ships, ships servicing the oil-rigs etc. Public viewing area adjoins docks. For a guide, phone 0493 551514.
Wells-next-the-Sea Coastal ships.
King's Lynn* Grain, coastal ships, ro-ro etc.

LINCOLNSHIRE
Boston* Timber, steel etc. Public access.

HUMBERSIDE
Grimsby* General cargo, ro-ro etc. For pass, phone 0472 59181.
Goole* Coal, general cargo, ro-ro etc. For pass, phone 0405 2691.
Hull* Grain, timber, container-ships and ro-ro; continental ferries. For pass, phone 0482 27171.

NORTH YORKSHIRE
Selby-on-the-Ouse Small shipyard, general cargo.
Scarborough* Timber, potatoes, barley, fish. Parts are accessible and there is an open day during August for Fishermen's Wives Fair. 0723 72351

CLEVELAND
Hartlepool* Base for North Sea gas and oil. Car imports etc. Guided tours. 0642 241121

DURHAM
Seaham Coal exports etc. View from north side of South Dock.

TYNE AND WEAR
Sunderland Shipbuilding etc. No access but good view from the road to **Washington.**

NORTHUMBERLAND
Blythe Coal, timber etc. Shipbreaking. Good views from Duncow Quay or South Foreshore.

Further reading
An excellent little book, full of drawings to explain what goes on in any typical small port is 'The Port of Poole at Work', obtainable from Poole Museum (see Chapter 5). For access to ports not usually open to the public contact the World Ship Society (c/o S. J. F. Miller, 35 Wickham Way, Haywards Heath, West Sussex), or the Yorkshire Ship Enthusiasts, 0532 648514. Most ports have free booklets describing what they do and some not ordinarily open to the public will accept groups and school parties.

31 Fishermen today

The techniques of fishing are as varied as the fish themselves. Some deep-water trawlers, equipped to process and freeze the fish on board, are floating factories that go out from great ports to very distant waters indeed, often trawling far afield in the Arctic.

At the other extreme are fishermen who never go to sea at all, like the fish farmers. And along the Humber estuary, for example, you may see someone on the muddy foreshore catching eels; cockling and shrimping in Morecambe Bay or the Dee estuary is done with tractors; and, if you go on a summer's evening to the old railway jetty at Bowness on the Solway estuary, you can watch salmon being caught in haaf nets ('haaf' is from a Norse word meaning sea). Here the fishermen (who may in fact follow other occupations most of the time, such as bus-driver or parson) wade out waist-deep to where there are deep pools in the narrow river-channel which, at low tide, is all that divides England from Scotland. Their skill lies in knowing what route the salmon will follow, so you will not be surprised to find them a very secretive lot, suspicious of too many questions. After that, each simply holds up his square net on its posts — like a football goal — and awaits results. It's a risky game, for there are quicksands out there, and every so often a fisherman loses his life. It would be safer to use fixed nets as in Scotland, but in England these are illegal. So the fishermen have to be on their guard, constantly shifting their weight from one foot to the other lest they get sucked down. The biggest hazard is tripping over, for once those thigh-boots fill with water the wearer is virtually doomed. Similar methods are used elsewhere — at Berwick-upon-Tweed, for instance.

Such activities as these, on foreshores and estuaries, are fairly easy to watch from the shore. Where the fishing-boats are concerned, their goings and comings

The traditional haaf nets are used by wading fishermen for catching salmon.

are more mysterious to the landsman. Yet, despite the arrival of modern techniques, many of their methods are centuries old. On Weymouth quay, I paused to watch the arrival of one boat laden with crabs and lobsters, a scene that has changed very little over the generations. There was a stack of traditional lobster-pots, a litter of nets and ropes lying in a tangle by an old bollard. The tall young fishermen, in dark blue smocks and black caps with peaks, heaved up their catch of blue-black lobsters and barnacle-encrusted crabs. Children gathered, half fascinated and half scared by the mass of claws waving in protest. There are plenty of fishing families today with the same surnames as fishermen listed in the Domesday Book, going out to the same fishing grounds. Most fishermen still make their own lobster-pots, and each man knows his own.

But not everything goes on as before. Natural causes, or overfishing, has sometimes brought some species almost to an end. The herring family (which includes pilchards and sprats) was once so abundant that fish merchants grew rich on it, and some magnificently endowed coastal churches were called 'herring churches' as a result. No more. The herring cellars of St Ives are now cafés, and no huer keeps a lookout to cry aloud the arrival of the shoals of fish. The great rollicking sprat feasts of Poole are over: it is said that the birthrate tended to peak some nine months after each of these annual saturnalia.

In what other ways has fishing changed? I sat eating crab in a fishermen's inn at Poole (Dorset), the 'King Charles', chatting to Sandy Wells. Now in his seventies, he has been a fisherman ever since he left school and still goes out regularly in winter, often at five in the morning, to find the skate and sole which are abundant some 30 km out. (In summer, he removes the winch and nets to convert his boat for taking visitors on harbour trips.) He said:

'When I was a lad, it was all sail — you had a seven h.p. engine if you were lucky. Now 16 or 18 h.p. is commonplace, and one boat covers more ground in a day than a whole fleet did before. Two boats have a net spread out between them, and may catch a tonne of fish . . . or nothing. We go whenever the weather is right, and that sometimes means you never see daylight.

'There's no shortage of young men wanting to come in. I used to go out alone, but I've more sense now, and I take a lad along to train him fresh from school — then he'll want to be off fishing from his own boat. When I first went out, there was nothing to help you. You had your cold tea in a bottle, bread-and-jam wrapped up in paper. Now every boat's got a cooker and radar to find your way home for you. If it wasn't for the hours, you'd call it an armchair job — yes, really, they've all got chairs in their boats!

'On my way back, I call up the dealer on my radio and tell him how many boxes to send down to the quay. The lorry will be waiting when I get in. If there are any sprats, they'll go for fishmeal — people can't be bothered with the cooking of them now, and the smell (they're very fishy fish). A lot of the skate goes to Belgium.

'I was ten when I first went fishing. Everyone in the family was in fishing, and in those days you were let off school to go winkle-picking when the tide was right.'

Sandy doesn't just catch fish, he also eats it with gusto, discussing cooking methods and recipes meantime. 'I never tire of it — I could eat it every day. Bass is the prime fish now (it can cost as much as salmon), and mullet. A pal of mine barbecued some mullet last week and it was the best I ever tasted. You need to put a few bayleaves with it.'

He disapproves of the tactics used by some fishermen in their powerful boats 'tearing the boulders out of place, the fish haven't a chance'.

Fishing is still flourishing in Dorset, but in many other places it is a different story. Harbours in the north which were once crowded with fishing-boats are almost empty, and great ports like Fleetwood and Hull are no longer synonymous with herrings or cod.

When I went to Craster (Northumberland), for the best kipper tea I've ever had, I was told by Alan Robson that the 3,000 herrings hanging in his smoke-house had not been fished locally as in years past (for there had been a government ban on catching herring) but brought by lorry from Loch Fyne in Scotland. Plump and fatty, each one a mature four- or five-year-old fish, they hung

Herrings hang for 14 hours in oak smoke before they are fully kippered, (Craster, Northumberland).

140

gracefully in pearly, gleaming rows high up in the old smokehouse, tier upon tier of them overhead. The fish are first split by machine and then soaked in warm brine for 20 minutes before being suspended there. On the floor were nine heaps of smouldering sawdust – whitewood topped with oak, for that distinctive flavour. No 'painted ladies' here – it is the oak smoke, not dye, which will turn the pale fish to a rich nutty brown. Every two-and-a-half hours (even through the night) Alan or his brother tend the sawdust fires until, after 14 hours, the herrings are well and truly kippered. Ever since 1856, herrings have been treated in exactly the same way and in this same tall smoke-house, its black interior now richly encrusted and gleaming with the tarry deposits from the smoke. In winter, the smokehouse is used for salmon, because herring then are 'spent' (that is, thin, after spawning).

Outside, a wisp of smoke curled up from the hole in the top of the smoke-house, joining a dense sea mist that was creeping in. A week later, the big box of kippers I had ordered arrived at my home by post, rich and succulent, as much of a delicacy as smoked salmon. (Try some! Just phone the Robsons, 066576 223, in summer or autumn.)

Like all fish, kippers keep well in a freezer. (Mine is now full of the harvest of the sea and of my travels in the course of writing this book: plaice from the Scillies, fluke from Morecambe Bay, Parkgate shrimps from the Dee estuary, lobsters and mullet from Dorset, and salmon from the Lune estuary.)

I found a treasure-house of salmon on the opposite (Lancashire) coast, by Glasson Dock at the mouth of the River Lune. John Price of Glasson Dock could hardly be more different from Alan Robson. He has no fishing family background but was an art teacher. He simply had a passion for the ancient craft of fish-smoking, and eventually gave up his teaching career for it. Four years ago, he bought a derelict, earth-floored building on the quay: now it is immaculate, with red-tiled floor, stainless steel worktops, white-tiled walls and the pleasant, fresh smell of fish. He is now one of the 12 commissioners who are responsible for this small port – almost unique in that, under a Victorian Act of Parliament, it is the locals who run it, are responsible for buoys and for dredging, and even own the nearby lighthouse, collecting dues from ships when they dock.

John showed me his smoking cabinet, a modern cupboard of stainless steel, automatically regulated and with an electric fan to distribute the smoke from the smouldering oak sawdust across the racks of salmon (or eel). After a day in the smoke, sides of a salmon that had weighed up to two-and-a-half kg will have been reduced to less than a kg each.

In the adjoining preparation-room, cool and spotless, were dozens of salmon that had just been delivered from the Lune: scales pearly-silver shading to blue-black, eyes bright, and on the sides of the huge fish, a sure token of freshness – harmless sea-lice still clinging. I touched the great mouth of one salmon: there were vicious teeth inside and a jagged tongue (to grip slippery sand-eels, John explained). In the walk-in freezer more salmon were stacked, with imported squid and giant prawns from Africa, local soles, potted shrimps and game (including venison).

Glasson Dock is picturesque, with cargo-ships and small sailing craft, lock-gates and watch-tower, capstans and black-backed gulls. An attractive spot in which to go shopping for fish and game, its story is well told in a booklet available locally called 'Glasson Dock through the Ages'. (To order smoked fish by post, phone 0524 751493.)

In smaller ports and harbours it is easy to watch what is going on and to find fishermen who enjoy talking about their way of life. But the big deep-sea trawlers bring their catch into huge ports where they unload behind high walls, the public rarely allowed inside. (For some exceptions, see list at end of chapter.) I learned about what goes on in these by visiting local museums, particularly the Town Docks Museum at Hull (Humberside). Not only are the displays there exceptionally good but, I discovered, many of the keepers are former trawlermen — like the one who said to me:

'I loved the life, except for the separation from my family. Usually you had only two days at home before going off for three weeks — or much longer if you had to go hundreds of miles to Newfoundland. The work was hard, though. Most deep-sea fishing was in Arctic waters. Once you found where the fish were, you'd have to keep trawling day and night, with lights on all the time because there's only half an hour of daylight up there during winter. You might get no rest for 30 hours. And sometimes there would be mountainous waves — we didn't stop fishing unless they were more than 6 m high, though. We'd return laden with 300 tonnes if we were lucky, through the White Sea and the Norwegian fiords.'

Things are different on the factory ships. About 20 of them go out from Hull and as many from Grimsby, each with twice the crew of the old trawlers — about 40 men. The nets, winched in over the stern, empty the fish into 'ponds' below deck, where they are sorted and gutted immediately before going on to be frozen into 45 kg blocks in readiness for the long journey back. Waste is turned into fishmeal on board.

Another new feature in the scene is the Fishery Protection Squadron of the Navy: ships like small frigates or mine-sweepers policing British waters (a 19 km width of sea around the coastline) to keep foreign trawlers out.

In the near waters are found plaice, to be trawled from the bottom of the sea, and haddock which swim near the surface and are caught in a seine net — rather like a huge bag. Further out in the North Sea cod are fished. There was a time when fishermen detected the presence of fish by indications like the colour of the water: now echo-sounders do this part of the job for them.

The White Fish Authority (031 225 2515) has an interesting free booklet 'Fish from the Sea' explaining the different types of fish and nets, with a map of the principal British fishing grounds and ports, and also recipes. ('White' fish is a term that is used to cover virtually everything except the herring family and freshwater fish.)

Many local museums (eg Bridlington, Hull, and Hartlepool,) have excellent booklets, too: see Chapter 11.

Where to see fishermen at work

The principal fishing ports are mostly on the east-facing coasts. You may see trawlers coming and going, but it is often impossible to enter the port itself, and in any case much of the activity takes place early in the morning. These ports are:

Fleetwood* (Lancashire): trawlers have an open day in late August, 03917 71141, and the Nautical College in June, 03917 79123. **Newlyn** and **Falmouth*** (Cornwall). **Plymouth*** and **Brixham*** (south Devon): the fish markets at these ports are open to the public, and **Brixham*** has a spectacular trawler race every summer. At **Lowestoft*** (Suffolk) there are guided tours of the harbour and fish market and sometimes one may be shown over a

trawler, 0502 62111, ext 104. A smokehouse in Raglan Street can also be visited. **Grimsby*** (Humberside) has open days at the docks during August. 0472 54084. So do **Hull*** (Humberside) and **North Shields*** (Tyne and Wear).

Smaller fishing harbours nearly all the way round the coast are more accessible. Some specialise in local inshore fish, others have their own local type of boat which can be seen in harbours or on beaches (examples are the cobles of the north-east and the luggers of **Hastings***). Often fishermen are willing to take visitors to sea with them.

Although much fishing takes place in the summer, you would have to visit the coast in winter if you wanted to see, for example, the activity when the shoals of sprats arrive off the north-east coast. What goes on at any particular time or place can change dramatically from one season to the next. Herrings have diminished in places where they were once abundant and most herring fishing was for some years under a temporary ban until stocks built up again; on the other hand, previously unknown beds of scallops and of clams have been discovered in recent years. The biggest fishery is now mackerel, caught in the south-west from November to March and, as the big trawlers work close to the shore, this is one of the few opportunities for seeing trawling in action. The boats assemble in Mounts Bay (**Penzance***) with the accompanying factory-ships in Falmouth Bay. They may go as far east as **Lyme Regis*** in Dorset. At **Newlyn** (Cornwall) you can see the smaller boats landing their mackerel.

You can see shellfish being landed in virtually any fishing port. The large, finned fish like cod usually arrive at the big ports, where the public are rarely admitted. Many ports have stalls where the fishermen's families sell freshly caught fish.

The general pattern of what's to be seen around the English coast is as follows:

North-west: sole, haddock, hake, cod, saithe The major port is **Fleetwood*** (Lancashire) but it is not open to the public. Some fishing-boats can be seen at **Whitehaven*** (Cumbria) and elsewhere.

South (Avon to Kent): sole, plaice, mackerel, turbot, pilchard, skate Most fish are found around Devon and Cornwall (crab is plentiful). The shallow Channel has sole and plaice, in particular. Oysters come from the Solent. You can go 'bouncing' with rod-and-line for codling at the Varne. The best ports at which to see fish being landed are **Newlyn** (Cornwall), **Brixham*** and **Plymouth*** (south Devon), **Folkestone*** (Kent) and **Hastings*** (East Sussex).

East: sole, plaice, cod, haddock, whiting In summer, dog fish (also known as flake, huss or rigg) is a main catch off Norfolk and Lincolnshire. Winter herring fishing, suspended after over-fishing, is being resumed in 1982; and a special herring fishery continues in the Blackwater estuary (Essex). The biggest fishery is of sole and plaice, much of it landed at **Lowestoft*** (Suffolk). Shellfish is abundant: from shrimps in The Wash and crabs off north Norfolk, down to oysters off Essex. **Grimsby*** (Humberside) is the leading port. It has a few deep-sea trawlers and many wooden-hulled seiners which go out singly or in pairs to net cod and haddock in their seine nets, which are like huge bags.

North of the Humber are the cod, haddock and whiting fisheries. Some specialities are the dabs of **Scarborough*** (North Yorkshire) and **Bridlington*** (Humberside); sea-caught salmon and salmon-trout at **Whitby*** (North Yorkshire); winter sprats from **North Shields*** (Tyne and Wear) down to the Humber; mussels and other shellfish along the Northumberland coast.

You can watch fish being landed at **Whitby***, **Scarborough*** and **Bridlington***; and see the biggest ships of all, the freezer-trawlers, approaching **Hull*** (the fish dock itself is not open to the public but there is a footpath around it). Some fishing ports or harbours that are interesting to visit are listed below.

CUMBRIA
Silloth* Shrimpers etc. Trips.
Whitehaven* Fish can be bought.

LANCASHIRE
Morecambe* Shrimp stalls.
Overton Salmon fishing with haaf nets.
Lytham St Anne's* Shrimpers; shrimps on sale (fresh and potted).

MERSEYSIDE
Southport* Tractors used for shrimping.

SOMERSET
Bridgewater Bay Shrimps.
Stogursey and **Watchet** Ancient fishing method: nets serviced by 'mud horses'.

DEVON (north)
Appledore Small trawlers.
Clovelly A few small boats in the harbour.

CORNWALL
Boscastle Small harbour.
Port Isaac Lobster storage tanks.
Padstow Lively port. Shellfish storage tanks.
St Ives* Harbour. Net-mending on quay.
Newlyn A leading fishing port. Auctions. Canning shellfish.
Porthleven Harbour. Fish processing.
Mullion Cove Small cove.
Cadgwith Beached boats in cove.
Coverack Small shellfishing harbour.
Penryn Small dock.
St Mawes Small harbour.
Gorran Haven Small cove.
Mevagissey Harbour.
Fowey* Fishing includes scallop-dredging and oysters.
Looe* Small harbour. Shark-fishing.

DEVON (south)
Beesands Small boats on open beach.
Dartmouth* South Hams Smokers Ltd can be visited.
Kingswear Shellfish.

Paignton* Crab processors can be visited.
Teignmouth* Fishing includes mussels.
Beer Beached boats.
Seaton* and **Axmouth** Beached boats.

DORSET

Lyme Regis* Boats moor at the Cobb.
Weymouth* Crabs and crabbers' race.
Poole* Trawlers. Crabs, oysters.
Mudeford Trawlers. Crabs, salmon.

HAMPSHIRE

Lymington Oysters and crabs.
Portsmouth* All kinds of fish at Camber
Docks.

WEST SUSSEX

Selsey Crabs (storage tank).
Worthing* Beached boats.

EAST SUSSEX

Newhaven* Fishing-boats in harbour.
Hastings* Fish can be bought on beach
where boats lie.

KENT

Dungeness Beached fishing-boats selling to
the public.
Folkestone* Has fish market and auctions
open to the public.
Ramsgate* Fishing-boats in harbour, fish
can be bought.
Whitstable* Oysters (visitors can go out
with local fishermen).
Seasalter Cockles.

ESSEX

Leigh On Sea Cockles; special sheds on
quay. Cockles and shrimps can be bought
from the fishermen.
Maldon Small fishing-boats moor in estuary.
West Mersea Oysters for quayside eating at
Mussetts. 020638 2871
East Mersea Oysters: beds can be visited
and oysters eaten. 020638 4141
Colchester Enterprising fish merchant sells a
wide variety of fish and gives talks: Peter
Green. 0206 76731

SUFFOLK

Felixstowe* Fish stalls in old part of town.

Orford Butley Oysterage: smoked fish too.
03945 277
Aldeburgh Fish and shellfish sold from
boats; sprats in winter.
Dunwich Sole etc sold from beached boats.
Southwold Fish can be bought from the
boats. Old smokehouse for kippers.
0502 81929

NORFOLK

Great Yarmouth* Bloater depot and several
fish merchants. 0493 2747
Cromer* Crabs can be bought from
fishermen's cottages. Boats drawn into the
sea by tractors.
Sheringham* Fish shop-cafés, specialising
in dressed crab, potted crab etc.
Cley-next-the-Sea Smokehouse.
026374 282
Wells-next-the-Sea Whelks from the
whelkhouse.
Brancaster Staithe Fishing-boats at the
quays or buy from merchant (Gurney's).
King's Lynn* Shellfish and other fish, boats
old and new.

HUMBERSIDE

Bridlington* Fish stalls round busy harbour.

NORTH YORKSHIRE

Filey* Traditional cobles on open beach,
hauled to sea by tractors; fish stalls.
Scarborough* Stalls on quays, auctions etc.
Whitby* Stalls on quays, auctions etc.
Staithes Traditional cobles.

CLEVELAND

Redcar Cobles, fish stalls etc.

TYNE AND WEAR

North Shields* Distant-water trawlers;
seine-netters come in about 6 p.m.

NORTHUMBERLAND

Newbiggin Lobsters brought in by coble.
Amble Light trawlers and seine-netters in
harbour.
Beadnell Shellfish from cobles.
Berwick-upon-Tweed* Salmon; see text.
Seahouses* Shellfish etc.

32 Maritime inns

Fishing is thirsty work. And voyagers have always needed places of refreshment,
for sad farewells or to celebrate joyous homecomings. Like the inland coaching-
inns — but often with origins far older than these — waterfront inns have a
particular flavour of their own. Many have stories to tell of smugglers or of

maritime heroes who once drank in their bars. Others have collected so many nautical mementos that they are virtually small museums.

One weekend, I set off on a waterfront pub-crawl – down the Thames estuary and the Kent coast. Of many downriver inns on Thames-side, I chose first the 'Mayflower' at Rotherhithe. Even though it was a Friday evening, the old inn was quiet, with just a few regulars seated on the oak settles or leaning over the rail of the small wood jetty at the back – the jetty from which the Pilgrim Fathers stepped onto the deck of the 'Mayflower' for the first time. The brown water slapped at great mooring posts; on the inn roof, a gilded 'Mayflower' on the weathervane veered slightly in the breeze. There was a salty tang in the air, and a solitary shelduck winged its way across the river.

The scene has changed a lot since the Pilgrim Fathers left these waters – with what feelings of hope or anxiety, relief or distress, one can only imagine. In their day the banks were green and the water full of fish – a local place-name, Shad Thames, refers to the shoals of shad (a kind of herring) that used to be fished nearby.

Groups of iron barges were moored out in the water; and by the bank, secured by frayed red hawsers, lay 'Leo' (once a river tug) and 'Nellie' (a fishing-smack brought from Falmouth), both in the process of being renovated for pleasure by local enthusiasts. On the opposite bank are great wharves and, slightly upstream, the headquarters of the river police. Above the modern buildings downstream, one of Hawksmoor's elegant church towers (St Anne's, Limehouse) shone white in the evening sun. This inn (or the nearby 'Angel' with its Captain Cook associations) is a good spot from which to view the summer barge-driving race, when huge barges (decorated for the occasion) compete against one another – sped along simply by means of colossal oars, and muscle-power (see Chapter 14).

Perhaps the inside is not greatly changed since the days of the Pilgrims. Light filters into the timbered interior through small lattice windows. A few carvings salvaged from ships decorate the walls, on one of which is displayed the long parchment will of Beatrice Brewing, mother of one of the Pilgrims, dated 1686. When a replica of the 'Mayflower' was built some years ago, detailed drawings of tools, sails and so on were made, and these now hang in one of the bars. But the inn's real treasure is its model of HMS 'Victory' above the brick fireplace: not just any model, but the one made before she was built – for the shipwrights to work from (plans on paper were not used in those days).

On the opposite bank lie other similar inns – the 'Prospect of Whitby', the 'Town of Ramsgate' and the 'Grapes', all with their feet in the water. Further downriver are the waterfront inns of Greenwich, of which my favourite is the one now known as the 'Cutty Sark' (originally the 'Union'). Here you can have a whitebait supper (or other dishes) upstairs in a room with pine-plank walls and a big bay window; the large bar downstairs has a stone-flagged floor, brick fireplace, great tarry baulks of timber supporting the ceilings, a curving oak stair rising up through the middle and chairs made from barrels. This is snug in winter, but in summer most people take their drinks out and lean on the sea-wall to watch the boats go by. There is often more activity here than at Rotherhithe because the Victoria Deep-Water Terminal is within view and container-ships can be seen coming and going. Steel-rod may be unloaded, mountains of scrap-iron taken on board, or a cable-layer pass by.

The next inn I visited does not have a waterfront view, though the Medway estuary is just behind it and it is frequented by seamen whose cargo-ships are berthed at Rochester's quays. It is called the 'North Foreland' after the famous lighthouse but its history goes much further back: one of its most striking features is a carved Jacobean fireplace, painted black and gold, with colourful figures. Once it was the house of a retired commander of Chatham dockyard, who started to brew — and then sell — his own ale, with such success that from his activities the brewery firm of Style & Winch developed. This old pub is a mini-museum, every inch of its walls crammed with nautical mementos. There are four tiny bars, low-ceilinged, with wood settles. Even the smoky Lincrusta ceiling is used for a collection of ships' pennants. Wherever you look there are ships' models, lamps, rope-knots, oars, a porthole, lifebuoys (with their ships' names — 'Beefeater' of London and 'Mammy Yoko' of Freetown). And in particular there is a huge collection of fading photographs, of HMS 'Dreadnought' and many other long-vanished battleships.

A little further on is Chatham and another (but much grander) house-turned-pub. This is the fine Georgian mansion known as Command House because it was once the official residence of the commander of the naval dockyard, which is close by. A flight of a dozen steps leads up to a handsome front door, and beyond is the principal bar (all blue velvet and gilt fringes — the brewery's interpretation of the nautical touch) which has some of the graceful marble fireplaces that were there in its heyday. Downstairs, the original kitchens and cellars have been less smartened up (the old range is still there, with copper pans). The floor is flagstoned and you can sit in any of the arched brick vaults to drink. But the best part of Command House is outside: it has lawns and wood tables (and a row of seven cannon) overlooking the estuary, its shipping and Rochester Castle beyond.

A short drive further into Kent, through its hopfields and orchards, and then, beyond Sittingbourne, comes the 'Ship' at Conyer. This tiny village, off the Swale channel, was once a centre of shipbuilding — many Thames sailing-barges were launched here (and three still sail in and out). It has two boatyards now, building pleasure-craft. Many of the 'Ship's' customers are sailing people and it gets busy at weekends. Mike Porter-Ward, a musician, used to live on a house-boat at Conyer and when the former landlord of the 'Ship' decided to sell up, he took over.

The buildings are nearly 400 years old, and originally comprised a forge and a bakery, becoming an inn after 1800. Mike has restored the inn to a traditional style — with boarded ceiling, log fire (with nautical iron fireback and fitments for mulling ale), wood settles and so forth. He collects marine antiques and old prints — fog-horns, a ship's wheel, lanterns and (built in as a lintel across the fireplace) a great hatch-combing from an old barge. I relinquished the pleasures of a fireside rocking-chair and a bowl of home-made soup to read one of several naval recruiting posters (from the time of the French Revolution) which he has found: 'Let us who are Englishmen protect & defend our good King & country against the designe of our natural enemies who intend in this year to invade old England, to murder our gracious King [George III] as they have done their own, to make whores of our Wives & Daughters. Royal Tars of old England now is the time to repair (all who hate the French & damn the Pope) to Lieutenant Stephens at Shoreham, where they will be allowed to enter for any Ship of War.'

The 'Ship' is cosy when wind and rain do their worst outside. People in jeans, anoraks and Guernseys press round the bar of varnished wood (hung with the regulars' pewter mugs) or crowd into a small back room when someone gets the pianola going. The talk is sailing 'shop', or the swapping of notes among people who come for the birdwatching — the Swale has a reserve.

In midsummer, Mike organises a 'mud day' to raise funds for the Lifeboat Institution: there are apparently plenty of masochists willing to participate in the tug-of-war, three-legged-races and so on which are held at low tide in the

An annual tradition: Roundheads and Cavaliers battle it out once again on the beach before the Royal Escape Race from Brighton (East Sussex) to Fécamp.

creek, when it is a slough of thick, soft, grey mud. Definitely a spectator sport for the less adventurous! (For dates, phone 0795 521404.)

This is a pretty way-out form of pub entertainment, but many waterfront inns run other activities of their own such as water sports, races and trips on boats or sailing-barges. One of the most exciting is the Royal Escape Race.

When Charles II (then prince) was on the run from the Roundheads in 1651, he escaped by sea to Fécamp in France with the help of a Brighton sea captain, Tettersell, whom he later rewarded. The reward enabled Tettersell to buy himself the 'Old Ship' tavern. The 'Old Ship' (which has a Tettersell bar filled with mementos of these events) now organises every May a Brighton-to-Fécamp race, controlled by the Royal Navy. Spectators gather outside the hotel to see some 90 yachts of various sizes gather on the sea facing it, and to watch a Roundhead v Cavaliers battle on the beach just before the race starts. (For dates and programme, phone 0273 29001.)

Live music in pubs is an endangered species; but there are some attempts to keep it going, which include efforts to revive the singing of sea shanties. Up to a century ago these songs were sung on ships while hauling on ropes or turning capstans — aboard merchant sailing-ships, not in the Navy — and it is this that gives them their particular rhythms, the rope-hauling ones differing from the capstan or windlass ones. One of the oldest, 'What shall we do with the drunken sailor?', is a rope-hauling shanty; 'Blow the man down' is a capstan shanty. 'Fire down below' was sung when pumping. The American 'Shenandoah' became adopted world-wide as a capstan shanty to sing when raising the anchor preparatory to setting sail.

Inns with maritime connections

CUMBRIA
Sandyside Ship Inn. On estuary, nautical fittings.

MERSEYSIDE
Liverpool* Baltic Fleet. Marine mementos and a publican who dresses up as Nelson.

SOMERSET
Porlock Weir Ship Inn. On rocky beach, nautical fittings; rooms to let.

DEVON (north)
Ilfracombe* Royal Britannia Hotel. On harbour; Nelson stayed here. George and

Dragon. Stone-flagged, fishermen's inn.
Clovelly Red Lion. Harbour views.

CORNWALL

St Ives* Sloop. Ancient inn on quay.
Zennor Tinners' Arms. Old pub; D. H.
Lawrence lived here for a while.
Sennen Cove Old Success Inn. Ocean
views; rooms to let.
Mousehole Old Coastguard Hotel. Lifeboat
mementos. Lobster Pot Hotel. Its dining room
overhangs the harbour.
Newlyn Tolcarne Inn. Granite fishermen's
inn.
Penzance* Turk's Head. Smuggling. Union
Hotel. Trafalgar victory was announced from
its gallery.
Madron near **Penzance*** William IV.
Trafalgar Day celebration in October with free
rum for naval band.
Helston Ship Inn, **Porthleven**. Old
harbourside inn.
Helford Shipwright's Arms. Old inn with
downriver views.
Falmouth* Pandora Inn at **Restronguet
Creek**. Beamy old yachting inn.
St Mawes Rising Sun. On harbour; rooms to
let.
Portloe Lugger Hotel. Cliff and cove views.
Polkerris near **Par** Rashleigh Inn. On beach,
nautical bars, sea views.
Bodinnick Old Ferry Inn. Splendid views.
Polperro Three Pilchards. Old fishermen's
inn.
Torpoint Edgcumbe Arms. By boatyard and
Cremyll ferry.

DEVON (south)

Plymouth* Edgcumbe Arms, **Cremyll**.
Reached by ferry, dockyard views.
Bigbury Island Pilchard Inn. Reached by
walking over sands at low tide.
Salcombe* Fortescue. Nautical bar. King's
Arms. Old waterfront inn.
Dartmouth* Ferryboat Inn, at **Dittisham**.
Yachting centre. Seale Arms. Model ships,
made of iron locally. Dartmouth Arms, in
Bayard's Cove. Has featured in films of
'Treasure Island' and others.
Brixham* Quayside Hotel. Harbour views.
Bullers' Arms. Bar like a boat. On waterfront.
Paignton* Olde Smokey House. Beamy with
sea views. Smugglers signalled by smoke
from it.
Dawlish* The Smugglers, at **Holcombe**. Bay
views.
Starcross Ship Inn. Beamy old inn over-
looking harbour.
Axmouth Harbour Inn. On estuary.

DORSET

Seatown near **Chideock** Anchor Inn.
Formerly fishermen's cottages, by the sea.
Charmouth Queen's Armes. Mediaeval;
visited by Catherine of Aragon and Charles II.
Weymouth* Smugglers' Inn, at **Osmington
Mills**. Rooms to let.
Swanage* Ship Inn. Good fish served here.

HAMPSHIRE

Lymington Ship Inn. On yachting quay.
Portsmouth* Thatched House at Milton
Locks. Lone Yachtsman. Sir Alec Rose
associations. Dolphin Hotel. Nelson
associations. Still and West Country. Stained
glass window of HMS 'Victory'; harbour
views.
Hayling Ferryboat Inn.

ISLE OF WIGHT

Shanklin* Fisherman's Cottage. Temporary
club membership needed. Crab Inn. Thatched;
over-popular!
Bembridge Crab and Lobster Inn. Stunning
views, seafood; rooms to let. Pilot Boat Inn.
Shaped like a boat.
St Helen's Ferryboat Inn.
St Catherine's Point Buddle Inn. Model of
nearby lighthouse.
Wooton Bridge Sloop Inn. By the harbour.
Whippingham Folly Inn. Boats moor
alongside.

WEST SUSSEX

Bosham Anchor Bleu. The sea comes right
up to it.
Chichester* **Dell Quay** Crown and Anchor.
By the harbour; smuggling associations.
West Itchenor Ship Inn. Ship models and
paintings; rooms to let.
Bracklesham Bay Lively Lady. Started by
Sir Francis Chichester; maritime exhibits; rum
pump.
Nyetimber Lamb Inn. Old inn near bird
reserve.
Felpham Fox Inn. Named after an excise
cutter.
Littlehampton* White Hart. Nelson and
other mementos.

EAST SUSSEX

Brighton* Fortune of War. Model ships.
Newhaven* Hope Inn. Sea and harbour
views.
Norman's Bay Star Inn. A 15th-century
sluice house to control haven waters; storm
and smuggling associations.

KENT

Dymchurch Ship Hotel. 14th-century
smuggling inn.

Dover* Albion. Frequented by sailing enthusiasts and swimmers.
Deal* Forester. Sea-rowing mementos. Royal Hotel. Nelson associations. Zetland Arms, at **Kingsdown**. Right on the beach; has many nautical photos and mementos.
Broadstairs* Tartar Frigate. On harbour, nautical mementos.
Herne Bay* Ship Inn. 17th-century smuggling inn on seafront.
Whitstable* Pearson's Arms. Oysters at the bar.
Sheerness* Royal Fountain Hotel. Has the beds of Nelson and Lady Hamilton.
Queenborough Old House at Home. Views of boats.
Rochester* Ship Inn. Paddle-steamer mementos.
Upnor Tudor Rose. Beside estuary and castle.
Lower Upnor Pier Inn. Views of yachts and (sometimes) sailing-barges.
Gravesend Three Daws. Waterfront inn, smuggling associations. Ship and Lobster, Denton Wharf. Smuggling and sailing-barge connections.

ESSEX
Leigh On Sea The Peter Boat. Tudor inn overlooking seafront.
Burnham-on-Crouch Old White Harte. Georgian inn, waterfront views.

SUFFOLK
Pinmill Butt and Oyster. Sailing-barges moor alongside it.
Ipswich* Bristol Arms, at **Shotley**. Views of shipping.
Waldringfield Maybush. Frequented by sailing enthusiasts.
Orford King's Head. Smuggling stories, good food including fish.
Aldeburgh Mill Inn. Frequented by fishermen.

NORFOLK
Sheringham* Two Lifeboats. Beamy old inn.
Burnham Thorpe Lord Nelson. Nelson mementos.
Hunstanton* Wash and Tope. Beach inn, full of nautical instruments; 'tope' is a shark.
Denver Sluice Jenkyns Arms. Sea on one side, fresh water on the other.

LINCOLNSHIRE
Skegness* Jolly Fisherman. With figure from the famous Skegness poster.

HUMBERSIDE
Grimsby* Barge Inn. A former barge.
Flamborough Royal Dog and Duck. 'Royal' because of a visit by Prince Louis of Battenburg, great-uncle of the Duke of Edinburgh. Seafood bar; rooms to let.

NORTH YORKSHIRE
Scarborough* Three Mariners. Full of smugglers' secret passages; collection of fishermen's jerseys.
Staithes Crab and Lobster. Smugglers' inn on a jutting rock, regularly eroded by storms.

CLEVELAND
Saltburn-by-the-Sea Old Ship Inn. Smuggling tales; has ship's figurehead. Ship Inn. Maritime mementos; local fish served.
Marske-by-the-Sea Ship Inn. Built with warships' timbers.

TYNE AND WEAR
South Shields* Marsden Grotto. A cavern-tavern with smuggler's ghost; overlooks bird reserve.

NORTHUMBERLAND
Seaton Sluice Astley Arms. Submarine mementos.
Beadnell Craster Arms. In an old pele tower, fort erected against the Scots.
Seahouses* Olde Ship Inn. On the harbour-side, marine mementos; rooms to let.

33 A taste of England-by-the-sea

This country has been described as an island surrounded by fish so, even though fishing is not what it used to be, it is natural that most coastal towns and villages can produce at least one good fish restaurant. At its best, there is nothing to beat that most traditional of English eating places — the fish-and-chip shop. There are so many good ones that I have not attempted to list them all.

Each coast tends to have its own local fish, described in the notes below, and sometimes its local fish recipes too. (Some ports, associated with imports from the American continent have other specialities — based, for instance, on rum and Barbados sugar — and these too are described below.)

One of the most unusual of traditional fish recipes is Star-Gazy Pie which comes from Cornwall, land of the pasty, and in particular from the fishing village of Mousehole. The story told at the 'Ship Inn', where a great pie is still served every 23rd December, is that before one Christmas when very few fish had been landed and all was gloom, tough Tom Bawcock put to sea despite the storms and came back with seven kinds of fish which were then used in one huge pie. The 'Ship Inn's' pie takes 50 kg of varied fish; but for smaller-scale pies the method is to blend cooked fish, mashed potato, herbs and seasoning, cover with pastry and (this is where the star-gazing comes in) poke pilchards' or herrings' heads into slits in the pastry before baking. As the pie cooks, the fatty heads enrich the pastry.

Other coastal specialities to look out for are listed at end of chapter.

If you want to taste fish at its freshest, seek out a fish restaurant near the coast and choose a dish that uses the local fish — caught close to the shore. (Sometimes cod, for example, is caught in deep waters thousands of kilometres away, and will have gone through wholesale markets before finding its way to shops or fish-and-chip-shops.)

Dover sole, for instance, reigns supreme on the south coast; and at 'English's' in Brighton they know 20 classic and delicious ways to serve it, such as these: Mornay — with cheese sauce; Newburg — with lobsters, egg yolk, cream and parsley; Walewska — with lobster and cheese sauce; Bonne Femme — with mushrooms, shallots and parsley; Dieppoise — with shrimps and mussels; Florentine — with spinach and cheese sauce; Vèronique — with grapes and white wine sauce; Cardinal — with lobster, mushrooms, cheese and brandy; Aux Huîtres — with oysters and white wine sauce; Caprice — grilled, with banana and chutney sauce; St Germain — grilled, with Bearnaise sauce; Colbert — deep-fried with a pat of parsley butter in its opened-up back. And there are many other ways too. But to my mind there is nothing to beat a simple Sole Meunière pan-fried in butter and served on the bone.

To some extent what is on or off the menu at 'English's' is dictated by wind, weather and the whereabouts of the fish during the last tide. Simon Leigh-Jones goes at 7 a.m. every morning to the local fish-market, buying the pick of the previous tide's catch. All along this stretch of coast, fishing-boats will have been coming in — to the harbours of Newhaven and Shoreham, onto the beaches at Brighton — to land their catch, often fishing by night in order to go out with the ebb and return on a high tide. On Simon's return, there is frenzied activity behind-scenes, as all the filleting is done in the restaurant's own kitchen. Sole is the most popular of the many fish on the menu, and on a busy day 100 will be cooked.

'English's' began as a fish shop run by the Brazier family when Victoria was still a very young Queen. It specialised in oysters (from the nearby River Adur, in those days) and in due course the manager, Mr English, married the proprietor's daughter and ultimately took over, steadily expanding the shop which now became known as 'English's Oyster Stores'. Fish was sold in the traditional way from a marble slab; and then an oyster bar was added at which a dozen could sit to eat (as they still can, at any hour from 10.30 in the morning). Son and then grandson inherited, and to the first fisherman's cottage (300 years old) was added the one next door. It was not until after the Second World War that the English dynasty ended and the Leigh-Jones family (with a background in Naval catering) took over.

They have kept the traditional style of the interior unchanged: the cream-painted Victorian Lincrusta on the walls, crimson velvet chairs, a little circular mahogany bar, and below the tables cast-iron pedestals with twined dolphins. *Fin-de-siècle* style paintings, like those in many old Parisian restaurants, show Brighton bathing-machines and pleasure-seekers of the 1890s.

Behind the oyster bar reigns one of Brighton's personalities, Ted Katkowski, large and jovial, a fund of anecdotes. Ted, a Pole, came here after fighting at Monte-Cassino and the only job he could then get was as a waiter. Now he is as much a part of 'English's' as the gilt and marble fixtures. He has opened half a million oysters so far (but has a long way to go before beating his predecessor, who topped a million and won one of the annual oyster-opening contests that are held at Galway). 'English's' gets through some 25,000 oysters every season — these days they all come from Colchester.

'English's' has been frequented for over a century by the great and the good (and not-so-good, too). Edward VII came to try the famous oysters, was asked to put out his cigar (you smoke at your peril in 'English's'), ate one oyster and departed in a huff. One of the more bizarre episodes in the restaurant's history is related in Harold Nicolson's diary. His mother-in-law, Lady Sackville, had requested in her will that her ashes should be scattered at sea. The family did not want the press pursuing them, and so: 'February 8, 1936. We go to the oyster shop of Mr English where the ashes have been preserved overnight. The urn is placed in the back of the car by Mr English who is slightly drunk but says he has a cold in the head. He is anxious to come with us in the boat but I am very firm on that point: "No, Mr English, we really should prefer to be by ourselves".' 'English's' even has a ghost story. Martha Gunn, a dipper (one of the women who used to help Regency bathers dip in the sea, for their health) lived close by. The dippers wore distinctive gear, including a rather conical hat, as worn by men at the time. A waitress and then, much later, a waiter have reported seeing just such a figure in the passages upstairs. After a little too much Muscadet, who knows what one might see?

The fish restaurant at the 'Dickens Inn' by the Tower is in complete contrast to 'English's'.

The Inn is part of one of Europe's most outstanding conservation successes, known as St Katharine's by the Tower. St Katharine's was a not-very-busy London dock before it was closed down in 1968. Now it is again a maritime centre, though of a very different kind.

The old quays have been carefully preserved with their original iron bollards bearing the emblem of St Katharine's (a seal with the saint, the wheel of her martyrdom and the Tower of London) and with their old cobbles, gas lamps, swing-bridges and locks: the work of Thomas Telford. But the craft that fill the dock-basins with activity are very different now — mostly smart white yachts; though you will usually find half-a-dozen sailing-barges also moored here, as well as the Maritime Trust's collection of old ships (see Chapter 6). The buildings, too, serve new purposes: handsome great warehouses have been restored and converted to provide flats, offices, shops — and restaurants.

When some new buildings were being planned, it was intended to demolish a down-at-heel brewery warehouse — then, behind the grimy brickwork was discovered a much older frame of colossal timbers, three storeys high, which dates from the 18th century. This great frame, after it had been moved some 65 m, was used in the construction of the Dickens Inn and it is the most striking feature inside the building. Outside, wood balconies have been built in the style of the galleried coaching-inns of the 18th century, from which plants now hang.

It is the top floor of the Inn that houses the fish restaurant. Here the roof-timbers have been left exposed; and the balcony is furnished with tables for outdoor eating when the weather is warm. From balcony or windows there is

A warehouse makes an unusual restaurant overlooking the old docks by the Tower of London: the Dickens Inn.

a gull's-eye-view of the sailing-barges and yachts below.

Even the tables are made from old planks five cm thick; and on the beams above are lodged boats, barge name-boards, coils of thick hemp rope, masts, wood oyster-tubs and all manner of ships' tackle: somebody must have spent many enjoyable days hunting for all this marine bric-à-brac.

At one end, fish are laid out on a chilled marble slab, fishmonger-style; in the great copper fish-kettle which awaits them, *court bouillon* simmers gently. There is a small room for private parties called Little Nell; the office is a 'counting house' called Scrooge & Marley. Whimsy? Yes, but carried out with style as well as humour.

As to the food, this is where to go for fish dishes that are different from the average. The Dickens Inn is not afraid to offer the less usual fish: for instance, John Dory, sea bream and salmon trout. And some of its recipes are equally unconventional — such as fish mousse flavoured with stem ginger, cockles and mussels in a hot garlic sauce, scallops wrapped in bacon, fish kebabs, and that Cornish speciality, star-gazy pie. I found the seafood pancake (listed as an *hors d'oeuvres*) so large as well as so excellent that it was almost a meal in itself. (For table bookings phone 01-488 9932.)

Afterwards, I walked along the quays. Spots of light sparkled through the dusk, and were twinkling on the water. It is quite possible that Dickens, who wrote so often of downriver Thames, perhaps most memorably in 'Our Mutual Friend', walked here too. From chinks between the great stones that make the side of each dock there were growing ragwort, valerian and toadflax, touching the water. Iron pillars, newly painted, shone white or jet-black. A perfect way to end a memorable meal.

Restaurants in a maritime setting which serve local fish

This list makes no pretence to be comprehensive, but is a cross-section of what is to be found – from shellfish bars to stylish restaurants, by the sea or in buildings of maritime interest.

CUMBRIA
Ravenglass* Pennington Arms. Local fish.
Biggar, Walney Queen's Arms. Local fish.

LANCASHIRE
Blackpool* Lobster Pot. Close to the famous Tower. 0253 293201 Robert's Oyster Bar. Five generations have served shellfish here, with draught champagne. Also home-soused herrings from Fleetwood. 0253 21226

MERSEYSIDE
Parkgate, Wirral The Ship. Overlooks estuary. 051336 3931

DEVON (north)
Clovelly New Inn. 02373 303

CORNWALL
Tintagel House on the Strand. Next to beach, in cove. 08404 326
Padstow Old Custom House Inn. On the quay. 0841 532359 Seafood Restaurant. Converted quayside granary. 0841 532485
Carbis Bay near **St Ives*** John Beck. Superb fish-and-chippery.
St Ives* Tilly's Café. Built high into cliff face, view of bay.

SCILLY ISLES
St Mary's* The Galley. Fishermen brothers catch and cook the fish. 0720 22602

CORNWALL
Lamorna near **Penzance*** Lamorna Cove Hotel. Overlooks valley and sea. 073673 411
Penzance* Admiral Benbow. Smugglers' inn; full of figureheads etc. 0736 3448
St Mawes Idle Rocks Hotel. Right on the harbour. 03266 771
Porthscatho near **Falmouth*** Smugglers Cottage. Thatched cottage near ferry. 087 258 309
Mevagissey Mr Bistro. Harbourside restaurant, with many fish dishes. 072 684 2432
Fowey* Riverside Hotel. Overhangs the river. 072 683 2215
Looe* Klymiarven Hotel. Manor house overlooking the fishing village. 05036 2333

DEVON (south)
Plymouth* The Cooperage. 18th-century barrel-makers' building, with fittings made from marine salvage. 0752 64288
Salcombe* South Sands Hotel. Right on sandy cove. Local fish served – even squid.

054 884 2791
Torcross near **Kingsbridge*** Start Bay Inn. On the beach. Seafood restaurant. 0548 580305
Dartmouth* The Steam Packet. Wine bar, specialising in seafood. 08043 3886
Teignmouth* Minadab. Unusual house built by one of Nelson's captains. 06267 2044
Budleigh Salterton* The Rum Hole. Fishermen's cottages near the beach. 03954 2628
Seaton* Ship Inn at Axmouth. 0297 21838

DORSET
Weymouth* The Spinnaker. In a former seamen's mission, on the quay. 0305 782767
Poole* Corkers. Quayside fish restaurant. 02013 4184
Wareham near **Poole*** Old Granary. On quay. 09295 2010
Bournemouth* Longi's. Haute cuisine fish cookery. 0202 296210
Christchurch* Fishermen's Haunt. 17th-century house with waterfront view. 0202 484071

HAMPSHIRE
Lymington The Slipway. On the quay. 0590 74545
Beaulieu* Master Builder's House Hotel. 059 063 253
Portsmouth* The Seagull. 0705 24866

ISLE OF WIGHT
Cowes (west) Flying Dutchman. By the sea; full of figureheads etc. 098 382 2508
Bonchurch near **Ventnor*** Bay House Café. On the beach. The owner catches the crabs and other fish himself. 0983 852464

EAST SUSSEX
Brighton* Allanjohns. Long-established jellied eels and shellfish. 0273 683087 Market Wine House. Wine bar, with local fish dishes. 0273 23829 Medina. Restaurant on a boat. 0273 697049

KENT
Deal* Royal Hotel. Frequented by Nelson; overlooks the Channel. 03045 5555
Broadstairs* The Mad Chef. Harbour bistro. 0843 65306
Herne Bay* Petit France. Shellfish bar. 02273 64888

ESSEX
Leigh On Sea La Bastille. Unusual fish dishes. 0702 555154
Southend* Cotgroves. Modern building, marine decor, fish a speciality. 0702 338155
Maldon Wheelers. 17th-century building

with ship's timbers inside. 0621 53647
Harwich* The Pier. On quayside.
02555 3363

SUFFOLK
Orford Butley Orford Oysterage. Seafood
served on marble-topped tables. 03945 277

NORFOLK
Great Yarmouth* Bloater Depot. Smoke-
house too. 0493 2747 Seafood Restaurant.
Former Victorian pub; staggering variety of
fish served. 0493 56009

Burnham Market Fishes. They smoke their
own fish. 032873 588

HUMBERSIDE
Hull* Waterfront Hotel. Old warehouse,
carefully conserved. 0482 227222

NORTH YORKSHIRE
Whitby* Magpie. Café with fresh local fish.
0947 2058

TYNE AND WEAR
Whitley Bay* Schooner Grill. Nautical
surroundings. Lobster and scallop dishes.
0632 533847

Index

Numbers in italics refer to
illustrations

Acknowledgements

Colour photographs
Aquila Photographics: E. Soothill, facing page 96; British Tourist Authority, facing pages 33, 64, 97; England Scene, facing pages 32, 128, 129; Island Cruising Club: Mike Smith, facing page 65.

Black-and-white photographs
Janet and Colin Bord 57, 112; British Insulated Callender's Cables Ltd and the Corporation of Trinity House 110; British Tourist Authority 20, 27, 33, 60, 72, 78, 93, 119, 138, 140, 152; British Transport Docks Board 134, 135; Chatham News and Standard: Ray Christopher 126; England Scene 98; David Hosking 87; Humber Keel and Sloop Preservation Society 31; Island Cruising Club: Ken Fraser 66; Magdalen College Cambridge 43; Mary Evans Picture Library 37, 40, 50, 55, 130; National Bus Company 95; Nature Photographers: T. Andrewartha 101, M. D. E. Oates 83, Bill S. Paton 103; The Old Ship Hotel 147; T. P. Roskrow and the Royal National Lifeboat Institution 121; Thames Barge Sailing Club: D. G. Wood 23; Andy Williams 46.